S P O

SOUTHEAST ALASKA

DON PITCHER

Contents

SOUTHEAST ALASKA

SOUTHEAST ALASKA

For many people, the name Alaska conjures up images of bitterly cold winters and sunshine-packed summers, of great rivers, enormous snowcapped mountains, and open tundra reaching to the horizon. If that's your vision of the state, you've missed its Garden of Eden, the Southeast. Almost entirely boxed in by British Columbia, Southeast Alaska's "Panhandle" or Inside Passage stretches 500 miles along the North American coast. Everything about this beautiful, lush country is waterbased: the rain that falls on the land, the glaciers that drop from giant icefields, and the ocean that surrounds it all. Gray-blue clouds play a constant game of hide-and-seek with the verdant islands; deep fjords drive up between snow-covered summits; waterfalls plummet hundreds of feet through the evergreen forests to feed rivers rich in salmon; brown bears prowl the creeks in search of fish; bald eagles perch on treetops beside the rugged, rocky coastline; and great blue glaciers press down toward the sea.

ORIENTATION

The Land

Nearly 95 percent of the Southeast is federal property, most of it within Tongass National Forest and Glacier Bay National Park. The Panhandle is composed of a mountainous mainland and hundreds of islands, varying from rocky reefs that barely jut out of the sea at low tide to some of the largest islands in North America. Collectively, these islands are called the Alexander Archipelago. This ragged shoreline stretches for more than 11,000 miles and

© DON PITCHER

HIGHLIGHTS

◖ Totem Bight State Historical Park: Ketchikan is home to several notable totem pole collections, but Totem Bight takes the prize with a gorgeous waterside setting, historic clan house, and lush forests (page 21).

◖ Misty Fiords National Monument: Almost always encased in clouds, this wilderness has spectacular cliffs that plummet into deep fiords. Tours by air and boat are offered from Ketchikan (page 32).

◖ The Stikine River: Jetboat trips from Wrangell are the main attraction for visitors to this mighty river with its hidden glaciers and relaxing hot springs (page 56).

◖ Sitka National Historical Park: This gem of a park encompasses Sitka's rich Tlingit and Russian heritage with historic buildings, totems bordering a wooded trail, and the chance to watch Native artisans at work (page 71).

◖ Mendenhall Glacier: Southeast's best-known drive-up glacier, Mendenhall has fine hiking trails and a fascinating visitor center. It's just a few miles north of Juneau (page 90).

◖ Tracy Arm – Fords Terror Wilderness: Almost unknown outside Alaska, this wilderness area is a popular destination for day tours by boat from Juneau. It's a great place to watch ice calving from the glacier or to see seals resting atop icebergs (page 106).

◖ Visiting Glacier Bay: Made famous by John Muir, this national park has towering mountains, thundering glaciers, abundant wildlife, fun day trips, and memorable sea kayaking adventures (page 113).

◖ Fort Seward: Looking more like a New England village than a fort, this picture-perfect collection of historic Haines buildings now houses a variety of artistic, commercial, and cultural endeavors (page 127).

◖ Klondike Gold Rush National Historical Park: The town of Skagway's gold rush heritage is preserved in a dozen classic –

LOOK FOR ◖ TO FIND RECOMMENDED SIGHTS, ACTIVITIES, DINING, AND LODGING.

and immaculately restored – downtown buildings that now hum with tourism all summer (page 139).

◖ White Pass & Yukon Route Railroad: Originally built to haul miners into the Klondike and gold back out, this narrow-gage railroad now fills with travelers and hikers. It may be the most scenic train ride in America (page 139).

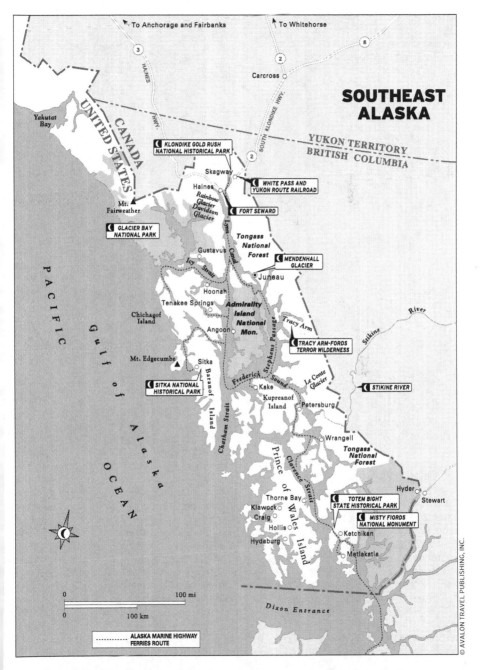

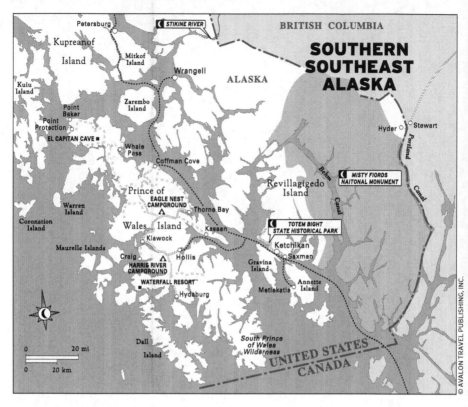

includes over 1,000 named islands, the largest being Prince of Wales, Chichagof, Baranof, Admiralty, Revillagigedo, and Kupreanof—names that reflect the English, Russians, and Spaniards who explored the area.

The Rainforest

Much of the Southeast is covered with dense rainforests of Sitka spruce (the state tree), western hemlock, Alaska yellow cedar, and western red cedar. Interspersed through these rainforests are open boggy areas known as "muskegs," with a scattering of stunted lodgepole pines and cedars. Above the tree line (approx. 2,500 ft.) are rocky peaks covered with fragile flowers and other alpine vegetation. Shorelines often sport a fringe of grass dotted with flowers during the summer.

The rainforests here are choked with a dense understory of huckleberry, devil's club, and other shrubs. Berry lovers will enjoy a feast in late summer as the salmonberries, red and blue huckleberries, and thimbleberries all ripen. If you're planning a hike, learn to recognize **devil's club,** a lovely, abundant plant with large maple-shaped leaves and red berries. Barbed spines cover the plants, and when touched they feel like a bee sting. The spines become embedded in your fingers and are difficult to remove, often leaving a nasty sting for several days. If you're planning a cross-country hike, wear leather gloves to protect your hands. Surprisingly, mosquitoes and other biting insects are not nearly as abundant in the Southeast as they are in, for example, Alaska's Interior. They can, however, make your life

© DON PITCHER

devil's club in rainforest near Ward Lake, Tongass National Forest

miserable some of the time, especially during no-see-um season.

Climate

Tourist brochures invariably show happy folks cavorting around gleaming glaciers under a brilliant blue sky. Photographers might wait weeks to capture all three elements: Southeast Alaska is rain country! Expect rain or mist at least half of the time. In much of the region, blue-sky days come once a week, if that. The cool maritime climate brings rain in summer, and rain and snow in winter. Most towns in the Southeast get 80 inches or more of precipitation, and of the major towns, Ketchikan takes top honors with 162 inches per year. The tiny fishing settlement of Port Alexander on the south end of Baranof Island drowns in 220 inches per year!

Weather patterns vary greatly in the Southeast; Skagway gets just 22 inches a year, but only a few miles away, precipitation tops 160 inches annually on the peaks bordering Canada. Fortunately, the driest months are generally June–August.

Residents learn to tolerate the rain, which they call "liquid sunshine." You won't see many umbrellas, but heavy raingear and red rubber boots are appropriate dress for almost any occasion. If you ask, locals will admit to a grudging appreciation for the rain; it not only creates the lush, green countryside and provides ample streamflow for the vital salmon runs, it also keeps the region safe from overcrowding by the drier-minded set.

The People

Southeast Alaska has only 70,000 people. Nearly half live in Juneau, with the rest spread over nearly two dozen isolated towns and settlements strung along the Inside Passage. Much of the economy is based upon fishing, logging, governing, and tourism. The towns are dependent upon the sea for their survival, not only for the fish it provides, but also as a way to transport huge log rafts to the mills. Fully 95 percent of the goods brought to the Southeast arrive by barge or ship, and most of the visitors arrive aboard cruise ships or state ferries.

The Southeast corresponds almost exactly to the ancestral homeland of the Tlingit (KLINK-it) Indians, and signs of their culture—both authentic and visitor-oriented—are common. Almost every town has at least one totem pole, and some have a dozen or more. Tlingit artwork generally includes carvings, beadwork, sealskin moccasins, and silver jewelry. It *doesn't* include the *ulus,* Eskimo dolls, and other paraphernalia frequently sold in local tourist shops.

PLANNING YOUR TIME

All the major Inside Passage towns are separated by water or mountainous coastlines, with planes, state ferries, and cruise ships providing the connections. This limitation is a blessing in disguise: a long ferry ride north allows time to soak up the scenery and plan adventures in the next port. Anyone traveling with a vehicle is limited to ferry travel, while others can mix and match ferries or plane flights with local car rentals when needed. Cruise ships, of course, offer the leave-the-driving-to-us version. Plan on at least a week in Southeast Alaska—and preferably more—unless you are simply taking the Alaska Air jet to Sitka (or another town) and stopping for a few days of exploration.

Rain-soaked Ketchikan is the southernmost port, and a very popular destination for travelers of all ages and incomes. Downtown's Creek Street forms a picturesque stop, while totem poles and Tlingit (KLINK-it) culture are the big draws at Saxman and **Totem Bight State Historical Park.** Day trips by air or sea to **Misty Fiords National Monument** provide a great introduction to a dramatic wilderness of high cliffs and deep inlets.

Nearby Metlakatla and Prince of Wales Island are off-the-beaten-path destinations, and to the north lie the fishing towns of Wrangell and Petersburg, with the mighty **Stikine River** (popular for jetboat trips) heading into the mountains of British Columbia. Stop in the old Native and Russian town of Sitka with its gem-like setting, **Sitka National Historical Park,** and the Alaska Raptor Center. Juneau is not just the state capital and third largest city, but also home to a fun tramway up Mt. Roberts, the

Alaska State Museum, and famous **Mendenhall Glacier.** Boat tours to the deep fjords and calving glaciers of **Tracy Arm** are popular day trips from Juneau, as are boat tours (and kayaking trips) into magnificent **Glacier Bay.** The quiet town of Haines is home to **Fort Seward,** where century-old homes surround the old parade grounds. The touristy town of Skagway has a gold-rush aura courtesy of the many buildings preserved within **Klondike Gold Rush National Historical Park.** Especially popular here are narrow-gauge train rides aboard the **White Pass & Yukon Route Railroad.**

GETTING THERE

Visitors come to the Southeast by three primary means: cruise ship, jet, and ferry (the Alaska Marine Highway). Cruise ships are easily the most popular method—more than 900,000 people travel this way each year—but also the most expensive and the least personal. The second option, air, is more popular with independent travelers. **Alaska Airlines** (800/426-0333, www.alaskaair.com) has daily flights from Seattle, with service to Juneau, Ketchikan, Wrangell, Petersburg, Sitka, Gustavus, and other Alaskan cities. Floatplanes connect these towns to smaller places and provide access to even the most remote corners of the Inside Passage, such as Elfin Cove, Tokeen, and Port Alexander.

The Ferry System

Only three Southeast towns (Haines, Skagway, and Hyder) are connected by road to the rest of the continent. All the others, including Juneau, the state capital, are accessible only by boat or plane. This lack of roads—hopefully they will never be built—has led to an efficient public ferry system, the best in the Western Hemisphere and the longest in the world. Most ferries sail between Prince Rupert, B.C., and Skagway, stopping along the way in the major towns. There is also weekly service from Bellingham, Washington, all the way to Skagway, a three-day voyage. In the larger towns, summer service is almost daily, but in the smallest settlements, ferries may be up to two weeks apart.

Get schedules and make reservations from the **Alaska Marine Highway** (907/465-3941 or 800/642-0066, www.ferryalaska.com). Since most travel in the Southeast centers around the ferry schedules, it's wise to check the ferry schedule before making any solid travel plans. Reservations for the summer can be made as early as December, and travelers taking a vehicle should book as early as possible to be sure of space.

The **Inter-Island Ferry Authority** (907/826-4848 or 866/308-4848, www.interislandferry.com) serves Prince of Wales Island, with service connecting the island with Ketchikan, Wrangell, and Mitkof Island (Petersburg). Travelers can use their ferries to create a side trip to Prince of Wales without backtracking. For example, you can take the state ferry to Ketchikan, then transfer to an Inter-Island ferry to Hollis on POW Island, drive up the island, and then catch another ferry to Wrangell and Mitkof Island, where you can continue north on the state ferry system.

Ketchikan

After the 36-hour ferry ride up from Bellingham, Ketchikan is many first-timers' introduction to Alaska. Along the way they've heard tales from sourdoughs (and those who claim to be), talked to Forest Service naturalists, and watched the logging towns and lush, green islands of British Columbia float past. As the ferry pulls into busy Tongass Narrows, an air of expectancy grows among the newcomers who are about to take their first steps in Alaska.

The state's fourth-largest city (pop. 8,000, plus another 6,000 in nearby areas), Ketchikan bills itself as "Alaska's First City," and even its zip code, 99901, seems to bear this out. Quite a few ferry passengers don't bother to stop here, instead hurrying on toward Juneau and points north. Because downtown is two miles away, they only have time for a superficial bus tour or a walk to the grocery store for provisions. But with its great scenery, fine local trails, the world's largest collection of totem poles, a bustling downtown, and the famous Misty Fiords nearby, Ketchikan certainly deserves a longer stay.

The Setting

Located 90 miles north of Prince Rupert, Ketchikan clings to a steep slope along Tongass Narrows, on Revillagigedo (ruh-VEE-ya-he-HAY-do) Island; locals shorten the name to "Revilla." Fortunately, it doesn't bear the one-time viceroy of Mexico's full name: Don Juan Vicente de Guemes Pacheco de Pedilla y Horcasitas, Count of Revilla Gigedo! Locals call the town "three miles long and three blocks wide." It forms a continuous strip of development along the waterfront from the ferry terminal to beyond Thomas Basin. Because of this, Tongass Avenue—the only through street—has long been one of the busiest in the entire state. A hilltop bypass opened a few years back, but traffic is still very heavy on Tongass Avenue.

Much of Ketchikan is built on fill, on pilings over the water, or on hillsides with steep, winding ramps for streets. Fishing boats jam the three boat harbors (there are almost as many boats as cars in Ketchikan), and the canneries and cold-storage plants run at full throttle during the summer. Floatplanes are constantly taking off from the narrows, cruise ships crowd the docks, and tourists explore the downtown shops and attractions.

Ketchikan is one of the rainiest places in Alaska, getting upward of 13 feet a year, or an average of half an inch per day. Luckily, May–August are the driest months, but expect to get wet nevertheless. Locals adapt with "Ketchikan sneakers" (red rubber boots) and Helly Hansen raingear; umbrellas are the mark of a tourist. Residents pride themselves on almost never

© DON PITCHER

Ketchikan

canceling baseball games, and enjoy weekend picnics at Ward Lake in a downpour. Weather predicting is easy in Ketchikan: If you can't see the top of Deer Mountain, it's raining; if you can, it's *going* to rain. For an only-in-Ketchikan sight, check out the Valley Park Grade School on Schoenbar Road. This unique school was built atop its own playground, creating an escape from the rain.

History

The name Ketchikan comes from *Kitcxan,* a Tlingit word meaning "where the eagles' wings are," a reference to the shape of a sandspit at the creek mouth. The sandspit was dredged in the 1930s to create Thomas Basin Boat Harbor. Rumor has it that several bodies were found then, and suspicious fingers were pointed toward the denizens of nearby Creek Street, the local red-light district.

One of Southeast Alaska's youngest major towns, Ketchikan began when the first of many salmon canneries at the mouth of Ketchikan

Creek opened in 1885. By the 1930s it had become the "Salmon Capital of the World" (13 canneries), and Alaska's largest town. Overfishing caused salmon populations to crash in the 1940s, and the fishing industry was supplanted in the 1950s by a new pulp mill that turned the town into a major logging center.

For several decades Ketchikan's pulp mill was the biggest employer in Southeast Alaska, processing spruce and hemlock for the production of rayon and cellophane. The pulp mill closed in 1997, just as Ketchikan's economy shifted full-bore into tourism.

The big story today for Ketchikan—as in Juneau and Skagway—is cruise ships. More than 900,000 cruise ship travelers step onto Ketchikan's docks annually, with four or five ships tied up along Tongass Narrows most summer days. The rough old downtown with its sawmill, flophouses, and bars has been transformed into rows of jewelry stores (63 at last count!) staffed by employees from the Caribbean, and trinket shops selling plastic totem

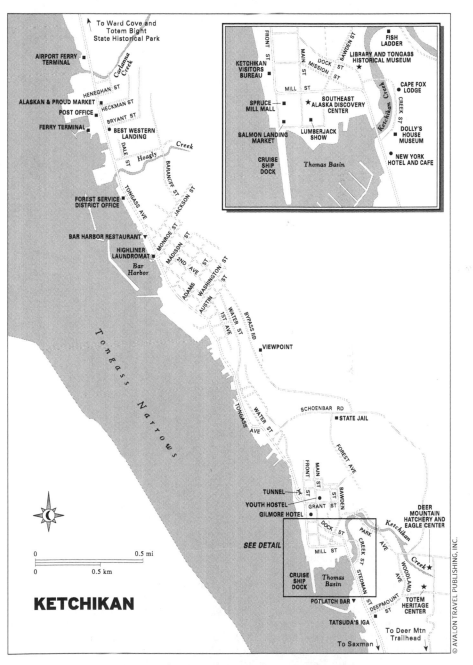

KETCHIKAN

To Ward Cove and Totem Bight State Historical Park

AIRPORT FERRY TERMINAL

Carlana Creek

HENEGHAN ST

ALASKAN & PROUD MARKET
HECKMAN ST
POST OFFICE
BRYANT ST
FERRY TERMINAL
BEST WESTERN LANDING

DALE ST
Hoagly Creek

BARANOF ST

TONGASS AVE

FOREST SERVICE DISTRICT OFFICE

JACKSON ST
MONROE ST

BAR HARBOR RESTAURANT ▼

HIGHLINER LAUNDROMAT
Bar Harbor

MADISON ST
2ND AVE ST
WASHINGTON ST
ADAMS ST
AUSTIN ST
1ST AVE
WATER ST
BYPASS RD

VIEWPOINT

Tongass Narrows

SCHOENBAR RD
WATER ST
STATE JAIL
TONGASS AVE

FOREST AVE

0 ___ 0.5 mi
0 ___ 0.5 km

TUNNEL
YOUTH HOSTEL
GILMORE HOTEL

FRONT ST
MAIN ST
GRANT ST
BAWDEN ST

DEER MOUNTAIN HATCHERY AND EAGLE CENTER

SEE DETAIL

DOCK ST
MILL ST

PARK AVE
CREEK ST
Ketchikan Creek ★
STEDMAN ST
WOODLAND AVE

CRUISE SHIP DOCK
Thomas Basin

TOTEM HERITAGE CENTER ★

POTLATCH BAR ▼
DEEPMOUNT ST

To Deer Mtn Trailhead

TATSUDA'S IGA

To Saxman ↓

Detail inset:

FRONT ST
MAIN ST
DOCK ST
MISSION ST
BAWDEN ST
FISH LADDER

KETCHIKAN VISITORS BUREAU
LIBRARY AND TONGASS HISTORICAL MUSEUM ★

MILL ST
CAPE FOX LODGE ●

SPRUCE MILL MALL
SOUTHEAST ALASKA DISCOVERY CENTER ★
Ketchikan Creek
CREEK ST
DOLLY'S HOUSE MUSEUM

SALMON LANDING MARKET
LUMBERJACK SHOW

CRUISE SHIP DOCK
Thomas Basin
NEW YORK HOTEL AND CAFE ●

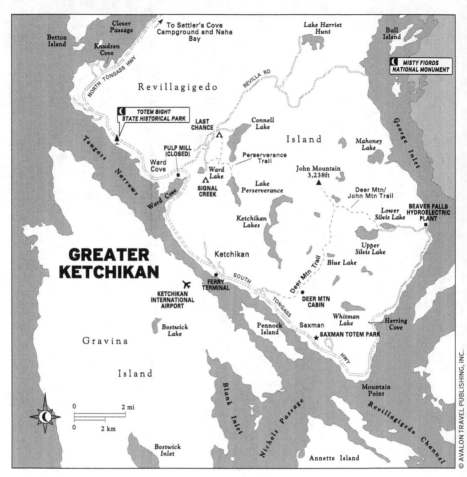

poles and stuffed animals made in China. Crossing guards at the intersections, horse-drawn wagon rides, amphibious "duck" tours, a pseudo-logging show, and thousands of befuddled cruise shippies add to what Edward Abbey labeled "industrial tourism." Sad, but it makes the cash registers ring, at least those businesses willing to accept kickback deals with the cruise lines in exchange for promotion onboard the ships. Fortunately, the cruise ships generally depart by early evening, allowing locals and overnight visitors to rediscover this fascinating town.

SIGHTS

Outside the library/museum is **Raven Stealing the Sun Totem,** and not far away stands the **Chief Johnson Pole** (an older version is inside the Totem Heritage Center). Tiny Whale Park occupies the intersection across from the Forest Service office and is home to the **Chief Kyan Totem,** raised in 1993 to replace an older version. The older one was reputed to reward those who touched it by bringing money within a day. It's worth a try on the new one, but don't head immediately to Las Vegas on the basis of this claim.

Check out some of Ketchikan's many long aerobic **stairways** up to hillside homes and outstanding vistas. The best ones start from the tunnel at Front and Grant streets, and from the intersection of Main and Pine streets. If you have a bike (or better yet, a skateboard), you may want to test your mettle on Schoenbar Road, the route blasted out of a steep hillside behind town. By the way, the Front Street **tunnel** is said to be the only one in the world that you can drive through, around, and over! Or so claims the *Guinness Book of World Records*.

Picturesque **Thomas Basin Boat Harbor** is just across the bridge over Creek Street. Walk out Thomas Street, past the Potlatch Bar (good for a game of pool or a beer with local fishermen), and out the jetty for a fine view back towards town.

Visitor Center

The **Ketchikan Visitors Bureau** (131 Front St., 907/225-6166 or 800/770-3300, www .visit-ketchikan.com) is right on the downtown dock. It's open whenever cruise ships are docked, which means daily 6:30 A.M.–6 P.M. most days May–September, and Monday–Friday 8 A.M.–5 P.M. the rest of the year. Pick up their free map that includes a walking tour of local sites. The building also houses booths for local tour companies.

Southeast Alaska Discovery Center

A great place to start your exploration of Ketchikan is the Southeast Alaska Discovery Center (50 Main St., 907/228-6220, www.fs.fed. us/r10, open Mon.–Sat. 8 A.M.–5 P.M. and Sun. 8 A.M.–4 P.M. May–Sept., and Tues.–Sat. 10 A.M.–4:30 P.M. the rest of the year, $5 adults, kids under 15 free). Operated by the U.S. Forest Service, it's filled with impressive exhibits—including a full-scale rainforest—that offer an educational portrait of the land and people of the Southeast. The 13-minute multimedia show "Mystical Southeast Alaska" is a must-see. Look through the spotting scope for mountain goats on Deer Mountain or

check out the video feed from the fish cam in Ketchikan Creek. The staff will help you with information on the outdoors, and the big gift shop features books, trail guides, and maps.

Logging Show

Located on Mill Street next to the cruise ship dock, the **Spruce Mill Complex** is the tourist shopping center for downtown Ketchikan, with retail stores, souvenir shops, galleries, and restaurants. Ketchikan's old spruce mill stood on this site for many years, so it is perhaps fitting to also find **The Great Alaskan Lumberjack Show** (907/225-9050 or 888/320-9049, www.lumberjackshows.com, three shows daily—rain or shine—May–Sept., $32 adults, $16 kids) here. This cornball 90-minute exhibition of old-time logging skills features ax throwing, bucksawing, springboard chopping, logrolling, and a speedy 50-foot tree climb. Covered grandstands protect the audience from the inevitable rain. If you're looking for a cheesy, Disneyfied imitation of old-time logging, this may be your ticket.

Tongass Historical Museum

The cramped Tongass Historical Museum (629 Dock St., 907/225-5600, www.city .ketchikan.ak.us, $2) shares the library building, and is open daily 8 A.M.–5 P.M. early May–September; and Wednesday–Friday 1–5 P.M., Saturday 10 A.M.–4 P.M., and Sunday 1–4 P.M. the rest of the year. The museum contains local historical items with changing exhibits that include examples of Native culture and commercial fishing. Look around for the model of a clan house, the 200-year-old Chilkat blanket, the dance paddle inlaid with abalone shell, the bentwood boxes, and the amusing totem pole with President Truman's features.

Creek Street

Ketchikan's best-known and most-photographed section features wooden houses on pilings along Ketchikan Creek. A boardwalk connects the buildings and affords views of salmon and steelhead in the creek. Now a collection of tourist shops, Creek Street once

Dolly's House Museum on Creek Street

© DON PITCHER

housed the red-light district; during Prohibition it was the only place to buy booze. Jokesters call it "the only place where both salmon and men came up from the sea to spawn." By 1946 more than 30 "female boardinghouses" operated here. Prostitution on Creek Street was stopped in 1954, and the house of Dolly Arthur was eventually turned into the **Dolly's House Museum** (907/225-2279, open daily all summer, $4). Inside are antiques, liquor caches, and risqué photos. Born in 1888, Dolly moved to Ketchikan in 1919, and worked at the world's oldest profession for many decades. When she died in 1975, her obituary was featured in newspapers across the West. Dolly's is fun to tour with grandmothers who would never otherwise step foot in such a place, and the fascinating collection of memorabilia makes it well worth a visit.

A **funicular car** ($2; free if you hike up and ride down) connects Creek Street with Cape Fox Lodge, where you'll discover impressive vistas over Ketchikan and Tongass Narrows.

Totem Heritage Center

One of the highlights of the Ketchikan area, the Totem Heritage Center (907/225-5900, www.city.ketchikan.ak.us, daily 8 A.M.–5 P.M. May–Sept., Mon.–Fri. 1–5 P.M. the rest of the year, $5 adults, kids under 12 free) is a quarter-mile walk up Deermount Street. The center was established in 1976 to preserve a collection of 33 original totem poles and house posts retrieved from abandoned village sites. Unlike other totems in the area, these works are not brightly painted copies or restorations, but were carved more than a century ago to record Tlingit and Haida events and legends. Guides answer your questions and put on a short video about the totem recovery program. Surrounding the building is a short trail with signs identifying local plants. Out front is the Fog-Woman pole by noted carver Nathan Jackson.

Deer Mountain Hatchery and Eagle Center

This small hatchery along Ketchikan Creek is just across a footbridge from the Totem Heritage

Center. Signboards illustrate the process of breeding and rearing king and coho salmon, and visitors can feed the young fish. The hatchery is run by the **Ketchikan Indian Council** (907/225-5158, www.kictribe.org, daily 8 A.M.–4:30 P.M. May–Sept., $9), with educational tours and a video on the life cycle of salmon. A large enclosure houses two eagles with permanent injuries—you might even see them catching salmon.

King salmon arrive from the Pacific Ocean to spawn at the hatchery late in the summer; look for them in the creek. A **fish ladder** to help them get past the falls is visible from the Park Avenue bridge. If too many fish return to spawn, the state opens Ketchikan Creek to dipnet fishing by locals, creating an astounding scene. Thousands of pink (humpback, or "humpies") salmon also spawn in the creek each summer. Another good place to see spawning humpies is **Hoadly Creek,** a half-mile south of the ferry terminal.

◖ Totem Bight State Historical Park

Located eight miles northwest of the ferry terminal, Totem Bight (907/247-8574, www.alaskastateparks.org, free) has 15 Haida and Tlingit totems and a realistic replica of a clan house, complete with a brightly painted facade and cedar-scented interior. Be sure to pick up the brochure describing the poles and their meanings. The totems, carved 1938–1941, are modeled after older poles. They are surrounded by a stand of young hemlock trees and a gorgeous view across Tongass Narrows. Drop by the gift shop for details on the poles or the informative weekly tours. Don't miss free performances by the **Haida Descendant Dancers** here the second Friday of each month at 6:30 P.M. Access to Totem Bight is easy and cheap: city buses stop at Totem Bight hourly on weekdays.

Saxman

This Native village (ironically named for a white schoolteacher) is a 2.5-mile walk via a paved path, a $2 city bus ride, or a $12 taxi ride south of Ketchikan. Saxman (pop. 400)

is crowded with the largest collection of standing totem poles in the world—more than two dozen. Most were brought from their original sites in the 1930s and restored by Native Civilian Conservation Corps (CCC) workers; others came from a second restoration project in 1982. The oddest pole is topped with a figure of Abraham Lincoln, and commemorates the settlement of a war begun by the U.S. revenue cutter *Lincoln*. Probably the most photographed is the Rock Oyster Pole, which tells the story of a man who drowned after his hand became caught in a large oyster. Behind the poles is a cedar **Beaver Clan House,** open most days.

Adjacent to the totem park is a **carving shed** (free admission) where you'll find local artisans completing totems, masks, and other pieces. You're welcome to drop in whenever a carver is at work, which is most weekdays in the summer. Renowned carver Nathan Jackson can often be found working here. Interested in having a pole carved? Expect to pay at least $2,000 per linear foot.

Cape Fox Tours (907/225-4846, www.capefoxtours.com, $35) guides 1.5-hour tours that include a visit to the carving shed, a video on Tlingit culture, and a performance by the Cape Fox Dancers. Get tickets at the Ketchikan Visitor Center or the **Saxman Village Store** (907/225-4421), which sells a mix of wares, including some locally made totems, masks, carved pieces. Two blocks downhill is the **Saxman Arts Co-op** (907/225-4166), with historic photos and local pieces.

Ziplines

Eight miles south of town at Herring Cove is **Alaska Rainforest Sanctuary** (907/225-5503, www.alaskarainfroest.com), where a former lumber mill serves as headquarters for a series of seven high ziplines (longest is 850 ft.) and three suspension bridges through the treetops. Three-hour guided tours cost $149 per person, or $160 with round-trip transportation from town. A gift shop and a half-dozen reindeer (!) are at the old mill site, and a boardwalk leads along the creek—a good place to watch black bears fishing for salmon most summer evenings.

TOTEM POLES

These largest of all wooden sculptures were carved in cedar by the Tlingit, Haida, Tsimshian, Kwakiutl, and Bella Bella peoples of the Pacific Northwest. Their history is not completely known, but early explorers found poles in villages throughout Southeast Alaska. Apparently, totem-pole carving reached its heyday in the late 19th century with the arrival of metal woodworking tools. The animals, birds, fish, and marine mammals on the poles were totems that represented a clan, and in combination, conveyed a message.

Totem poles were very expensive and time-consuming to produce; a clan's status could be determined in part by the size and elaborateness of its poles. In a society without written words to commemorate people or events, the poles served a variety of purposes. Some totem poles told a family's history, others told local legends, and still others served to ridicule an enemy or debtor. In addition, totems were used to commemorate the dead, with a special niche at the back to hold the ashes of a revered ancestor.

Totem poles were never associated with religion, yet early missionaries destroyed many, and as recently as 1922, the Canadian government outlawed the art in an attempt to make the Natives more submissive. Realizing that a rich heritage was being lost because of neglect, skilled Native carvers worked with the Civilian Conservation Corps during the 1930s to restore older totems and create new ones. Today, active carving and restoration programs are taking place in Saxman, Ketchikan, Sitka, and Haines. Other good places to find totems include the Southeast towns of Hydaburg, Klawock, Kasaan, Juneau, Wrangell, and Kake.

Saxman Village is one of the best places to see totem poles.

ENTERTAINMENT AND EVENTS

A local theater group, First City Players (1716 Totem Way, 907/225-4792), puts on the light-hearted melodrama, *Fish Pirate's Daughter* Friday evenings in July. The show has been going on since 1966, and tickets cost $40 with an all-you-can eat crab dinner. Catch a movie downtown at the **Coliseum Twin Theater** (405 Mission St., 907/225-2294).

Ketchikan's live music scene changes each year, but something is always happening downtown; just follow your ears. **First City Saloon** (830 Water St., 907/225-1494) tends to bring in the better bands, and is the main dance spot in town. More rock at the **Arctic Bar** (907/225-4709), near the Front Street tunnel, where a pleasant patio hangs over Tongass Narrows. Shock your friends back home with one of its risqué baseball caps. If Dave Rubin and his rockin' Potlatch Band are playing at the **Potlatch Bar** (907/225-4855), next to Thomas Basin, make tracks in that direction. You won't regret it. The finest bar views are from **Cape Fox Lodge,** overlooking town above Creek Street. It's a nice place to get romantic.

Ketchikan's fun **4th of July** celebration includes the usual parade and fireworks, plus a **Timber Carnival** with ax throwing, pole climbing, and a variety of chainsaw contests, ending with a dramatic pole-felling event. In the first week of August, check out the **Blueberry Arts Festival,** complete with slug races, pie-eating contests, a fun run, arts and crafts exhibitions, and folk music. Ketchikan also has king and silver salmon fishing derbies and a halibut derby each summer. The **Winter Arts Faire** on the weekend after Thanksgiving is a good time to buy local arts and crafts. **Festival of the North** arrives in February, complete with music, art shows (including edible art!), and various workshops for the entire month.

SHOPPING

The **Spruce Mill Mall** is the primary focal point for shopping in downtown Ketchikan. Cruise ships dock directly in front, disgorging their passengers to feed the hungry cash registers of such places as Caribbean Gems or Tanzanite International. Needless to say, locals would never step foot in these jewelry stores owned and staffed by Outsiders cashing in on the tourists. Fortunately, many of the other downtown shops—including a number of places in Salmon Landing Marketplace—are locally owned and worth a visit.

Locals do much of their shopping at **Plaza Mall,** centering around Safeway and McDonald's, and the **Wal-Mart** (907/247-2156) five miles north of town. There's even a free summertime shuttle from downtown to Wal-Mart; it's mainly for cruise ship workers, but is also popular with cheapskate travelers

Arts and Crafts

A surprisingly creative town, Ketchikan is home to a number of fine artists. The center of Ketchikan's art action is the historic 5-Star building on Creek Street, where the artist Ray Troll holds down the fort at **Soho Coho** (907/225-5954 or 800/888-4070, www.trollart.cosm), with his weird and fishy T-shirts and prints. Other artists—including the wonderfully prolific printmaker Evon Zerbetz—also display their works here. The same building houses **Alaska Eagle Arts** (907/225-8365 or 800/308-2787, www.marvinoliver.com), with colorful T-shirts, jewelry, and prints, along with samples of the stunning Native designs by world-famous sculptor and printmaker Marvin Oliver.

Herring Cove Originals Studio and Gallery (229 Stedman St., 907/247-2693, www.sharronhuffman.com), has fish-print T-shirts and distinctive linocuts and block prints. Other downtown galleries worth a visit include **Exploration Gallery** (633 Mission St., 907/225-4278, www.explorationgallery.com), **Blue Heron Gallery** (123 Stedman St., 907/225-1982, www.blueheronalaska.com), **Eagle Spirit Gallery** (310 Mission St., 907/225-6626 or 866/867-0976, www.eaglespirit alaska.com), **Scanlon Gallery** (318 Mission St., 907/247-4730 or 888/228-4730, www .scanlongallery.com), **Crazy Wolf Studio** (607 Mission St., 907/225-9653 or 888/331-9653, www.crazywolfstudio.com), and **Dockside**

Gallery (907/225-2858, www.alaskanart.net) inside Salmon Landing.

For additional artwork, visit the **Mainstay Gallery** at the Ketchikan Area Arts & Humanities Council (716 Totem Way, 907/225-2211, www.ketchikanarts.org) near Creek Street. Exhibits change monthly, and they produce the *Ketchikan Arts Guide* with brief bios of local artists, plus descriptions of galleries, museums, and other places to find creative works. In the winter, their Monthly Grind brings fun events to the Saxman Tribal House.

RECREATION

The Ketchikan area is blessed with an abundance of hiking trails and remote wilderness cabins maintained by the U.S. Forest Service. If you arrive in Ketchikan unprepared for a cabin stay, **Alaskan Wilderness Outfitting** (907/225-7335, www.latitude56.com) rents outboard motors, coolers, stoves, and dishes (but not sleeping bags). It even has a "cabin outfit" set up with the supplies you'll need at a Forest Service cabin.

Take in a **panoramic view of Ketchikan** from the short trail that climbs from the high-point along Bypass Road (Forest Ave.). The road takes off from Schoenbar Road on the south end.

Deer Mountain

The best hike from Ketchikan is up to the 3,000-foot summit of Deer Mountain (6 miles round-trip). Begin by heading a half-mile uphill from Deermount and Fair streets. Take the first left—the road to Ketchikan Lakes, source of the city's drinking water—and then an immediate right to the trailhead. The trail climbs along an excellent but strenuous path through dense Sitka spruce and western hemlock forests. There's an incredible view in all directions from the top of Deer Mountain, but right into July you'll have to cross snowbanks to reach the summit. (Rain gear works fine for sledding down again.)

Just before the final climb to the peak, a trail to the left leads around the north slope and on to tiny **Blue Lake** and **John Mountain** (3,238 ft.). Entirely above the tree line, this portion

Ketchikan, with Deer Mountain in the background

© DON PITCHER

can be hazardous for inexperienced hikers. Carry a map and compass since it's easy to become disoriented if the clouds drop down. Ambitious hikers can do a 12-mile trek over the top, ending at Beaver Falls powerhouse, at the end of South Tongass Highway. Free **shelter cabins** (no reservations) are atop Deer Mountain and at Blue Lake; get current trail info at the Discovery Center.

Ward Lake Area

Several good trails are near the Forest Service campground at Ward Lake, eight miles north of downtown via Revilla Road. The 1.3-mile **Ward Lake Nature Trail** is an easy loop with interpretive signs and good summertime fishing for steelhead and salmon. **Ward Creek Trail** starts across from the day-use area and follows the creek 2.5 miles to Last Chance Campground. It's built for wheelchairs, with a couple of short spur paths leading to platforms over this beautiful creek.

Perseverance Trail climbs two miles to Perseverance Lake following a "stairway-to-heaven" boardwalk, passing through several muskegs along the way. Beyond this, you can take the **Minerva Mountain Trail** all the way to Carlanna Lake. Contact the Forest Service for details on the latter since this is a newly built trail.

Settler's Cove State Recreation Site, 16 miles north of Ketchikan, has a one-mile trail through the rainforest, with a pretty waterfall and spawning pink salmon in mid-summer.

Nearby Cabins

The Naha River watershed, 20 miles north of Ketchikan, contains one of the finest trail and cabin systems in the Southeast. The river once supported astounding runs of sockeye salmon and is still a popular salmon, steelhead, and trout fishing area for locals. At one time the town of **Loring** (established 1888) at its mouth had the world's largest fish cannery and was the main point of entry into Alaska. Today, it's a tiny settlement of retirees and vacation homes. **Heckman Lake,** six miles upriver, supported the world's largest and most costly

salmon hatchery at the turn of the century. The hatchery failed, however, and all that remains are the overgrown ruins.

The pleasant six-mile **Naha River Trail** begins at Naha Bay, follows the shore of Roosevelt Lagoon, then climbs gently up to Jordon and Heckman Lakes. At the mouth of Roosevelt Lagoon is an interesting salt chuck where the direction of water flow changes with the tides. Covered picnic tables are nearby. More picnic tables are two miles up the trail at a small waterfall—a good place to watch black bears catching salmon late in the summer. There's a Forest Service cabin on Jordan Lake and two cabins on Heckman Lake (one wheelchair accessible); all three have rowboats and cost $35. Reservations can be made at 518/885-3639 or 877/444-6777, or online at www.reserveusa.com. Access to the Naha area is by sea kayak, floatplane, or skiff. Contact **Knudsen Cove Marina** (907/225-8500 or 800/528-2486; www.knudsoncovemarina.com) for skiff rentals or dropoffs.

Lake Shelokum, 40 miles north of Ketchikan, has a free three-sided shelter near a hot springs. A two-mile trail stretches from the shelter to Bailey Bay, passing the scenic lake and an impressive waterfall. Other cabins well worth visiting include **Lake McDonald, Reflection Lake, Helm Creek,** and **Blind Pass.** Get details at the Discovery Center in Ketchikan.

Sea Kayaking and Canoeing

The Discovery Center has detailed information on sea kayaking in the waters near Ketchikan, including Misty Fiords and a circumnavigation of Revilla Island. **Southeast Sea Kayaks** (907/225-1258 or 800/287-1607, www.kayakketchikan.com) leads a variety of kayak trips, starting with a 2.5-hour paddle along Tongass Narrows ($79), and a four-hour trip ($149) that includes a boat ride to a cove on Gravina Island and the chance to explore this quiet area by kayak. An all-day trip to Misty Fjords ($389) includes the boat ride over and back, lunch, and four hours of paddling.

Southeast Exposure (515 Water St.,

907/225-8829, www.southeastexposure.com) has easy paddles for the cruise ship crowd, including a 2.5-hour waterfront tour ($50), and a 4-hour trip to Tatoosh Islands ($76) by bus, boat, and kayak. Both companies also offer multi-day trips to Misty Fiords and kayak rentals.

Ketchikan Parks and Recreation Department (2721 7th Ave., 907/225-9579) rents canoes and sports equipment, as well as skis and snowshoes in the winter.

Fishing, Boating, and Diving

Many Ketchikan companies offer charter fishing trips in search of salmon or halibut; see the visitors bureau for a complete listing. Rent skiffs and fishing gear to head out on your own from **Knudsen Cove Marina** (13 miles north of town, 907/247-8500 or 800/528-2486, www.knudsoncovemarina.com) If you're just looking to try your luck with all the locals who fish from the Creek Street bridge, rent a pole a block away from the little stand across from the Federal Building. **Mountain Point,** 5.5 miles south of Ketchikan, is a good spot to try your luck at salmon fishing from the shore.

The **Ketchikan Yacht Club** (907/225-3262, www.ketchikanyachtclub.org) sponsors low-key races on Wednesdays at 5:30 P.M. in the summer, and the skippers are always looking for volunteer crew. It's a fun way to sail with the locals for free.

ACCOMMODATIONS

For an up-to-date listing of local lodging places, browse over to the Ketchikan Visitors Bureau website (www.visit-ketchikan.com).

Hostel

The **Ketchikan Youth Hostel** (907/225-3319, June–Aug.), downtown in the basement of the Methodist church at Grant and Main, costs $15. It's open 6 P.M.–9 A.M., and the doors are locked at 11 P.M. If your ferry gets in after that, call the hostel promptly upon arrival and they'll open for you. The hostel isn't fancy—we're talking simple cots—but is friendly and clean, with kitchen facilities and showers. It's a good place to meet other budget travelers. There's a four-night maximum stay.

Hotels and Motels

Built in the 1930s and now on the National Register of Historic Places, the centrally located **Gilmore Hotel** (326 Front St., 907/225-9423 or 800/275-9423, www.gilmorehotel.com), exudes an old-fashioned ambience, but has been updated with modern furnishings. Rates are reasonable: $120 d for cramped rooms, $130 d for larger rooms with two beds and a harbor view, or $140 d for the suites. Amenities include courtesy van service, a light breakfast, free Wi-Fi, and parking. Rooms over the bar may get noisy at night.

Cozy **❰ New York Hotel** (207 Stedman St., 907/225-0246 or 866/225-0246, www.thenewyorkhotel.com) has been painstakingly restored to its Roaring '20s heyday. It's a great location—facing the harbor and just a few steps off Creek Street—and the downstairs café is one of the best in town. Free airport and ferry shuttles, too. The eight rooms in the historic main building are small but nicely furnished: $109 s or $119 d with private baths and queen beds. Also available are four luxury suites with covered waterside decks along Creek Street for $179 d (plus $15 for each additional guest). The latter units feature lofts with spiral stairs, full kitchens, and jetted tubs. Book early for the popular suites.

The Narrows Inn (907/247-2600 or 888/686-2600, www.narrowsinn.com, $130–145 d) sits four miles north of Ketchikan along Tongass Narrows. Rooms are small, but modern, bright, and nicely appointed. Free Wi-Fi and continental breakfast too. Waterside rooms (ask for room 1209) have small balconies where you can watch the parade of boats and planes, and three larger suites are available. A steak and seafood restaurant is also on the premises, and the staff is very accommodating.

Ketchikan's largest lodging place, **Best Western Landing** (3434 Tongass Ave., 907/225-5166 or 800/428-8304, www.landing hotel.com) sits right across from the ferry terminal. The 107 rooms are newly refurbished and include microwaves and fridges; $180 s or $190 d in standard rooms, $210 s or $220 d for suites. Also on the premises are two restaurants, a fitness center, courtesy van, and free Wi-Fi.

At the top end of Ketchikan's lodging spectrum is the elaborate **Cape Fox Lodge** (800 Venetia Way, 907/225-8001 or 866/225-8001, www.capefoxlodge.com, $200 d, $251 d for a two-room suite). This attractive hilltop hotel overlooks Tongass Narrows, and has spacious, modern rooms. A funicular car takes guests to the Cape Fox from Creek Street.

Fishing Lodges

Many fishing lodges can be found in the Ketchikan area, particularly on nearby Prince of Wales Island; see www.visit-ketchikan.com for a complete listing.

Located 17 miles north of Ketchikan, **Salmon Falls Resort** (907/225-2752 or 800/247-9059, www.salmonfallsresort.net, open mid-May–mid-Sept.), has modern rooms and a dramatic shoreside setting. Fishing packages start at $1,100 per person for three nights, or $1,550 with a guide.

Yes Bay Lodge (907/225-7906 or 800/999-0784, www.yesbay.com) is a remote fishing lodge near Lake McDonald on the Cleveland Peninsula north of Ketchikan. The setting is wonderful, and the fishing is great, most notably a famous steelhead stream adjacent to the property. Rates start at $6,000 d for a four-night all-inclusive package.

Also check out **Naha Bay Outdoor Adventures** (907/247-4453, www.nahabay outdooradventures.com), a 20-minute boat ride from Knudson Cove Marina. Good fishing, hiking, sea kayaking, and more, starting at $1,800 d for three nights.

B&Bs and Vacation Rentals

You'll find links to Ketchikan B&Bs at www.visit-ketchikan.com, or contact **Ketchikan Reservation Service** (907/247-5337 or 800/987-5337, www.ketchikan-lodging.com) or **Alaska Travelers** (907/247-7117 or 800/928-3308, www.alaskatravelers.com) for assistance in booking a room, cabin, or guest house.

Captain's Quarters B&B (325 Lund St., 907/225-4912, www.ptialaska.net/~captbnb, $100–110 d) has three rooms with private baths, harbor views, and continental breakfasts; no kids.

Two miles north of the ferry terminal, **Black Bear Inn B&B** (907/225-4343, www.stayinalaska.com, $150 d) is an elegant, newly built four-bedroom house with an outdoor hot tub, plenty of privacy, and tall windows facing Tongass Narrows. A separate apartment ($200 d) on the top floor has its own entrance and porch. A make-it-yourself breakfast is provided.

Lundberg's South Shore Inn (907/225-0909, $125 d with continental breakfast), has a private two-bedroom apartment with kitchenette, woodstove, large deck, and private beach. The very comfortable home is seven miles southeast of town near Mountain Point.

Located four miles south of town, and right on the water, **Anchor Inn by the Sea** (907/247-7117 or 800/928-3308, www.alaskatravelers.com, $125–135 d) is a fine option for families, with three large suites with kitchenettes. All of these feature private baths and entrances. A five-night minimum stay is required.

Located close to downtown, **Madame's Manor** (324 Cedar St., 907/247-2774 or 877/531-8159, ext. 2484, www.madamesmanor .com, $149–169 d) is a hillside B&B with three lavish Victorian-style suites with private baths. The deck overlooks the harbor and Tongass Narrows, making this a delightful spot to sip your tea or enjoy a filling gourmet breakfast. Also available are two downstairs apartments ($115–125 d, $25 for additional guests) that are popular with families; breakfast not included. A two-night minimum is required.

Located along picturesque George Inlet eight miles south of Ketchikan, **Waypoint Inn at Herring Bay** (907/225-8605, www.way pointinn.com, $175 d) is a studio apartment with a big deck for relaxing and a full kitchen. There is a minimum four-night stay.

Alaska's Hidden Cove Vacation Rentals (907/225-7934, www.akhiddencove.com) has two lovely places north of town: a three-bedroom home ($210 d; 4-night minimum) and a one-bedroom suite ($125 d; 3-night minimum).

CAMPING

There are no campsites in town, but the Forest Service operates two summer-only campgrounds ($10) in the scenic Ward Lake area—a world away from the craziness of downtown Ketchikan when the cruise ships are in port. Get there by heading five miles north from the ferry terminal and turning right up Revilla Road. Ward Cove is a good place to see eagles, so stop for a look before heading to the lake. The most popular camping area is scenic **Signal Creek Campground,** along Ward Lake. Another mile and a half north is **Last Chance Campground.** Both campgrounds have running water, and can be reserved (518/885-3639 or 877/444-6777, www.reserveusa.com, $9 extra).

Settler's Cove State Recreation Site (16 miles north of the ferry, $10) has campsites beneath the trees. The beach is a popular spot for summer picnics, and a trail takes you through the rainforest to a small waterfall.

Clover Pass Resort (907/247-2234 or 800/410-2234, www.cloverpassresort.com, open mid-May–Sept.), 15 miles north of Ketchikan, has RV hookups for $29–31, plus a restaurant on the premises.

FOOD
Breakfast and Lunch

Housed within the historic New York Hotel, the bizarrely named **That One Place Cafe/ The Other Place Lounge** (207 Stedman St., 907/225-8646) has big windows facing Thomas Basin Harbor. Lunchtime salads, soups, and sandwiches give way to a $5-per-plate tapas menu in the evening, including chicken satay, gorgonzola fries, coconut prawns, and tempura vegetables to name a few.

Dockside Diner (1287 Tongass Ave., 907/247-7787) is a hometown place with burgers, halibut and chips, hot beef sandwiches, liver and onions, and fried chicken, plus a big

selection of pies. Breakfast is available all day, and the covered deck provides a view of busy Tongass Narrows and escape from the thick cigarette smoke inside.

Located right across from the ferry terminal, **The Landing Restaurant** (3434 Tongass Ave., 907/225-5166), fills with locals and travelers in search of a filling breakfast.

A fine little fish and chips stand called **Alaskan Surf** attracts tourists and locals to its shipside location on the downtown dock. An order of halibut and fries is $11. It's owned by the folks from Bar Harbor Restaurant, so you know the fish is fresh and tasty. Find the best local chicken sandwiches, salmon burgers, and hamburgers at the tiny **Burger Queen** (907/225-6060) just north of the Front Street tunnel. **McDonald's** is in the Plaza Mall 0.75 mile south of the ferry, and the local **Subway** (415 Dock St.) is downtown.

Coffee and Sweets

Several places serve espresso downtown, but the best is probably **Ketchikan Coffee Company** right on the dock. If you just want to relax and enjoy looking over busy Tongass Narrows, stop by **Coffee Connections** (521 Water St., 907/247-0521) for a cup of espresso or a pastry. **KetchiCandies** (315 Mission St., 907/225-0900 or 800/225-0970, www.ketchicandies.com) makes hand-dipped chocolates, and will ship your purchases.

Dinner

Upstairs in the Spruce Mill Mall, **Steamers** (907/225-1600, $15–40) is a large and noisy tourist restaurant where you'll find fresh seafood, pasta, and steaks, along with 31 brews (half of these Alaskan beers) on draft. The featured attraction is crab (all you can eat for $30), but all the seafood is good, and servings are ample. Try the po' boy oyster sandwich, chicken pasta, or seafood tacos. Make reservations for a window seat facing Tongass Narrows, though the view is usually blocked by one of those honking cruise ships.

Ocean View Restaurant (1831 Tongass Ave., 907/225-7566, $11–20) is a favorite of locals, and with good reason. The food is varied and nicely prepared, the atmosphere is classy, prices are reasonable, and delivery is free. The menu encompasses pasta (including halibut fettuccine), steaks, seafood, burgers, and best-in-town pizzas, but Mexican dishes are the real attraction, and all meals come with chips and a dose of Mexican tunes over the speakers.

Next to the footbridge on the north end of Creek Street, **Good Fortune Chinese Restaurant** (907/225-1818) has upstairs seating overlooking the water. It's authentically Chinese, but also reasonable, including a $7 lunch of sweet and sour pork or spicy Kung Pao chicken. A la carte dinners are $12–14. Service is quick and friendly, but the setting is unpretentious. Not far away—and also overlooking the creek—**On's Thai House** (127 Stedman St., 907/225-8424)—serves Thai and Chinese dishes.

Fine Dining

With its 1920s-style decor, **Annabelle's Keg and Chowder House** (326 Front St., 907/225-6009, www.gilmorehotel.com) wins the "best atmosphere" prize among Ketchikan restaurants. The menu features seafood (including four kinds of chowders), steaks, salads, and sandwiches, along with prime rib on weekends. There are daily specials, plus cocktails, espresso, and a jukebox. Located in the historic Gilmore Hotel, this is a good place to impress a friend.

◖ Bar Harbor Restaurant (2813 Tongass Ave., 907/225-2813, www.barharborketchikan.com, $16–25) fills a tiny building south of the ferry terminal, and the back deck provides outdoor dining with a view of this busy harbor if it isn't raining too hard. The food is dependably good, and includes such specialties as clams a la Karl, bleu steak salad, crab cakes, and weekend prime rib. Free Wi-Fi too. Open Monday–Saturday for dinner only; reservations recommended.

Héen Kahídi Restaurant and Lounge (800 Venetia Way, 907/225-8001, www.capefoxlodge.com, $20–40) inside Cape Fox Lodge, serves seafood and steak dinners—try the

pepper steak or halibut Olympia—in a quiet and romantic setting. Reserve ahead to get a window seat for an evening sunset over town.

Located 17 miles north of Ketchikan, **Salmon Falls Resort** (907/225-2752 or 800/247-9059, www.salmonfallsresort.net, dinners May–Sept. only) is a large octagonal restaurant specializing in steaks and seafood, with blackened halibut, king crab, steaks, lobster, and other filling fare for $22–36. The building vaults 40 feet overhead, with an impressive waterfall and views across Clover Passage.

Groceries

The closest grocery store to the ferry is **Alaskan & Proud Market** (907/225-1279 or 800/770-8258) right across the road, while **Safeway**, 0.75 mile south of the ferry, has a salad bar and the biggest selection of groceries. **Tatsuda's IGA** (633 Stedman, 907/225-4125) is on the south edge of town.

Salmon Etc. (907/225-6008 or 800/354-7256 outside Alaska, www.salmonetc.com), has two locations: on Creek Street, and downtown at 322 Mission Street. It sells high-quality canned, smoked, or frozen salmon, halibut, crab, clams, and other sea critters.

INFORMATION AND SERVICES

The two primary information centers are the Ketchikan Visitors Bureau and the Southeast Alaska Discovery Center, described in *Sights*. Forest Service offices for **Ketchikan and Misty Fiords** ranger districts (3031 Tongass Ave., 907/225-2148, www.fs.fed.us/r10/tongass) are a half-mile south of the ferry terminal.

Showers are available at **Highliner Laundromat** (2703 Tongass Ave.) and **Thomas Wash Basin** (989 Stedman St.). A better option is to head up Madison Street to the **high school swimming pool** (2610 4th Ave., 907/225-2010), where a swim, sauna, and shower cost $5.

Get fast cash from ATMs at First Bank and Wells Fargo downtown, and at the Safeway and A&P grocery stores.

The main post office is next to the ferry terminal on the north end of town, and a branch post office is downtown in the Great Alaskan Clothing Company (422 Mission St.).

Ketchikan General Hospital (3100 Tongass Ave., 907/225-5171, www.peacehealth.org) is the largest in southern Southeast Alaska. **Ketchikan Medical Clinic** (3612 Tongass Ave., 907/225-5144) is out near the ferry terminal.

Books and Internet Access

Ketchikan's woefully small **public library** (629 Dock St., 907/225-3331, www.firstcitylibraries. org) is a great place to relax, with big windows overlooking Ketchikan Creek. Unfortunately, this may be the only Alaskan library where the computer terminals are off-limits to non-residents.

A book-lover's bookstore, **Parnassus Bookstore** (907/225-7690) is upstairs above Soho Coho on Creek Street. Sit down and talk with the friendly owner, Lillian Ference, about the latest Ketchikan news. Parnassus stocks an especially impressive collection of women's books. The other bookstore in town is **Waldenbooks** (907/225-8120) in Plaza Mall.

Surf the web for a fee at **Seaport CyberStation** (Salmon Landing Mall, 907/247-4615 or 888/295-0965, www.seaport cyber.com) or **The Crows Nest** (308 Grant St., 907/225-6119) next to the tunnel. Quite a few places have free Wi-Fi; try Annabelle's Restaurant, The Edge (Salmon Landing Mall), Thomas Basin Harbor, plus the airport and the ferry terminal.

GETTING THERE
Ferry

Ketchikan's ferry terminal is two miles northwest of downtown, and is open Monday–Friday 9 A.M.–4:30 P.M. and when ships are in port. Call 907/225-6182 or 907/225-6181 for recorded arrival and departure times. During the summer, ferries provide almost-daily runs to Prince Rupert, Metlakatla, Wrangell, and points north. Ferry service to Bellingham is once a week. Contact the **Alaska Marine Highway** (907/465-3941 or 800/642-0066, www.ferryalaska.com) for the current schedule and prices.

The **Inter-Island Ferry Authority** (907/826-4848 or 866/308-4848, www .interislandferry.com) operates from the same building, with daily service to Hollis on Prince of Wales Island.

Air

Ketchikan Airport is on Gravina Island, directly across Tongass Narrows from the ferry terminal. In 2005, Ketchikan became a national laughingstock when Alaska's congressional delegation rammed through a bill that included funding for a pair of bridges to the otherwise-uninhabited island. The notorious "bridge to nowhere" became a national symbol of pork barrel politics before the funding was hurriedly cut off. There really isn't a need for bridges since an **airport ferry** (907/225-6800, $4 one-way plus $6 for vehicles) operates every half-hour daily 6:15 A.M.–9:30 P.M. Several companies provide van service from the airport to downtown for around $20 (including ferry fare). If you're heading downtown and don't have a rental car, a better option is the **Tongass Water Taxi** (907/225-8294); Rich Schuerger takes you directly from the airport to Thomas Basin in the heart of Ketchikan for $18 s or $25 d. He meets most flights and can be found next to the baggage claim.

Alaska Airlines (800/426-0333, www .alaskaair.com) has flights from Ketchikan to Juneau, Petersburg, Sitka, Wrangell, and other cities in Alaska and the Lower 48.

Three air taxi operators, **ProMech Air** (907/225-3845 or 800/860-3845, www .promechair.com), **Pacific Airways** (907/225-3500 or 877/360-3500, www.fly pacificairways.com), and **Taquan Air** (907/225-8800 or 800/770-8800, www.taquanair.com), have daily service to Prince of Wales Island and Metlakatla, while **L.A.B. Flying Service** (907/772-4300, www.labflying.com) flies from Ketchikan airport to Klawock.

ProMech, Pacific Airways, and Taquan also do flightseeing trips around Ketchikan. Other air taxi operators include **Carlin Air** (907/225-3036 or 888/594-3036, www.carlinair.com), **Family Air Tours** (907/247-1305 or 800/380-1305, www.familyairtours.com), **Island Wings Air Service** (907/225-2444 or 888/854-2444, www.islandwings.com), **Misty Fjords Air and Outfitting** (1285 Tongass Ave., 907/225-5155 or 877/228-4656, www.mistyfjordsair.com), **Alaska Seaplane Tours** (907/225-1974 or 866/858-2327, www.alaskaseaplanetours .com), **Seawind Aviation** (907/225-1206 or 877/225-1203, www.seawindaviation.com), and **Southeast Aviation** (907/225-2900 or 888/359-6478, www.southeastaviation.com). Especially popular is a two-hour flightseeing trip to Misty Fiords National Monument that includes a landing on a lake for around $220. Some of these companies include a half-hour on land as part of the tour, providing a good chance to stretch your legs and take in the wild country.

GETTING AROUND

The Bus (907/225-8726, www.borough.ketchikan.ak.us, $2 each direction) runs throughout Ketchikan, south to Saxman, and north to Totem Bight approximately every hour daily 7 A.M.–7 P.M. Schedules are available at the visitors bureau and ferry terminal, or find a bus stop and wait.

The local taxi companies are **Alaska Cab Co.** (907/225-2133), **Sourdough Cab** (907/225-5544, www.ketchikantaxicabtours.com), and

Yellow Taxi (907/225-5555). They charge about $11 from the ferry to downtown, $12 from downtown to Saxman, or $75 an hour for tours (up to six people).

Tours

The downtown visitors bureau houses booths from companies promoting their trips, including two-hour city tours for $30. Most of these—including an embarrassing "Duck Tour"—are for cruise ship travelers. Also popular are two-hour waterfront cruises offered by **Alaska Cruises** (907/225-6044 or 800/228-1905, www.mistyfjord.net, $50 adults, $25 kids) and visits to Saxman village from **Cape Fox Tours** (907/225-4846, www.capefoxtours.com, $35).

Car Rentals

Because Ketchikan's sights are so spread out, renting a car is a good idea. Rental rates (with unlimited miles) are around $60 from **Alaska Car Rental** (2828 N. Tongass Ave., 907/225-5000 or 800/662-0007, www .akcarrental.com) and **Budget** (4950 N. Tongass Ave., 907/225-6004 or 800/478-2438, www.budget.com). Both companies have cars at the airport and on the Ketchikan side of Tongass Narrows; it's a $6 ferry ride each way to transport a vehicle.

Vicinity of Ketchikan

⟨ MISTY FIORDS NATIONAL MONUMENT

The 2.2-million-acre Misty Fiords National Monument is the largest national forest wilderness in the United States, covering the east side of Revillagigedo Island, the adjacent mainland all the way to the Canadian border, and the long narrow Behm Canal that separates island and mainland. Misty contains a diversity of gorgeous scenery—glaciers, rainforests, narrow fjords, and rugged mountains—but is best known for the spectacular cliffs that rise as much as 3,000 feet from the ocean. Almost unknown until its establishment in 1978, Misty Fiords is today one of the highlights of an Alaskan trip for many visitors. Be forewarned, however, it's an expensive highlight.

The name "Misty" comes from the wet and cloudy conditions that predominate throughout the summer. Rainfall averages almost 160 inches per year, so be sure to bring rubber boots and raingear. Because of all this rain the land exhibits a verdant beauty, even when clouds drape the mountain slopes.

Flightseeing and Boat Tours

On any given summer day, flightseeing planes constantly take off from Tongass Narrows for trips over the monument. One-hour-and-fifteen-minute flightseeing trips cost around $220 (including a water landing) and are offered by all the local air taxis listed in *Getting Around.*

Another excellent way to see Misty is by boat from either **Alaska Cruises** (907/225-6044 or 800/228-1905, www.mistyfjord.net, 6.5 hrs., $130 adults, $80 kids) or **Allen Marine Tours** (907/225-8100 or 877/686-8100, www.allenmarinetours.com, 4 hrs., $149 adults, $99 kids). Both companies oper-

floatplane and cruise ship, Tongass Narrows

© DON PITCHER

ate catamaran cruises into Misty Fiords in the summer. Along the way, the boats pass towering cliffs, peaceful coves, and dramatic New Eddystone Rock, which juts straight out of the water from a tiny island in the midst of Behm Canal. The tours turn around in Rudyerd Bay before returning to Ketchikan. A delicious and filling lunch is included, and the onboard naturalist is exceptionally knowledgeable. When the weather cooperates, this is one of the best side trips you can take anywhere in Alaska. Alaska Cruises also offers a faster 3.5-hour trip—most folks choose this version—that includes a flightseeing return to Ketchikan (or vice versa) for $260 adults or $220 kids.

Sea Kayaking Tours

The best way to see Misty Fiords is from a kayak. You can paddle there from Ketchikan, but only if you're experienced and adequately prepared. Two Ketchikan companies offer guided, multi-day sea kayaking trips in Misty Fiords: **Southeast Sea Kayaks** (907/225-1258 or 800/287-1067, www.kayakketchikan.com) and **Southeast Exposure** (907/225-8829, www.southeastexposure.com). Both companies also rent kayaks and set up transportation into Misty for those who prefer to paddle independently. Kayakers should be warned that flightseeing planes and cruise ships may impact your wilderness experience in Rudyerd Bay, but other areas get far less use.

Hiking and Cabins

Misty Fiords National Monument has 14 recreation cabins (518/885-3639 or 877/444-6777, www.reserveusa.com, $35). Those near magnificent **Rudyerd Bay** are very popular, and reservations must be made months in advance. There are also 10 trails that take you from saltwater to scenic lakes, most with cabins or free three-sided shelters. Two of the best trails lead up to shelters at Punchbowl and Nooya Lakes. The three-quarter-mile **Punchbowl Lake Trail** switchbacks up from Rudyerd Bay, passing spectacular Punchbowl Creek Waterfall on the way. Punchbowl is one of the finest short hikes in Southeast Alaska, and there's a canoe and

skiff at the lake. Both brown and black bears may be encountered on any of these trails, so be certain to make plenty of noise and to hang all food.

Before heading out on any overnight trips into Misty, talk with staff at the District Office (1817 Tongass, 907/225-2148, www.fs.fed. us/r10/tongass). They can provide information on trail conditions, campsites, and what to expect. Be sure to request a copy of their Misty Fiords map.

METLAKATLA

Twelve miles southwest of Ketchikan on the western shore of Annette Island is the community of Metlakatla (pop. 1,500). Metlakatla (it means "saltwater channel" in Tsimshian) is Alaska's only Indian reservation, a status that was reaffirmed in 1971 when its residents refused to join other Native groups under the Alaska Native Claims Settlement Act. This quiet, conservative town—the only predominantly Tsimshian settlement in Alaska—has a strong religious heritage and the air of a pioneer village. Large frame houses occupy big corner lots, while vacant lots yield abundant berry crops. There seems to be a church on every corner—eight in all, none of them Catholic. Metlakatla boasts a flourishing cannery, cold-storage facility, fish hatchery, rock quarry, and a sawmill. Most of Annette Island is wooded, mountainous terrain reaching up to 3,500 feet, but the town of Metlakatla spreads out across a large, relatively flat portion of the island that contains many muskegs and lakes. Although Metlakatla is only a dozen miles away from Ketchikan, it gets 118 inches of precipitation per year, 44 inches less than Ketchikan.

History

In 1887, a Tsimshian Indian group left Canada in search of religious freedom in Alaska. They discovered an abandoned Tlingit settlement on Annette Island offering a sheltered bay, gently sloping beaches, and a beautiful nearby waterfall. Under the direction of Anglican missionary William Duncan (who established a similar community in Metlakatla, Canada), 823 Tsimshian

Yellow Hill on Annette Island, near Metlakatla

followers began clearing a town site. The converts took new Christian names, dressed in suits, and abandoned much of their cultural heritage. At Metlakatla, Alaska, the settlers established a sawmill to produce lumber for the construction of houses and the first cannery.

The most ambitious building erected was a 1,000-seat church, "The Westminster Abbey of Alaska." It burned in 1948 but was replaced by a replica six years later. In 1891, the U.S. Congress granted the Tsimshians the entire 86,000-acre island as a reservation, a right they jealously guard to this day. Duncan maintained his hold over most aspects of life here until 1913 when a government school opened. (Duncan's paternalism extended in other directions, too: Rumors persist that the bachelor fathered many Metlakatla children.) He opposed the school, preferring that education remain in the hands of his church. The ensuing conflict led to intervention by the U.S. Department of the Interior in 1915, which seized the sawmill, cannery, and other facilities that had been under his personal control. Duncan died

three years later, but his memory is still revered by many, and his influence can still be seen in the healthy little Indian settlement of today. For a fascinating account of Father Duncan and the two Metlakatlas, read Peter Murray's *The Devil and Mr. Duncan* (Sono Nis Press, Victoria, B.C.).

During World War II, the U.S. Army constructed a major military base seven miles from Metlakatla on Annette Island. The base included observation towers (to search for Japanese subs), a large airfield, hangars, communications towers, shore batteries, and housing for 10,000 men. At the time the airport was built, it was the most expensive one ever constructed by the government—everything kept sinking out of sight into the muskeg. Until construction of an airport on Gravina Island in 1973, this airfield was used for jet service to Ketchikan, forcing passengers to land on Annette and fly by floatplane to Ketchikan. With the area's notorious weather, delays were common; many times it took longer to get the last dozen miles to Ketchikan than the 600 miles from

Seattle to Annette Island. Today, the Air Force is slowly constructing a 14-mile road across the northern end of the island to what will eventually (possibly by 2010) become a new dock for the ferry to Ketchikan.

Sights and Events

Father Duncan's Cottage (907/886-8687)—where the missionary lived from 1894 until his death in 1918—is open as a museum when cruise ships are in port or by appointment. The old photographs of Metlakatla and the fascinating assortment of personal items owned by Duncan make a stop here a must. Unique items housed within these walls include old glass fire extinguishers, an 1890 flag with 38 stars, and the second Edison phonograph ever made. Operated by a sewing machine treadle, it was given to Duncan by Edison. Duncan's tiny bed (he stood just over five ft. tall), old medical books, and medicines line the wall. The rather run-down **William Duncan Memorial Church** (built in 1954) stands at the corner of 4th Avenue and Church Street. Duncan's grave is on the left side.

A traditional **longhouse** (open Mon.–Fri. afternoons in summer) has been erected on the waterfront to stimulate local arts and crafts and to help recover the cultural traditions lost because of Duncan's missionary zeal. The back of the building has three totem poles, and the front is decorated with Tsimshian designs. Native dance performances take place when cruise ships are in port. Inside is a small library and a model of one of the floating fish traps that were used on the island for many years. An adjacent **Artists' Village** has booths selling locally made crafts, and is open when cruise ships are in port.

Metlakatla Tours (907/886-8687, www.metlakatlatours.net) leads tours that include the Duncan house, artist village, and a dance performance at the longhouse. These often fill with cruise ship folks, but space may be available if you call ahead.

Locals celebrate the establishment of Metlakatla each year on **Founder's Day,** August 7. As with most other American towns, Metlakatla also has a parade and other events on the 4th of July.

Recreation

Unlike almost everywhere else in Alaska, there are no bears on Annette Island, a relief to those who fear encounters with bruins. A short hiking trail runs from the corner of Milton Street and Airport Road on the southeast edge of town along **Skaters Lake,** a large pond where native plants and ducks can be observed. **Yellow Hill,** a 540-foot-tall fragment of 150 million-year-old sandstone, is unique in Southeast Alaska. The rock is rich in iron and magnesium, giving it a lovely desert-like yellow color set off by gnarled old lodgepole pines. An easy boardwalk trail (20 min. each way) leads up to its summit where you catch panoramic vistas of the western side of Annette, along with the snowcapped peaks of nearby Prince of Wales Island. Get there by walking or hitching 1.5 miles south from town on Airport Road to the signed trailhead on the right side. Some people claim to see George Washington's profile in a nearby mountain visible from Yellow Hill.

Two trails access alpine lakes in the mountains east of Metlakatla. The **Chester Lake Trail** starts at the end of the road, 0.25 mile beyond the ferry terminal. From the trail you get views over the impressive **Chester Lake Falls,** which first attracted Duncan's flock to Annette Island. The trail climbs steeply up steps and a slippery path along a waterline used for power generation. Plan on 45 minutes to reach beautiful Chester Lake, where there's a small dam. From this point, the country is above the tree line and it's possible to climb along several nearby ridges for even better views. Good camping sites are available, but be careful coming up the steep, slippery path with a pack.

Farther afield and not quite as scenic is the **Purple Lake Trail.** Take Airport Road four miles south of town and turn left near the Quonset huts at the unmarked Purple Mountain Road. Follow it two miles to the power plant. The unmarked trail heads directly up a steep jeep road. After a 30-minute climb, you reach a saddle and from there you can head up adjacent ridges into the alpine or drop down to Purple Lake (10 min.). Another place worth a look is the aptly named **Sand Dollar Beach** on the southwest end of the island. Ask locally for directions.

The flat country around Metlakatla contains a labyrinth of dirt roads built during World War II, and if you have a mountain bike or car, they're well worth exploring. You'll find abandoned structures of all types: huge communications towers, strangely quiet empty hangars, old gun emplacements, and a major airport with no planes. From the south end of the road network are excellent views of Prince of Wales and Duke Islands, as well as the open sea beyond Dixon Entrance. This is the southernmost road in Alaska.

Accommodations and Food

Metlakatla Hotel and Suites (3rd Ave. and Lower Milton St., 907/886-3456, www .metlakatlainn.com, $98 s or d) has standard motel rooms with microwaves, fridges, and a guest computer. Meals and car rentals are available.

Tuck'em Inn B&B (907/886-6611, www.alaskanow.com/tuckem-inn, $75 s or $85 d) has six comfortable and well-kept bedrooms in two houses on the same street. A continental breakfast is included.

Get huge portions of burgers, fish and chips, and other greasy fare at the **Mini Mart.** No wonder half the local population seems obese! There's a little espresso stand near the floatplane dock, or head to **Leask's Market** for groceries. Check the bulletin board here for such items as hand-carved fossil ivory or fresh Ooligan grease (if you don't know what it is, you probably won't like it). Metlakatla is a dry town, so alcoholic beverages are not allowed.

Services

Drop by the **municipal building** (907/886-4868), for local information. Camping is discouraged, and visitors who want to stay on Annette Island more than five days must obtain a special permit from the city. A local sponsor is required, and fishing is not allowed. The **Lepquinum Wellness Center,** next to the high school, houses an Olympic-size swimming pool, plus a weight room, racquetball, sauna, and showers. Out front is **Raven and the Tide Woman Totem,** with a descriptive plaque.

Getting There

The ferry *Lituya* provides daily runs between Metlakatla and Ketchikan, stopping at the **ferry terminal** (907/465-3941 or 800/642-0066, www.alaska.gov/ferry) a mile east of town.

ProMech Air (907/225-3845 or 800/860-3845, www.promechair.com) and **Taquan Air** (907/225-8800 or 800/770-8800, www.taquanair.com) have daily floatplane service between Ketchikan and Metlakatla for $80 round-trip.

HYDER AND STEWART

The twin towns of Hyder, Alaska, and Stewart, British Columbia, lie at the head of the long, narrow Portland Canal that separates Canada and the United States. The area's remoteness has kept it one of the relatively undiscovered gems of the entire Pacific Northwest coast. Most people arrive via the stunning 41-mile drive down Highway 37A from Meziadin Junction into Stewart, passing beautiful lakes, majestic glaciers, high waterfalls, spectacular mountain peaks, the narrow Bear River Canyon, and finally the mountain-rimmed, water-trimmed towns.

The town of Stewart (pop. 800) lies at the mouth of the Bear River, while tiny Hyder (pop. 90) is two miles down the road next to the mouth of the Salmon River. They are as different as two towns could possibly be. Stewart is the "real" town, with a hospital, churches, schools, a museum, a pharmacy, a bank, and the other necessities of life; it bills itself as Canada's northernmost ice-free port. In contrast, Hyder, "the friendliest ghost town in Alaska," makes the most of its flaky reputation. Between the two settlements lies an international boundary that seems of little importance; border checks are only made when re-entering Canada. Residents send their kids to school in British Columbia. Everyone uses Canadian currency and the Canadian phone system (area code 250). You can, however, mail letters from a post office in either country, saving postage and the hassles of shipping parcels internationally. Hyder is officially on Alaska Time, but everyone except the postmaster sets their watches one hour later, to Pacific Standard Time.

History

In 1793, Captain George Vancouver, searching for the fabled Northwest Passage, turned into Portland Canal. For days his men worked their boats up the narrow fjord, but when they reached its end after so many miles he was "mortified with having devoted so much time to so little purpose." Over a century later the area finally began to develop. In 1896, Captain David Gilliard of the Army Corps of Engineers (for whom Gilliard Cut in the Panama Canal was later named) explored the region and left behind four stone storehouses, Alaska's first masonry buildings. Prospectors soon arrived and found an incredible wealth of gold, silver, and other minerals in the nearby mountains. Stewart received its name from two of its earliest settlers, Robert and John Stewart. The adjacent Alaskan town was initially named Portland City, but postal authorities, wary of yet another Portland, vetoed it. Instead, the town was named after Frederick B. Hyder, a Canadian mining engineer.

Gold fever and the prospect of a transcontinental Canadian railway terminus attracted more than 10,000 newcomers to the area. The steep, mountainous terrain was difficult to build on; much of Hyder was constructed on pilings driven into the mudflats. The planned railroad made it only a few miles out of town, but in 1919 prospectors struck it rich. The Premier Gold and Silver Mine was, until its 1948 closure, the largest gold mine in North America. After it shut down, the local population dwindled to less than a thousand until development of the Granduc copper mine in the 1960s. To reach the rich Leduc ore vein, workers dug the longest tunnel ever built from one end— 10 miles. A devastating avalanche in 1965 buried 40 men in a tunnel entrance, killing 27 of them. The mine operated until 1984 when it was closed down and dismantled, and the site was restored to a relatively natural condition.

The spectacular Stewart/Hyder area has served as the location for several Hollywood movies: *Insomnia, Bear Island, The Thing, Iceman,* and *Leaving Normal.* Recent years have also seen sporadic promises of new gold, silver, coal, or asbestos mines, but times have been hard of late. As one local told me, "The Moose Park Graveyard is full of people still waiting for Hyder to boom."

Sights

Housed in a Fire Hall from 1910, **Stewart Historical Society Museum** (Columbia and 6th Sts., 250/636-2568, www.stewartmuseum. homestead.com, daily July and Aug., C$5) has wildlife specimens on the first floor as well as numerous historical items both upstairs and out front.

On the U.S. side of the international border stands a tiny **stone storehouse** built in 1896 by Captain Gilliard. The building looks like an old jail and once served that purpose, but for much of its life it was a shoe repair shop. On the mudflats in front of Hyder are hundreds of old pilings, remnants of what was once a town of 1,000 people. The straight row of pilings in front of Stewart is all that remains of the aborted transcontinental railroad.

About eight kilometers (5 miles) out of Hyder (turn right at the end of the main drag) is **Fish Creek Wildlife Viewing Area.** From late July to mid-September the creek is filled with pink salmon, along with some of the world's largest chum salmon—some weighing as much as 35 pounds. A viewing platform here provides an excellent vantage point for watching the black and brown bears that feast on the salmon. Forest Service (250/636-2367) staff are on hand to ensure the safety of bear-watchers and to answer questions; see bear photos at www.fishcreek.org.

The road beyond Fish Creek is well worth driving, but before heading out, be sure to ask about road conditions and snow levels; travel by RV is not recommended. Just a quarter-mile beyond Fish Creek are remains of an old brothel operated by Dolly, Ketchikan's best-known madam. Continuing north, the road

FISH TRAPS

The floating fish trap was developed in 1907 and quickly proved an amazingly efficient way to catch salmon. The traps were constructed with heavy wire netting that directed migrating salmon into progressively smaller enclosures. All one had to do was wait. The traps were hated by most Alaskans because they were owned by "outsiders" who could afford the high construction and maintenance costs, and because their efficiency took jobs from local fishermen. Their efficiency also robbed many streams of needed brood stock.

For many years these traps brought in over half of Southeast Alaska's salmon catch. Locals got even by stealing fish from the traps, and those who did often became folk heroes. As a territory, Alaska had no say in its own affairs, but when statehood came in 1959, the first act of the state legislature was to outlaw all fish traps. Only the Annette Island Reservation (which manages all waters within 3,000 feet of the island, and sets its own fish and game regulations) was allowed to continue operating the floating fish traps after statehood, but the last of these was closed in the 1990s.

follows the Salmon River, passes the remains of a covered bridge that once provided access to a remote mine, then begins a torturous climb, re-entering Canada along the way. The first glimpses of stunning **Salmon Glacier** come into view 17 miles from Hyder, but the views improve as the ever-narrowing road climbs above the tree line to a lookout point 23 miles from town. Beyond the glacier is **Tide Lake**, site of the world's greatest yearly snowfall: 88 feet in 1971.

Gorgeous **Bear Glacier**, 20 miles east of Stewart on Highway 37A, should not be missed. Like its more famous cousin, Juneau's Mendenhall, it is a "drive-up glacier" with the highway passing close to its base. The small lake in front is often filled with icebergs.

Accommodations

Ripley Creek Inn (on 5th Ave., 250/636-2344, www.ripleycreekinn.homestead.com, C$110–120 d) in Stewart is the finest local lodging choice, with a dozen large and nicely furnished rooms, including access to the sauna and exercise room. The lobby houses **Toastworks Museum,** an offbeat collection of some 600 antique kitchen appliances. The owners also run Bayview Hotel, with simple but clean rooms for C$45–60 d.

A new home in the center of Hyder, **Kathy's Korner B&B** (250/636-2393, summers only, $60–75 s or d) has four rooms, shared or private baths, continental breakfasts, and a large deck. Other options include **King Edward Hotel/Motel** (250/636-9160 or 800/663-3126, www.kingedwardhotel.com, C$79–99 s or C$89–109 d) in Stewart, and two seasonal Hyder places: **Grandview Inn** (250/636-9174, www.grandviewinn.net, $60 s or $65 d) and **Sealaska Inn** (250/636-9006 or 888/393-1199, www.sealaskainn.com, C$58 s or C$64 d).

Stewart's city-run **Rainey Creek Campground** (250/636-2537 or 888/366-5999, open May–Sept.) is quietly situated on the edge of town and has a cookhouse, firewood, and pay showers. Park RVs at **Camp Run-A-Muck** (250/636-9006 or 888/393-1199, www.sealaskainn.com, C$20 RVs, C$12 tents) in Hyder, or **Bear River RV Park** (250/636-9205, www.stewartbc.com/rvpark, C$21 RVs, C$12 tents) in Stewart.

Food and Drink

Several places serve meals in Stewart, but your best bet is **Bitter Creek Café** (5th Ave., 250/636-2166, May–Sept., www.bittercreek.homestead.com) with gourmet pizzas, pasta, seafood, Mexican, burgers, and homemade breads and desserts, along with espresso and nightly specials. An outside deck is a good place for a beer on a summer day. Inside, a 1930 Pontiac is the centerpiece for an eccentric collection of antiques.

Hyder has three bars for fewer than a hundred inhabitants, and getting "Hyderized" at the **Glacier Inn** (250/636-9248) is an experience that attracts folks from all over the world. It's cheap and lasts a lifetime (you even get an official card), but could also prove expensive if you fail the test. Warning: It involves Everclear. The walls of the Glacier Inn are papered with thousands of dollars in signed bills left by drinkers, creating the "world's most expensive wallpaper." The tradition began when prospectors would tack up a dollar bill on the wall, in case they were broke next trip into town.

Information and Services

Stewart/Hyder International Chamber of Commerce operates the **Stewart Visitor Information Centre** (250/636-9224 or 888/366-5999, www.stewart-hyder.com, daily 9 A.M.–6 P.M. mid-May–Sept.) in Stewart, at the west end of 5th Avenue.

The U.S. Forest Service has a summertime office/information center in Hyder; stop here for details on bear-viewing up the road. For swimming, showers, and a weight room, head to **Stewart High School pool** on 9th Avenue.

The public library is also at the high school. There are no U.S. banks in the area, but Stewart has a branch of the Canadian Imperial Bank of Commerce with an ATM.

Canada Day (July 1) and the American Independence Day (July 4) provide the opportunity for a four-day party in Stewart and Hyder. **International Days,** as it's called, features a parade of pets, daily pancake breakfasts, and culminates in a fireworks display in Hyder as darkness falls on the fourth.

Getting There and Around

There is no ferry service to Hyder. **Taquan Air Service** (250/636-9150 or 907/225-8800, www.taquanair.com) flies every Monday and Thursday between Ketchikan and Hyder. This is also the only time mail goes in or out of the Hyder post office.

Seaport Limousine (250/636-2622, www.seaportnorthwest.com) has vans between Terrace and Stewart, as well as guided tours of the area, including to Fish Creek and Salmon Glacier.

Prince of Wales Island

With more miles of roads than the rest of Southeast Alaska combined, a beautifully wild coastline, deep U-shaped valleys, rugged snow-topped mountains, hidden caves, and a wealth of wildlife, you might expect America's third-largest island (after Kodiak and Hawaii) to be a major tourist attraction. But Prince of Wales Island (POW) has thus far remained off the tourist path for a number of reasons, the primary one being logging. Much of the land has been heavily logged, with huge clear-cuts gouged out of the hillsides, particularly along the extensive road network. Logging has slowed markedly in recent years as the Forest Service shifts to a more diverse land-management policy, and as the Native corporations run out of trees to cut.

Actually, POW's notoriety is its saving grace as well: The towns are authentically Alaskan, with no pretext of civility for the tourists. The

7,000 or so people who live here are friendly, and the roads offer good opportunities for a variety of recreation—including mountain biking—not available elsewhere in the Southeast. The island is very popular with hunters, and the roads provide easy access to many bays for fishing. Black bears and deer are common sights, and wolves are occasionally seen. As logging has declined on POW, tourism—especially from those looking to catch halibut and salmon—has increased. Most of the main roads are now paved, and a ferry provides daily service between Ketchikan and Hollis.

Prince of Wales Island's largest settlement is Craig, on the west coast, but Klawock, Thorne Bay, and Hydaburg each have several hundred people. Rainfall on POW ranges 60–200 inches per year, depending upon local topographic conditions. As an aside, this is one of four Prince of Wales Islands on the planet. The others are in Canada's Northwest Territories, in Australia, and in Malaysia.

Located in Klawock, the **Prince of Wales Chamber of Commerce** (907/826-3870, www.princeofwalescoc.org, Tues.–Fri. 10 A.M.–3 P.M. year-round) is a good source for local info, and their website features links to many island lodging places and fishing resorts.

CRAIG

Just across a short bridge from the western shore of POW Island, the town of Craig (pop. 1,500) overflows Craig Island. Named after Craig Miller—founder of an early fish cannery here—it was originally even more prosaically called "Fish Egg," for the herring eggs that are considered a Tlingit delicacy. Fishing and logging are the mainstays of Craig's econ-

omy, giving it a likable feeling. The town has two fish-processing plants and a number of sportfishing lodges. No real "sights" in town, but as you enter Craig you pass the **Healing Heart Totem Pole.** Black bears and bald eagles are often seen at the dump, a mile north of town.

Hidden in the J. T. Brown Industrial Park a mile north of town, is **Stone Arts of Alaska** (907/826-3571, www.stoneartsofalaska.com), an unpretentious stone yard and gallery space where you can watch Gary McWilliams as he works on one-of-a-kind pieces—all created from stones he collected in Southeast Alaska. The gallery/stone yard is open daily in the summer, and includes both functional pieces (tables, benches, bowls, and garden art) and fine art—the finest of which sell for upwards of $40,000.

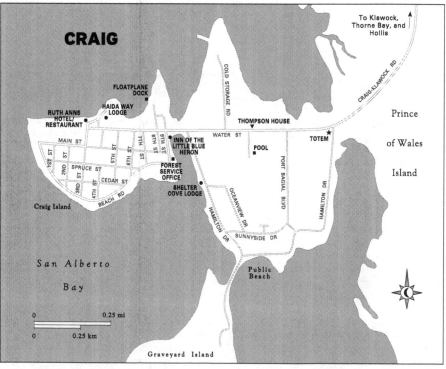

Accommodations

Find quaint, cozy rooms (some with kitchenettes) at **Ruth Anns Hotel** (907/826-3378, $95–115 d), and a suite that includes a private hot tub $(127 d). Nearby is **Haida Way Lodge** (907/826-3268), which charges $110 s or $125 d for standard rooms, or $135 d for rooms with whirlpool tubs. Wi-Fi is available.

Facing the south boat harbor, **Inn of the Little Blue Heron** (907/826-3608, www.little blueheroninn.com) has four rooms with private baths and fridges. The back deck overlooks the boat harbor, and a continental breakfast is served. One room contains two twin beds ($79 s or $89 d), and the other rooms ($99–115 d) have double beds. Also available is a new two-bedroom waterfront home ($155 d or $295 for up to six guests).

Located above Voyageur Bookstore, **Water Street Apartments** (907/826-2333, www.slentzrentals.com, $125 for up to six) consists of two efficiency units with small kitchens and Wi-Fi.

Dreamcatcher B&B (1405 Hamilton Dr., 907/826-2238, www.dreamcatcherbed andbreakfast.com, $105 d) is a modern home with three attractive rooms, all with private baths. A continental breakfast is served in the morning, and Wi-Fi is free.

If you have the money and like to fish, **Waterfall Resort** (907/225-9461 or 800/544-5125, www.waterfallresort.com), will put you in seventh heaven. Located on the south end of POW in a beautifully refurbished fish cannery, Waterfall is extremely popular with the elite crowd. Pampered guests stay in tiny Cape Cod–style cottages along a remote stretch of coast, and are treated to great fishing with a personal fishing guide, plus three sumptuous meals daily. It's not cheap: two people should be ready to drop $7,000 for three nights, but this does include floatplane fare from Ketchikan and all expenses.

Right in Craig, **Shelter Cove Lodge** (907/826-2939 or 888/826-3474, www.shelter covelodge.com) has package lodging-and-fishing trips from a modern and comfortable lodge.

RainCountry RV Park (907/826-3632) is on JS Drive.

Food and Services

Meal prices are high on POW; your best bet may be to stock up in Ketchikan or at the grocery store in Craig, **Thompson House** (907/826-3394), which has a deli. The historic **J. T. Brown's General Store** (907/826-3290) is a classic heart-of-town place with groceries, fishing gear, and other supplies. Right next door in another historic structure is **Ruth Anns Restaurant** (907/826-3377, $20–32), a classy place with an old-time atmosphere. You'll find good food three meals a day with a front-row view of the harbor from the dining room. The diverse menu includes seafood, chicken, and steaks for dinner, plus burgers, salads, halibut, fish and chips, and sandwiches for lunch. Dinner reservations are advised if you want a window seat. The building also houses a popular but minuscule bar.

Also downtown is **Dockside Café**, with reasonable breakfasts— available all day—plus tasty lunches and great pies. It's extremely popular with chain-smoking locals, so be ready to gag on the smoke. The $11 fish and chips are the most expensive item on the menu.

Craig's fine-dining experience, **Shelter Cove Lodge** (703 Hamilton Dr., 907/826-2939 or 888/826-3474, www.sheltercovelodge.com, daily June–Aug., $22–30 entrées) has tall windows facing the boat harbor, and a dinner-only menu of fine seafood, steaks, ribs, pasta, and nightly specials.

Very good pizzas—including a pesto and artichoke version—can be had at **Papa's Pizza** (907/826-2244), which also serves chicken and lasagna.

For fresh-roasted coffees, espresso, and pastries—plus books, gifts, CDs, computer rentals, and free Wi-Fi—head to **Voyageur Bookstore** (907/826-2333), across from the grocery store on Cold Storage Road. This is a fine spot to hang out.

Located along the south boat harbor, the Forest Service's **Craig District Office** (907/826-3271, www.fs.fed.us/r10/tongass) has maps and

Ruth Anns Restaurant in Craig

recreational information, including a listing of more charter fishing operators. ATMs can be found at the Wells Fargo and First Bank offices in Craig, and at the Thompson House grocery store.

Craig has an indoor **swimming pool** (907/826-2794) complete with water slide, hot tub, sauna, and weight room. **Log Cabin Sporting Goods** (1 Easy St., 907/826-2205 or 888/265-0375) sells outdoor gear.

KLAWOCK

Six miles from Craig is the Tlingit village of Klawock (pop. 700), home to the oldest cannery in Alaska (1878), along with a bustling sawmill, state fish hatchery, and POW's only airport; all other POW settlements have floatplane service. Klawock is best known for its 21-pole **Totem Park,** which dominates the center of town. These brightly painted poles—all originals—were moved from the old abandoned village of Tuxekan (20 miles north) in the 1930s and restored. The **Prince of Wales**

Hatchery (907/755-2231, www.powhasalmon. org) in Klawock raises coho and sockeye salmon, and has a 250-gallon aquarium filled with coho fry. Free tours are offered Monday–Saturday 1–5 P.M. in the summer. **Stan Snider Park** is a pleasant picnic spot beneath the trees.

Practicalities

Log Cabin Resort and RV Park (907/755-2205 or 800/544-2205, www.logcabinresort andrvpark.com) has a variety of lodging options, starting with basic cabins that share a bathhouse for $70 d. Three suites with kitchenettes in the modern main lodge are $120 d, and a separate log house with a full kitchen is $120 d or $150 for five guests. RV sites ($25) are also available, along with canoe and skiff rentals, and charter fishing.

Although primarily geared to weekly fishing packages, **Southeast Retreat Lodge** (907/755-2994, www.southeastretreat.com) has a furnished apartment with full kitchen for

$250 for up to four, including use of a 4WD vehicle. The lodge sits along Salt Lake.

Fireweed Lodge (907/755-2930, www.fire weedlodge.com), is a full-service fishing lodge in Klawock. Other lodging options include **Klawock Bay Inn** (907/755-2929, www.klawockbayinn.com) and **Changing Tides Inn** (907/755-2305, www.changing tidesinn.com).

Dave's Diner (907/755-2986) serves breakfasts, subs, soups, and sandwiches, or buy groceries and baked goods from **Klawock IGA** (907/755-2722). Next door is **Alaska Kustom Kayaking** (907/209-7082, www .alaskakustomkayaks.com) with guided tours and kayak rentals.

OTHER TOWNS
Thorne Bay

The settlement of Thorne Bay (pop. 600) was for many years the world's largest logging camp, and there's still a bit of logging going on, but the focus has shifted to fishing and tourism.

Thorne Bay isn't the most beautiful place, but it does have all the basics, including a grocery store, gas, lodging, a large and underpopulated high school, and a Forest Service district office (907/828-3304, www.fs.fed.us/r10/tongass).

McFarland's Floatel B&B (907/828-3335 or 888/828-3335, www.mcfarlandsfloatel.com) has modern two-bedroom log cabins that sleep four for $260. No TVs or phones, but the units do have full kitchens, baths, and Wi-Fi. Car and skiff rentals are also available.

Right in town, **Welcome Inn B&B** (907/828-3940 or 888/828-3940, www.lodginginn alaska.com, $75 s or $95 d) has three rooms. A full breakfast is included. Two businesses offer packages that include lodging, a vehicle, and your own skiff: **Adventure Alaska Southeast** (907/828-3907 or 877/499-3474, www.fishorhunt.com) and **The Landing at Otter Cove** (907/247-3528 or 888/424-5445, www.otterinlet.com).

Boardwalk Lodge (907/828-3918 or 800/764-3918, www.boardwalklodge.com)

© DON PITCHER

Thorne River, near Thorne Bay

is a luxurious fishing lodge near Thorne Bay, with access by boat or air.

Ten miles north of town on Forest Highway 30 is **Sandy Beach Picnic Area,** an attractive sandy beach (rare in the Southeast) where you can pitch a tent. The road is narrow and slippery after a rain.

Get very good pizzas from **Dale's Pizza** (907/828-8222), groceries from **Thorne Bay Market** (907/828-3306), and booze from **Riptide Bar** (907/828-3353). **Some Place to Go** has burgers and other fast food.

Thorne Bay's **Prince of Wales Island Logging Show and Fair** takes place the last weekend of July, with fun logging contests, a fair, and vendor booths. Even though logging is becoming less and less important on the island, this is still the island's biggest annual event.

Hydaburg

Hydaburg (pop. 400), 42 miles south of Craig, is the largest Haida settlement in Alaska. The Haida Indians are relative newcomers to the state, arriving in this Tlingit land around 1700. Originally from Canada's Queen Charlotte Islands, the Haida were given parts of POW in compensation for the accidental killing of a Haida chief by the Tlingits. Hydaburg was established in 1911 when three nearby Haida villages combined into one. Hydaburg has the prettiest setting on POW, situated along scenic Sukkwan Strait. Most of the houses, however, are very plain BIA-style boxes. The newly paved road to Hydaburg was only completed in 1983, opening the town to the outside world. In town is a nice row of totems restored by the CCC in the 1930s, along with a newer one erected in 1991. For food, head to **Do Drop In Groceries** (907/285-3311). Ask locally for rooms to rent.

Kasaan

The Tlingit village of Kasaan (pop. 50) is a rough 16-mile drive off the main road between Klawock and Thorne Bay. This is a wonderful out-of-the-way settlement, and just a 15-minute walk from the community hall are a beautiful **clan house** and a number of totem poles set in the woods. The poles were mostly carved in the

1930s and '40s, and the clan house belonged to Chief Son-i-hat, who is buried nearby. (Try to ignore the logging that has been allowed almost right up to the graves.) Older totems are in the abandoned village of Old Kasaan, accessible only by boat.

Logging and Fishing Villages

Several tiny communities (mostly former logging camps) are along the road network on the north end of POW Island.

The little settlement of **Coffman Cove** (pop. 200) is 53 miles north of Klawock. Visitors will find a restaurant and a general store (The Riggin Shack) with groceries, gas, and other essentials. Coffman Cove boasts several lodging options, all on the Web at www.coffmancove. org. They include **Coffman Cove Bunkhouse** (907/329-2219), **Coffman Cove Cabins** (907/329-2251), and **Oceanview RV Park/ Campground** (907/329-2226), which has beach-front campsites, a coin laundry, and showers. The InterIsland Ferry Authority (see the *Getting There* section) has summer-only service four days a week connecting Coffman Cove with the town of Wrangell.

Sixty-five miles north of Klawock is **Whale Pass** (pop. 60), with a general store and gas. Find lodging at **Northend Cabin** (907/846-5315) and **Bear Valley Lodge** (907/247-8512 or 800/936-9600, www.bearvalleylodgealaska.com).

On the far northern end of POW are a couple of minuscule fishing/retirement villages. A long boardwalk connects the homes of **Port Protection** (pop. 50), where **Wooden Wheel Cove Lodge** (907/489-2288 or 888/489-9288, www.woodenwheellodge.com) has fishing-lodge accommodations by the day or week. **Point Baker** (pop. 50) has a small general store and the nation's only floating post office.

RECREATION
Hiking, Camping, and Cabins

There are only a few trails on POW. One of the best and most accessible is the 1.5-mile **One Duck Trail** southwest of Hollis. The trailhead is on the east side of the Hydaburg Road, two miles south of the junction with the Craig–Hollis Road. The path climbs sharply to an Adirondack shelter (free) on the edge of the alpine where the scenery is grand and the hiking is easy. Be sure to wear rubber boots since the trail can be mucky.

The **Soda Lake Trail** (marked) begins approximately 14 miles south of the junction along the Hydaburg Road. This 2.5-mile trail leads to a pungent collection of bubbling soda springs covering several acres. There are colorful tufa deposits (calcium carbonate, primarily) similar to those in Yellowstone, but on a vastly smaller scale. **Control Lake,** at the junction of the Thorne Bay and Big Salt Lake Roads, has a nice cabin ($45) with a rowboat. There are 20 other Forest Service cabins (reservations: 518/885-3639 or 877/444-6777, www.reserveusa.com) scattered around POW, most accessible only by floatplane or boat.

For world-class steelhead and salmon fishing, reserve one of the four cabins in the Karta River area north of Hollis. The five-mile-long **Karta River Trail** connects Karta Bay to the **Salmon Lake Cabin** ($35) and provides panoramic views of surrounding mountains. This is part of the 40,000-acre **Karta Wilderness.**

You can camp almost anywhere on POW's National Forest land, but avoid trespassing on Native lands (these are generally quite easy to identify since the trees have been scalped for miles in all directions). **Eagle's Nest Campground** ($8) is just east of the intersection of the Klawock–Thorne Bay Road and Coffman Cove Road. Also here is a pleasant pair of lakes (Balls Lakes—named for, well, you figure it out) with a short path down to tent platforms overlooking the water. This is a good place for canoeing. **Harris River Campground** ($8) is 19 miles west of Hollis on the road to Klawock. Eagle's Nest and Harris River campground sites can be reserved (518/885-3639 or 877/444-6777, www.reserveusa.com, $9 extra).

Spelunking

Prince of Wales Island has the best-known and probably the most extensive system of caves in Alaska, and spelunkers keep discovering more.

In **El Capitan Cave** explorers found a treasure trove of bones from black bears, brown bears, river otters, and other mammals, the oldest dating back more than 12,000 years. The cave is located on the north end of the island at Mile 51 near Whale Pass. Free Forest Service tours (907/828-3304, www.fs.fed.us/r10/tongass) are offered three times a day in the summer. Bring flashlights, warm clothing, and hiking boots; hard hats are provided. Reservations are required at least two days in advance; no kids under seven.

Three miles south of El Capitan is another underground wonder. A stream flows out of Cavern Lake, and then underground for a few hundred feet before emerging from **Cavern Lake Cave.** You can wade up the waters into the cave for 150 feet or so.

Canoeing

The **Sarkar Canoe Trail** is an easy 15-mile loop route with boardwalk portages connecting seven lakes. The trailhead is at the south end of Sarkar Lake, on the northwest side of Prince of Wales, off Forest Road 20.

A more strenuous route is the 34-mile-long **Honker Divide Canoe Route.** This paddle-and-portage route begins near Coffman Cove at the bridge over Hatchery Creek on Forest Road 30, and works up Hatchery Creek to Honker Lake, which has a Forest Service cabin ($25). You may need to pull the canoe up shallow sections of the creek. The route then continues over Honker Divide on a mile-long portage to the upper Thorne River before heading downstream all the way to Thorne Bay. There is a two-mile portage to avoid dangerous rapids and falls. The route is strenuous and should only be attempted by experienced canoeists. For more information on either of these routes, contact the Thorne Bay Ranger District (907/828-3304, www.fs.fed.us/r10/tongass).

Sea Kayaking

With its hundreds of miles of rugged coastline, and numerous small islands, inlets, and bays, POW offers tremendous opportunities for sea kayakers. One of the wildest areas is

TONGASS NATIONAL FOREST

Three times larger than any other national forest in the country, Southeast Alaska's Tongass National Forest is America's rainforest masterpiece. Within these 17 million acres are magnificent coastal forests, dozens of glaciers, snowcapped peaks, an abundance of wildlife, hundreds of verdant islands, and a wild beauty that has long since been lost elsewhere.

Originally named Alexander Archipelago Forest Reserve in 1902, the area became Tongass National Forest in 1907 by proclamation of President Theodore Roosevelt. It was later enlarged to include most of the Panhandle. For more information, visit the Forest Service Tongass website (www.fs.fed.us/r10/tongass) or contact the Southeast Alaska Discovery Center (907/228-6220) in Ketchikan.

RECREATION

The Tongass is a paradise for those who love the outdoors. It has dozens of scenic hiking trails and over 1,000 miles of logging roads accessible by mountain bike (if you don't mind the clear-cuts and can avoid the logging trucks and flying gravel). The islands contain hundreds of crystal-clear lakes, many with Forest Service cabins on them. Fishing enthusiasts will enjoy catching salmon, cutthroat trout, and other fish from these lakes, the ocean, and the thousands of streams that empty into bays.

The Inside Passage is composed of a wonderful maze of semiprotected waterways, a sea kayaker's dream come true. Particularly popular with kayakers are Misty Fiords National Monument, Admiralty Island National Monument, Glacier Bay National Park, and the waters around Sitka and Juneau, but outstanding sea kayaking opportunities can be found throughout the Southeast. If you have a sea kayak, access is easy, since they can be carried on the ferries (extra charge). Ask the Forest Service recreation staff in the local district offices for information on nearby routes and conditions.

WILDERNESS AREAS

Less than 5 percent of the Tongass has been logged or otherwise developed, so it isn't necessary to visit an official wilderness area to see truly wild country. However, 21 wilderness areas total well over five million acres in the national forest, offering outstanding recreational opportunities. The largest are **Misty Fiords National Monument** (2.1 million acres) near Ketchikan and **Admiralty Island National Monument** (956,000 acres) near Juneau. Other major wildernesses include **Tracy Arm-Fords Terror** (653,000 acres) south of Juneau, **Stikine-LeConte** (449,000 acres) near Wrangell, **Russell Fiord** (349,000 acres) near Yakutat, **South Baranof** (320,000 acres) south of Sitka, and **West Chichagof-Yakobi** (265,000 acres) near Pelican.

Several wilderness areas, such as the remote the 98,000-acre **South Prince of Wales Wilderness,** but access is difficult and much of the area is exposed to fierce ocean storms. Nearby **Dall Island** has exploring possibilities, but parts of it have been logged. On beaches exposed to the open sea, you'll occasionally find beautiful Japanese glass fishing floats that have washed ashore.

Three other wilderness areas along POW's outer coast—**Maurelle Islands, Warren Island,** and **Coronation Island**—offer remote and rarely visited places to see whales, sea otters, and nesting colonies of seabirds. You're likely to see a few fishermen, but nobody else.

GETTING THERE
Ferry

The **Inter-Island Ferry Authority** (907/826-4848 or 866/308-4848, www.interislandferry.com) operates two vehicle and passenger ferries connecting POW with other parts of Southeast Alaska. The M/V *Prince of Wales* provides daily connections between Ketchikan and the tiny spot called Hollis (no services other than phones and toilets). It's 25 miles from Hollis to Klawock, the nearest town. Reservations for vehicles on this ferry are highly recommended. The M/V *Stikine* connects Coffman Cove on the north end of Prince of Wales with islands off the west coast of Prince of Wales (Coronation, Maurelle, and Warren Islands) are exposed to the open ocean and are inaccessible for much of the year, even by floatplane. Others, such as the Stikine-LeConte, Admiralty Island, Russell Fiord, and Petersburg Creek-Duncan Salt Chuck wilderness areas are relatively accessible. There are developed trails or canoe/kayak routes within the Misty Fiords, Admiralty Island, Stikine-LeConte, Tebenkof Bay, and Petersburg Creek-Duncan Salt Chuck wilderness areas.

FOREST SERVICE CABINS

Tongass National Forest has 150 public recreation cabins scattered throughout Southeast, providing a wonderful way to see the *real* Alaska. Most cabins are rustic, one-room Pan-Adobe log structures 12 by 14 feet in size, with bunk space for 4-6 people. They generally have a woodstove with cut firewood (some have oil stoves), an outhouse, and rowboats at cabins along lakes. You'll need to bring your own bedding, cookstove, cooking and eating utensils, Leatherman or Swiss army knife, food, playing cards, candles, flashlight, matches, and mousetraps. (Some of this will probably be there, but it's better to be sure by bringing your own.) No cell phone coverage, so you're generally on your own when it comes to emergencies.

Many Forest Service cabins can only be reached by floatplane. These flights can be very expensive, but even those on a tight budget should plan to spend some time at one of these cabins. A few can be reached by hiking from towns (Ketchikan, Petersburg, Juneau, and Skagway), cutting out the expensive flight. If you're considering a flight-seeing trip anyway, make it to one of these remote cabins where you get to see what the country is really like. This is one splurge you won't regret!

CABIN RESERVATIONS

The Forest Service charges $35-45 a night for these cabins, with all fees going toward their maintenance. Reservations are on a first-come, first-served basis up to six months in advance; some of the most popular cabins are even chosen by lottery. The Forest Service publishes brochures describing recreation facilities, and can also supply Tongass National Forest maps showing cabin locations. Both the **Forest Service Information Center** (907/586-8751) at Centennial Hall in Juneau and the **Southeast Alaska Discovery Center** (907/228-6220) in Ketchikan, can provide cabin information, as can the ranger district offices scattered around the Southeast. All cabin rentals are made through **Reserve USA** (518/885-3639 or 877/444-6777, www .reserveusa.com.) There is no extra charge for cabin reservations.

Wrangell and the south end of Mitkof Island (home to the town of Petersburg), with service Thursday–Sunday late May to mid-September; no winter service on this route.

Prince of Wales Transportation (907/957-2224) provides shuttle vans from the ferry in Hollis to Craig ($25 per person) and from Craig to the ferry in Coffman Cove ($75 per person). Call a day ahead for reservations.

Air

On a rainy midsummer day when the clouds were almost to the water, I sat in Craig waiting to fly back to Ketchikan. The weather looked marginal to me, but when I asked at the air taxi counter if they were flying, the woman glanced outside and nonchalantly responded, "Oh sure, it looks pretty good today." We flew. Three air taxi operators, **ProMech Air** (907/225-3845 or 800/860-3845, www.promechair.com), **Pacific Airways** (907/225-3500 or 877/360-3500, www.fly pacificairways.com), and **Taquan Air** (907/225-8800 or 800/770-8800, www.taquanair.com) have daily floatplane service from Ketchikan to Craig, Hollis, and Thorne Bay. Taquan also flies to smaller settlements scattered across the island. **L.A.B. Flying Service** (907/826-5220, www.labflying.com) flies between Ketchikan airport and Klawock.

GETTING AROUND

For a good road map, pick up the *Prince of Wales Road Guide* at Forest Service offices in Ketchikan, Craig, or Thorne Bay. In the last few years the roads have improved dramatically, and the most-used sections are now paved and in good condition, including roads connecting Hollis, Craig, Klawock, Thorne Bay, and Coffman Cove. Some 1,500 miles of rough gravel roads, most built for logging operations, remain on POW, providing lots of interesting mountain bike rides—if you don't mind the old clearcuts and soggy weather.

Rent cars in Craig from **Wilderness Car Rental** (907/755-2691 or 800/949-2205, www.wildernesscarrental.com) or **Shaub-Ellison Tire & Fuel** (907/826-3450).

Wrangell

Quiet, friendly, and conservative, the settlement of Wrangell (pop. 2,000) sits on an island near the mouth of the Stikine River. The streets are full of folks in pickup trucks, with their dogs hanging out the back and country tunes on the radio. Wrangell is quite unlike its neighbor, prim and proper Petersburg. Wrangell's inner harbor resonates with salmon- and shrimp-processing plants, fishing boats, and seaplanes, while totem poles guard historic Chief Shakes Island. Surrounding the harbor are old buildings on piles, wooded hillsides, and snowcapped mountains. Wrangell is compact enough that visitors can hoof it around to the most interesting sites in an hour or two and still have time to buy beer for the ferry. To see the area right, however, you should spend a couple of days, or longer if you're interested in exploring the mighty Stikine River.

HISTORY
Redoubt St. Dionysius

Third-oldest community in Alaska, Wrangell is the only one to have been governed by four nations: Tlingit, Russia, Britain, and America. Tlingit legends tell of an ancient time when advancing glaciers forced them to abandon their coastal life and move to what is now British Columbia. As the ice retreated after the last ice age, the Stikine River was their entryway back to the newly reborn land. When the Tlingits discovered that the river suddenly disappeared under a glacier, they sent old women to explore, expecting never to see them again. One can only imagine their astonishment when the women returned to lead canoes full of people out to the coast.

For many centuries the Tlingits lived in the Stikine River area, paddling canoes upstream to catch salmon and trade with interior tribes. Similarly, the river figured strongly in Wrangell's founding. Russians began trading with Stikine Indians in 1811; by 1834 the British were trying to move in on their lucrative fur-trading monopoly. To prevent this, Lieutenant Dionysius Zarembo and a band of men left New Archangel (present-day Sitka) to establish a Russian fort near the Stikine River mouth. The settlement, later to become Wrangell, was originally named Redoubt St. Dionysius. When the British ship *Dryad* anchored near the river, the Russians boarded the vessel and refused to allow access to the Stikine. The *Dryad* was forced to return south, but a wedge had been driven in Russia's Alaskan empire. Five years later, the Hudson's Bay Company acquired a long-term lease to the coastline from the Russian government. Redoubt St. Dionysius became Fort Stikine, and the Union Jack flew from town flagpoles.

Gold Fever

The discovery of gold on Stikine River gravel bars in 1861 brought a boom to Fort Stikine. Hundreds of gold-seekers arrived, but the deposit proved relatively small and most

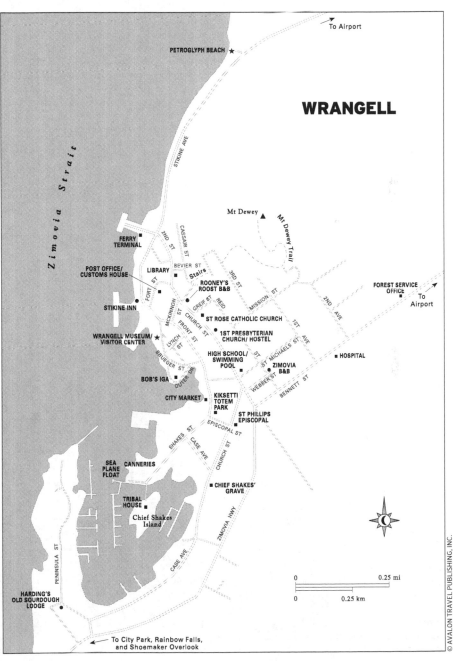

To Airport

PETROGLYPH BEACH ★

WRANGELL

Zimovia Strait

Mt Dewey ▲

Mt Dewey Trail

FERRY TERMINAL ■

2ND ST

CASSAR ST

POST OFFICE/ CUSTOMS HOUSE ■

LIBRARY ■

BEVIER ST

Stairs

3RD ST

ROONEY'S ROOST B&B ●

GREIF ST

REID

MISSION ST

FOREST SERVICE OFFICE ■

To Airport

FORT ST

MCKINNOH ST

2ND AVE

STIKINE INN ●

ST ROSE CATHOLIC CHURCH ●

CHURCH ST

FRONT ST

1ST PRESBYTERIAN CHURCH/ HOSTEL ●

1ST AVE

WRANGELL MUSEUM/ VISITOR CENTER ★

LYNCH ST

HIGH SCHOOL/ SWIMMING POOL ■

ST MICHAELS ST

HOSPITAL ■

BRUEGER ST

ZIMOVIA B&B ●

WEBBER ST

BENNETT ST

BOB'S IGA ■

OUTER DR

CITY MARKET ■

KIKSETTI TOTEM PARK ■

ST PHILLIPS EPISCOPAL ●

EPISCOPAL ST

SHAKES ST

CASE AVE

CHURCH ST

SEA PLANE FLOAT

CANNERIES

CHIEF SHAKES' GRAVE ■

TRIBAL HOUSE ■

Chief Shakes Island

ZIMOVIA HWY

CASE AVE

PENINSULA ST

HARDING'S OLD SOURDOUGH LODGE ●

To City Park, Rainbow Falls, and Shoemaker Overlook

0   0.25 mi

0   0.25 km

© AVALON TRAVEL PUBLISHING, INC.

prospectors soon drifted on to other areas. With the transfer of Alaska to American hands in 1867, Fort Stikine was renamed Wrangell, after Baron Ferdinand Petrovich von Wrangel, governor of the Russian-American Company. Its population dwindled until 1872 when gold was again discovered in the Cassiar region of British Columbia. Thousands of miners quickly flooded the area, traveling on steamboats up the Stikine. Wrangell achieved notoriety as a town filled with hard-drinking rabble-rousers, gamblers, and shady ladies. When the naturalist John Muir visited in 1879 he called it "the most inhospitable place at first sight I had ever seen... a lawless draggle of wooden huts and houses, built in crooked lines, wrangling around the boggy shore of the island for a mile or so in the general form of the letter *S*, without the slightest subordination to the points of the compass or to building laws of any kind."

By the late 1880s, the second gold rush had subsided and lumbering and fishing were getting started as local industries. The Klondike gold rush of the late 1890s brought another short-lived boom to Wrangell as the Stikine was again tapped for access to interior Canada, but Skagway's Chilkoot Trail became the preferred route. With its rowdy days behind, Wrangell settled into the 20th century as a home to logging and fishing operations, still mainstays of the local economy. Rebuilt after destructive fires in 1906 and 1952, much of downtown is now on rock-fill and pilings. Today, Wrangell is searching for a more prosperous future—and tourism is right at the forefront of that quest—while getting by on the remaining industries: fishing, construction, and small timber operations. It's an easygoing, slow-paced, and friendly town, and a good place to unwind.

SIGHTS

Wrangell is home to the oldest Protestant church building in Alaska, the **First Presbyterian Church,** as well as the oldest

totem pole and Tribal House of the Bear, Chief Shakes Island

© DON PITCHER

Roman Catholic parish, **St. Rose of Lima Catholic Church.** Appropriately located on Church Street, both were founded in 1879. The large, red neon cross atop the Presbyterian church is one of only two in the world used as a navigational aid (the other is in Rio).

Keep your eyes open for local kids selling **garnets** for $0.25 to $10 depending upon the size. They put up tables at the museum and on the cruise ship dock when ships are in port. These imperfect but attractive stones come from a garnet ledge along the Stikine River, deeded to the Boy Scouts in 1962 by a former mayor. At one time the mine was owned by the Alaska Garnet Mining and Manufacturing Company, the world's first women-only corporation.

Chief Shakes Island

This is the centerpiece of picturesque Wrangell harbor. A footbridge at the bottom of Front Street near Wrangell's cannery and cold-storage plant gives access to the island. Here you'll find the **Tribal House of the Bear** (907/874-2023, $2), a Native log house built in 1939–1940 by the CCC. Inside are various artifacts, including beautifully carved houseposts that date from 1835. The house is only open when cruise ships are in port or by appointment. Surrounding the house are seven totems, reproductions of older poles from the area. Shakes Island is especially beautiful at night, surrounded by the town and harbor.

The Shakes lineage was established more than three centuries ago, after the Stikine Tlingits defeated Niska invaders and then forced the vanquished chief, We-Shakes, to give away his name in exchange for peace. **Chief Shakes V's gravesite** is on Case Avenue opposite the Hansen Boat Shop. A white fence surrounds it, and two carved killer whales watch silently. (Surprisingly, Chief Shakes isn't really buried in this grave.)

Several impressive totem poles, carved by the CCC, stand in front of the Library on 2nd Street. Wrangell's small **Kiksetti Totem Park,** next to the City Market along Front Street, has four poles that were carved without the aid of power tools.

Wrangell Museum and Visitor Center

Given the size of Wrangell, its museum (296 Outer Dr., 907/874-3770) is a delightful surprise. Housed in the spacious and modern Nolan Center, it's open Tuesday–Saturday 10 A.M.–5 P.M. May–September, and when cruise ships are in port. The rest of the year, hours are Tuesday–Saturday 1–5 P.M. Admission is $5 adults, $3 seniors, $2 ages 6–12, free for younger children, and $12 for families. Professional exhibits take you through Wrangell's rich past with an in-depth look at the Tlingit, Russian, English, and American peoples who all called this place home. Petroglyphs, Native baskets, old photographs, and local relics are crowded into this provocative museum. Of particular interest are the original houseposts from the Chief Shakes house. Carved in the 1740s—before contact with whites—they are the oldest Tlingit houseposts in existence. The gift shop has a fine selection of books.

Also within the Nolan Center is the **Wrangell Visitor Center** (907/874-3901 or 800/367-9745, www.wrangell.com), staffed Monday–Friday 9 A.M.–3 P.M., and whenever cruise ships are in port. Winter hours are Tuesday–Friday 9 A.M.–3 P.M. You can pick up brochures here if the museum is open, and a computer is available to check your email (fee).

Petroglyphs

Hundreds of ancient petroglyphs (rock carvings) are found on Wrangell Island, but precisely who carved them or when is uncertain. They may date back more than 8,000 years. The best nearby carvings are only a 20-minute walk from town. To get there, turn left (north) from the ferry terminal and walk two-thirds of a mile to a small parking area on the left. A newly built boardwalk provides access to the beach, where you will find a dozen petroglyph rocks along upper parts of the beach, especially those on the right side (facing the water). One of the best, a killer whale, lies on the edge of a grassy lawn to the right of the path. Most petroglyphs face seaward and are near the high-tide line. They may be covered by water if the tide is over

THE PETROGLYPH MYSTERY

Petroglyphs (ancient rock carvings) are found along the coast from Kodiak to the Columbia River, although the greatest concentration is between Sitka and Puget Sound. The coastal type is very different from the petroglyphs of the interior plateau and central Oregon, but has similarities to carvings in the Amur River region of Siberia. Although a single style can be followed down the coast, no one knows who carved the petroglyphs, when they were carved, or why. Contemporary Natives have no knowledge of them. Many petro-glyphs – such as those in Wrangell – face west and were carved on rocks below the high-tide mark. Were they territorial boundary signs? Greetings to returning salmon? Sacred places? As with Stonehenge, we can only speculate. Some have posited that the petroglyphs were just the idle doodles of some ancient graffiti artist. This is unlikely not only from a cultural perspective, but also because of the difficulty of pecking out a design in these hard, fine-grained rocks using only stone tools.

Petroglyph Beach in Wrangell

© DON PITCHER

10 feet. To protect the originals, the state has set up several stone reproductions of the petroglyphs along the boardwalk for those who want to make rubbings. Rubbings are made by placing rice paper—available in local stores—over the copies and rubbing the surface with crayons, ferns, or charcoal. Other petroglyphs are in the Wrangell Museum and in front of the library. Do not make rubbings of the originals.

Mt. Dewey

An excellent half-mile boardwalk/trail winds up Mt. Dewey (actually more of a hill) from 3rd Street behind the high school. It's a steep 15-minute climb up to the top where a platform provides a vantage point over Wrangell. You could probably find a place to camp up here in a pinch. On a wild stormy night in 1879, John Muir did just that. He, however, also decided to build a huge bonfire atop the hill, its flames dancing off the clouds. Muir later wrote, "Of all the thousands of camp-fires I have elsewhere built none was just like this one, rejoicing in triumphant strength and beauty in the heart of the rain-laden gale." To the Native people below, however, the fire ignited fears of evil spirits, and as Muir's partner noted, "the Tlingits ever afterward eyed Muir askance, as a mysterious being whose ways and motives were beyond all conjecture."

ANAN CREEK WILDLIFE VIEWING SITE

Anan Creek, 30 miles south of Wrangell on the mainland, is a fine place to watch black and brown bears catching salmon and steelhead. A half-mile boardwalk leads from saltwater to an observation platform above the creek, and a three-sided blind sits closer to the falls where most of the action takes place. The best time to visit is the peak of the pink salmon run, mid-July–mid-August. Forest Service personnel are at the trailhead and observation area to provide information. No food is allowed along these trails, and flash photography is discouraged. The creek is shaded by tall trees and it's often raining, making photography a challenge.

Because of Anan Creek's popularity, permits ($10) are required, and a maximum of 60 visitors are allowed per day in July and August. If you're traveling on your own, get the permit from the Forest Service office in Wrangell (907/874-2323, www.fs.fed.us/r10/tongass). If you're in a guided group, the guide already has your permit.

The Forest Service's **Anan Bay Cabin** (518/885-3639 or 877/444-6777, www.reserveusa.com, $35) is just a mile away on a good trail, but is often booked months in advance; reserve early.

Many visitors to Anan Creek arrive on flights by **Sunrise Aviation** (907/874-2319 or 800/874-2311, www.sunriseflights.com) in Wrangell or **Taquan Air** (907/225-8800 or 800/770-8800, www.taquanair.com) from Ketchikan.

A number of companies offer guided boat trips to Anan Creek, including **Alaska Vistas** (907/874-3006 or 866/874-3006, www.alaskavistas.com), **Alaska Waters** (907/874-2378 or 800/347-4462, www.alaskawaters.com), **Alaska Charters and Adventures** (907/874-4157 or 888/993-2750, www.alaskaupclose.com), and **Breakaway Adventures** (907/874-2488 or 888/385-2488, www.breakawayadventures.com). Expect to pay $200 per person for a trip that includes four hours on the ground at Anan.

Those with a sea kayak may want to paddle along the east side of Wrangell Island to Anan Bay. En route, be sure to visit scenic **Berg Bay,** an area rich in moose, mountain goats, grizzlies, deer, geese, and other wildlife. A Forest Service cabin ($35) is available here, and a trail leads from the cabin along Berg Creek for several miles into a cirque basin with old mine ruins.

EVENTS

Wrangell's **Stikine River Garnet Festival** in late April celebrates the arrival of spring with natural history presentations, eagle-watching tours, live music, and even garnet bingo. From mid-May to mid-June, pull out your fishing pole for the **King Salmon Derby**—top prize is $6,000. The main summer event is the town's **July 4th** celebration, with a parade, logging show, log rolling contests, tug of war, tugboat races, street dance, and fireworks. All this is funded by a handful of teenagers and their families who run downtown food booths in June.

RECREATION

Rain Walker Expeditions (907/874-2549, www.rainwalkerexpeditions.com) rents bikes, canoes, and kayaks, plus a floating cabin near Anan Creek, from its office across from Stikine Inn. Owner Marie Oboczky leads informative nature hikes and bus tours, from two hours to all day. They're fun and geared to your area of interest, whether it's petroglyphs or rainforests.

A paved **walking/biking path** runs from Wrangell for six miles to the trailhead for Rainbow Falls at Shoemaker Bay.

Alaska Vistas (907/874-3006 or 866/874-3006, www.alaskavistas.com) guides sea kayaking day trips and multi-day adventures in the

Wrangell area. **Klondike Bike** (502 Wrangell Ave., 907/874-2453, www.klondikebike.com) has quality mountain bikes for rent.

Muskeg Meadows Golf Course (907/874-4653, www.wrangellalaskagolf.com) is an attractive nine-hole course with putting greens, a pro shop, and driving range.

Wrangell's **swimming pool** (907/874-2444) is at the high school. Fishing and sightseeing **charters** are available through a number of local outfits; get brochures from the visitor center.

Boat Tours

Wrangell is the primary starting point for fun and fast jetboat tours to watch bears at Anan Creek (see the *Anan Creek Wildlife Viewing Site* section) or to motor up the mighty Stikine River (see *The Stikine River* section). Three companies also offer excellent all-day jetboat trips to LeConte Glacier and Petersburg: **Breakaway Adventures** (907/874-3455 or 888/385-2488; www.breakaway adventures.com), **Alaska Waters** (907/874-2378 or 800/347-4462, www.alaskawaters .com), **Alaska Vistas** (907/874-3006 or 866/874-3006, www.alaskavistas.com).

Hiking

Scenic **Rainbow Falls Trail,** a moderately steep 0.75-mile hike (710 stairsteps!), begins across the road from Shoemaker Bay Campground, five miles south of town. More ambitious bodies can continue three miles up the trail to **Shoemaker Overlook** (1,500 ft.). The trail accesses large, ridge-top muskeg areas and ends at a three-sided Adirondack-style shelter offering a panoramic vista of Zimovia Strait. The trail and shelter provide an excellent opportunity for an overnight camping trip. The trail is steep and often muddy, but has boardwalk in places.

Logging roads crisscross most of Wrangell Island, providing cycling opportunities for mountain bike enthusiasts—if you enjoy seeing cut-over land. Those with wheels may want to visit several areas on the island. **Long Lake Trail,** 28 miles southeast of Wrangell along Forest Road 6271, is a half-mile boardwalk

that ends at an Adirondack shelter complete with a rowboat, fire grill, and outhouse. In the same vicinity is a 300-foot path to **Highbrush Lake,** where you'll find a small boat in which to practice your rowing skills. Individuals with disabilities may want to try fishing at **Salamander Creek,** 23 miles south of town on Forest Road 6265, where ramps lead right up to a pad along the creek. Good fishing for king salmon here, along with three campsites. For information on cabins and other trails around Wrangell, visit the Forest Service's **Wrangell Ranger District Office** (525 Bennett St., 907/874-2323, www.fs.fed.us/r10/tongass).

Cabins

There are 21 different Forest Service cabins (info: 907/874-2323; reservations: 518/885-3639 or 877/444-6777, www.reserveusa.com; $35) near Wrangell, including several described in the *Stikine River* section. The closest is at **Virginia Lake,** accessible by floatplane—and another nearby cabin is at **Kunk Lake,** across Zimovia Strait from the south end of the Wrangell Island road system. Access is by kayak, or skiff if you can get someone to run you across. A 1.5-mile trail climbs to a three-sided shelter at the lake. From here, it's a relatively easy climb into high-elevation muskeg and alpine areas that cross Etolin Island.

ACCOMMODATIONS

Housed within the Presbyterian church, Wrangell's **Youth Hostel** (220 Church St., 907/874-3534, $18 per person) is open late May–early June. It's clean and well-managed, but nothing fancy, with air mattresses for sleeping, along with kitchen and shower facilities. A private room ($40 s or d) is also available if you call ahead, along with a family room ($18 per person). The hostel is open all day, so you don't need to be out during the day.

New owners brought major improvements to the centrally located **Stikine Inn** (107 Stikine Ave., 907/874-3388 or 888/874-3388, www .stikineinn.com). Standard rooms cost $95–105 s, $105–115 d, and suites with kitchenettes cost $120 d. Be sure to request a remodeled room.

Zimovia B&B (319 Webber St., 907/874-2626 or 866/946-6842, www.zimoviabnb.com, $85 d) has a quiet, edge-of-the-woods location in a cedar-shingled home just a few blocks from downtown. The two guest rooms each have private baths and entrances, and one includes a sauna. The light breakfast includes home baked goods. Free Wi-Fi and van transport around town.

Rooney's Roost B&B (206 McKinnon, 907/874-2026, www.rooneysroost.com) has five comfortable guest rooms for just $80 d with shared bath, or $100 d with private baths. The attractive home contains avian collectibles, and a gourmet breakfast is included. Friendly owners, too.

Located two miles south of town, **Grand View B&B** (907/874-3225, www.grandviewbnb.com, $95–105 d) is a nice hillside home facing Zimovia Straits. The three guest rooms have private baths and the breakfast is filling.

Wrangell's most unique lodging option is **Rain Haven Houseboat** (907/874-2549, www.rainwalkerexpeditions.com), a surprisingly cozy little place with room for five, plus cooking and bath facilities. During July and August it's located in remote and beautiful Bradfield Canal, southwest of Wrangell. Take the canoe to nearby Berg Bay for a hike, or it's an hour paddle to the bears at Anan Creek. Three-day stays are $575 d, including transportation from Wrangell and a Stikine River jetboat trip; add $100/day for use of a skiff. The rest of the year the houseboat is docked at Shoemaker Bay, five miles south of Wrangell, where it rents for $85 d, including transportation from town and a bike to explore nearby trails.

CAMPING

Free tent camping is allowed (no RVs) at **City Park** just beyond the ball field, two miles south of the ferry on the water side of Zimovia Highway. The official limit is 24 hours, but this is not strictly enforced. Showers are available at a coin laundry near Chief Shakes Island, and at the high school swimming pool.

You'll find additional camping at the city-run **Shoemaker Bay RV Park** (907/874-2444, RVs $25), five miles south of town and right alongside the highway. Open all year. Guests get a pass to the city pool for showers and a free swim, and the area is near trails to Rainbow Falls and Shoemaker Overlook. The Forest Service's free **Nemo Campground** is 14 miles south of town and up Forest Roads 16 and 6267; impressive views across Zimovia Strait.

Alaska Waters RV Park (241 Berger St., 907/874-2378 or 800/347-4462, www.alaska waters.com, RVs $25) is on the south side of the harbor.

FOOD

Wrangell eating places deliver old-fashioned American meals without pretense. The **Garnet Room** inside Stikine Inn (107 Stikine Ave., 907/874-3388) has Zimovia Strait views from the dining room, with three meals a day; try the tender New York steak.

Get espresso—and use the free Wi-Fi—at the seasonally open **Java Junkie** next to the downtown dock. Nearby is **Memories,** a little trailer where you'll find tasty fish and chips and fresh oysters.

Zak's Café (316 Front St., 907/874-3355) offers a good variety of food: pasta, stir-fries, and steaks for dinner ($15–20), and lunchtime salads, sandwiches, and wraps. The setting is simple and clean, with fast service.

The **Elks Club** (9126 Front St., 907/874-3716) is open to the public for reasonably priced dinners most nights, including Saturday-night steak specials.

Bob's IGA (on Outer Dr., 907/874-2341) has a deli with inexpensive sandwiches. **City Market** (on Front St., 907/874-3336) is Wrangell's other grocery store. Both are closed on Sundays.

Locals hang out in **Marine Lounge** (274 Shakes St., 907/874-3005)—a.k.a. the Hungry Beaver—which has the best pizzas in town. The **Totem Bar** (116 Front St., 907/874-3533) also serves burgers and other pub fare; these smoke-filled bars are the only places serving meals after 8 P.M.

SERVICES

The Forest Service's **Wrangell Ranger District Office** (525 Bennett St., 907/874-2323, www.fs.fed.us/r10/tongass) is three-quarters of a mile from town on the left side of the road. It has information on local hiking trails, the Stikine River, and nearby recreation cabins.

Adjacent to the Stikine Inn is **River's Edge Fine Arts and Gifts** (907/874-3508, www.marineartist.com), selling locally made clothing, carved wooden bowls, pottery, and jewelry, plus the distinctive marine art of owner Brenda Schwartz.

The **library** (124 2nd Ave., 907/674-3535) has a good collection of books about Alaska and a couple of petroglyphs out front, along with computers for Internet access. Head to the Nolan Center theater for weekend movies.

Located out Airport Road, the **Wrangell Medical Center** (907/874-3356, www.wrangell medicalcenter.com) has physicians on staff.

GETTING THERE AND AROUND

Wrangell's **ferry terminal** (907/874-2021; 907/874-3711 for departure times) is right in town. **Alaska Marine Highway** (907/465-3941 or 800/642-0066, www.ferryalaska.com) ferries head both north and south almost daily during the summer, but the terminal is open only for vessel arrivals and departures.

The **Inter-Island Ferry Authority's** (907/826-4848 or 866/308-4848, www.inter islandferry.com) M/V *Stikine* connects Coffman Cove on the north end of Prince of Wales with Wrangell, and continues northward to the south end of Mitkof Island, where a good gravel road continues to the town of Petersburg. This ferry operates Thursday–Sunday late May–mid-September; no winter service.

The airport is 1.5 miles from town on Bennett Street. **Alaska Airlines** (800/426-0333, www.alaskaair.com) has daily flights from Wrangell to Juneau, Ketchikan, Petersburg, and Sitka. **Sunrise Aviation** (907/874-2319 or 800/874-2311, www.sunriseflights.com) provides flightseeing trips and charter flights to nearby Forest Service cabins and Anan Creek.

They often have seat fare rates if someone else has already set up a charter; this can be a fast and reasonable way to fly to Petersburg or Prince of Wales.

Rent cars at the airport from **Practical Rent-A-Car** (907/874-3975) for $50 a day. Both **Northern Lights Taxi** (907/874-4646) and **Star Cab** (907/874-3622) charge $5 from the airport to town.

◖ THE STIKINE RIVER

Seven miles north of Wrangell is the Stikine River, one of the top 10 wild rivers of Canada, and the fastest navigable river in North America. The river begins its 330-mile journey to the sea high inside British Columbia's Spatsizi Wilderness Park. The 55-mile-long **Grand Canyon of the Stikine,** just above Telegraph Creek, B.C., has thousand-foot walls enclosing fierce white water. River travel is easier below Telegraph Creek all the way to Wrangell, between high peaks of the coast range, past glaciers and forested hills. At one spot on the river, 21 different glaciers are visible! These glaciers dump tons of silt into the river, coloring it a milky gray; at the mouth of the Stikine, the sea takes on this color for miles in all directions. So much for the advertisements about glacially pure water.

Each spring, upward of 1,500 bald eagles flock to the river mouth to eat "hooligan" (eulachon), an oily fish that spawns here from late March to early May. The fish also attract hundreds of thousands of gulls and kittiwakes, plus harbor seals, Steller sea lions, and even killer whales.

River Tours

Several Wrangell charter boat operators provide fun jetboat trips up the Stikine River with a lunch break at Shakes Glacier and fast runs up the back sloughs. Three of the larger operators are **Breakaway Adventures** (907/874-3455 or 888/385-2488; www.breakawayadventures .com), **Alaska Waters** (907/874-2378 or 800/347-4462, www.alaskawaters.com), and **Alaska Vistas** (907/874-3006 or 866/874-3006, www.alaskavistas.com). All of these do a great job of showing the sights, but the Break-

Stikine River, near Wrangell

away and Alaska Vistas trips are cheaper ($150 versus $179 for a 6-hour trip) and also include a soak at Chief Shakes Hot Springs.

Running the River

The Stikine River is a popular destination for kayakers, canoeists, and river rafters. (It's even more popular with local jetboaters, so don't expect peace and quiet in the lower reaches.) Most folks choose to float down the river, after being transported up from Wrangell by boat or plane. You will need to go through customs (907/874-3415) at the Wrangell airport if you cross the border. In addition, a Canadian agent is frequently stationed along the river just across the border. The Forest Service publishes a helpful guide to canoeing or kayaking the Stikine River; it's available from the Wrangell Ranger District (907/874-2323, www.fs.fed .us/r10/tongass).

Stikine Riversong Lodge (250/235-3196, www.stikineriversong.com) in Telegraph Creek 160 miles upriver from Wrangell, has lodging, supplies, and a pleasant café. The owners also offer river tours, canoe and kayak rentals, and will help you set up trips down the Stikine.

In Wrangell, rent kayaks and canoes from **Rain Walker Expeditions** (907/874-2549, www.rainwalkerexpeditions.com) or **Alaska Waters** (907/874-2378 or 800/347-4462, www.alaskawaters.com); they can also set up jetboat transportation to Telegraph Creek. **Alaska Vistas** (907/874-3006 or 866/874-3006, www.alaskavistas.com), leads nine-day raft trips down the Stikine River.

Camping and Cabins

The lower Stikine is a multi-channeled, silt-laden river nearly a mile wide in places. The route is spectacular, wildlife crowds the banks, campsites are numerous, and 13 Forest Service cabins (reservations: 518/885-3639 or 877/444-6777, www.reserveusa.com, $35) are available. One of the finest is the **Mount Rynda Cabin** along crystal-clear Andrew Creek, a spawning area for king salmon. You may also want to stay in one of the two extremely popular cabins near **Chief Shakes Hot Springs.** At the springs you'll discover beautifully maintained wooden hot tubs (one enclosed to protect you from the mosquitoes); these are great places to soak those aching muscles. The area gets mighty busy on summer weekends, so you probably won't have it to yourself, and things can get rowdy after the locals pop a few beers. Escape the crowds at the main hot springs by finding your own undeveloped springs nearby.

The upper portion of the Stikine is a vastly different river, with less noise and development than on the U.S. side of the border and a drier, colder climate. The vegetation reflects this. The historic settlement of **Telegraph Creek** is accessible by road from the rest of British Columbia, or you can charter a small plane or jetboat from Wrangell. The upper river above here is some of the wildest white water anywhere; canoeists and kayakers intent on running the river would do best to begin at Telegraph Creek.

Petersburg

Southeast Alaska's picture-postcard town, Petersburg (pop. 3,200) sits at the northern tip of Mitkof Island along Wrangell Narrows. Great white walls of snow and ice serve as a dramatic backdrop for the town. "Peter's Burg" was named after Peter Buschmann, who built a sawmill here in 1897, followed by a cannery three years later. With ample supplies of fish, timber, and glacial ice, the cannery proved an immediate success—32,750 cases of salmon were shipped that first season. Unlike boom-and-bust Wrangell, the planned community of Petersburg has kept pace with its expanding fishing base. A number of the present inhabitants are descended from Norwegian fishermen, who found that the place reminded them of their native land. The language is still occasionally heard on Petersburg's streets, and Norwegian *rosemaling* (floral painting) can be found on shutters of the older homes.

Petersburg is a prosperous and squeaky-clean town with green lawns, tidy homes, and a hardworking heritage that may appear a bit cliquish to outsiders. The country around Petersburg is filled with opportunities for exploration by those who love the outdoors, but this off-the-beaten-path community still views tourism with a degree of skepticism. Although Petersburg has a lumber mill, fishing remains the main activity, with salmon, halibut, herring, crab, and shrimp all landed. The odor of fish hangs in the air, and bumper stickers proclaim "Friends don't let friends eat farmed salmon." Petersburg has the most canneries in Southeast Alaska (four) and is home to a large halibut fleet.

Wrangell Narrows

Between Wrangell and Petersburg the ferry passes through tortuous Wrangell Narrows, a 46-turn nautical obstacle course that resembles a pinball game played by ship. This is one of

humpback whale sign, Petersburg

© DON PITCHER

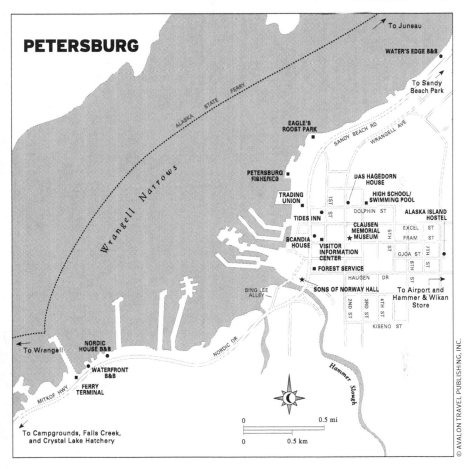

PETERSBURG

To Juneau

WATER'S EDGE B&B

To Sandy Beach Park

SANDY BEACH RD

WRANGELL AVE

EAGLE'S ROOST PARK

Wrangell Narrows

ALASKA STATE FERRY

PETERSBURG FISHERICO

DAS HAGEDORN HOUSE

HIGH SCHOOL/ SWIMMING POOL

TRADING UNION

1ST ST

DOLPHIN ST

ALASKA ISLAND HOSTEL

TIDES INN

5TH ST

EXCEL ST

FRAM ST

CLAUSEN MEMORIAL MUSEUM

SCANDIA HOUSE

VISITOR INFORMATION CENTER

GJOA ST

7TH ST

6TH ST

FOREST SERVICE

HAUGEN DR

BING LEE ALLEY

SONS OF NORWAY HALL

To Airport and Hammer & Wikan Store

2ND ST

3RD ST

4TH ST

KISENO ST

NORDIC HOUSE B&B

To Wrangell

NORDIC DR

Hammer Slough

WATERFRONT B&B

FERRY TERMINAL

MITKOF HWY

To Campgrounds, Falls Creek, and Crystal Lake Hatchery

0   0.5 mi

0   0.5 km

© AVALON TRAVEL PUBLISHING, INC.

the highlights of the Inside Passage trip and is even more exciting at night when the zigzag course is lit up like a Christmas tree. Be up front to see it. The larger cruise ships are too big to negotiate these shallow waters between Kupreanof and Mitkof Islands, thus sparing Petersburg from the tourist blitz and glitz that most other Southeast towns endure.

SIGHTS
In Town

Petersburg's main attraction is its gorgeous harbor and spectacular setting. The sharply pointed peak visible behind Petersburg is **Devil's Thumb,** a 9,077-foot mountain 30 miles away on the U.S.–Canadian border. Built in 1912, the large **Sons of Norway Hall** (907/772-4575) stands on pilings over scenic Hammer Slough, and is adorned with traditional Norwegian *rosemaling* designs. Next to Sons of Norway is the surprisingly small *Valhalla,* a replica of the original Viking boat. It was built in 1976 and sailed in the parade of ships bicentennial celebration in New York Harbor. A memorial to fishermen lost at sea stands next to the Sons of Norway Hall. Walk up the wooden street along **Hammer Slough** to see old homes hanging over this tidal creek.

Valhalla, replica of a Viking boat, in front of Sons of Norway Hall

The boat harbors usually have several Steller sea lions cruising around.

Clausen Memorial Museum (2nd and Fram Sts., 907/772-3598, www.clausenmuseum .alaska.net, $3, free for kids under 13) is open Monday–Saturday 10 A.M.–5 P.M. May–early September; call for winter hours. Inside are exhibits on commercial fishing—including the world's largest king salmon (a 126-pound monster) and chum salmon (36 pounds)—plus the Cape Decision lighthouse lens, a 200-year-old Tlingit dugout canoe, bentwood box, and other historical exhibits. Outside is *The Fisk*, a fishy sculpture and fountain by Carson Boysen.

Nearby

A good place to watch for America's national bird is **Eagle's Roost Park,** north of the Petersburg Fisheries cannery. Upward of 30 eagles can be seen along here when the tide is low. Whales, seals, and sea lions are frequent sights in Frederick Sound near **Sandy Beach Park**

north of town. Covered picnic tables and a playground add to the allure, and by late summer, pink salmon spawn in the tiny creek that flows through the park. Hike to the west side of Sandy Beach Park to discover ancient petroglyphs on the rocks. Icebergs from LeConte Glacier are common along the north side of Frederick Sound and sometimes drift across to Petersburg, especially in winter.

Heading out the Road

South of town, the main road is paved for 18 miles, with a gravel road continuing another 16 miles to the southeast end of Mitkof Island. From this point you have excellent views of the nearby Stikine River mouth and the white-capped peaks of the Coast Range. Canoeists or kayakers (with transportation) may want to start their trip up the Stikine from here rather than at Wrangell.

Approximately eight miles out is a small turnoff to **Falls Creek,** a pleasant picnic spot. Stop here to look at the fish ladder (built in 1959) used by coho and pink salmon, as well as steelhead.

Located 15 miles south of town, the **Blind River Rapids Trail** is an easy half-mile boardwalk that leads through the muskeg to a three-sided shelter overlooking the saltwater rapids. Bring your fishing pole. The trail loops back through the muskeg for a total distance of nearly a mile.

A **trumpeter swan observatory** is set up on Blind Slough 16 miles south of Petersburg. A dozen or so of these majestic birds overwinter here, and other waterfowl abound during spring and fall migrations. The state-run **Crystal Lake Fish Hatchery** (907/772-4772), 18 miles south of Petersburg, produces king and coho salmon. The kings return in June and July, while the coho come back to spawn from mid-August through September. Blind Slough flows away from the hatchery and is a great place to explore by canoe or kayak. The water gets swimmably warm by mid-summer, and picnic tables sit in the trees. The Forest Service's Ohmer Creek Campground is three miles farther down the road.

LECONTE GLACIER

LeConte Glacier, the southernmost tidewater glacier in North America, dips into LeConte Bay on the mainland, 25 miles east of Petersburg. Part of the vast Stikine Icefield, its glacial ice was once used by local fishermen to keep their catches cold on the way to market in Seattle. Today, locals use it to cool their drinks. LeConte Bay is home to 2,000 harbor seals. The entire area is included within the 448,841-acre **Stikine-LeConte Wilderness.**

There are no Forest Service cabins in LeConte Bay, but an excellent one is on **Mallard Slough** (reservations: 518/885-3639 or 877/444-6777, www.reserveusa.com, $35), near its entrance. A 1.5-mile trail connects the cabin and Le Conte Bay, where you're likely to find icebergs high and dry at low tide. A fine trip for experienced sea kayakers is to head up the Stikine River from Wrangell and then into LeConte Bay, 10 miles north, before crossing Frederick Sound and continuing on to Petersburg. Total distance is approximately 50 miles (longer if you explore the Stikine River or LeConte Bay).

Getting There

The visitor center has a complete listing of boat charters for glacier sightseeing, whale-watching, and fishing. Good companies include **Kaleidoscope Cruises** (907/772-3736 or 800/868-4373, www .petersburglodgingandtours.com), **Hook & Eye Adventures** (907/772-3400, www.alaska .net/~hookeye), and **Whale Song Cruises** (907/772-9393, www.whalesongcruises.com). **Kupreanof Flying Service** (907/772-3396, www.kupreanof.com), **Nordic Air** (907/772-3535), **Pacific Wing** (907/772-4258, www.pacificwing.com), and **Temsco Helicopters** (907/772-4780 or 877/789-9501, www.temscoair.com) all offer flightseeing tours over the glacier.

ENTERTAINMENT AND EVENTS

Petersburg's **Little Norway Festival,** held each year on the weekend nearest Norwegian Independence Day (May 17), is the town's biggest event. The three-day festivities include a parade, crafts, pageant, and a big seafood feast. The **American Independence Day** (July 4) is another time for fun and games, and the annual king salmon derby in late May is always popular with locals.

The **Petersburg Canned Salmon Classic** is a contest to guess the number of cans of salmon packed by local canneries each year; $2,000 goes to the person who comes closest. It's awarded in mid-August.

Live music, booze, cigarette smoke, and a clientele of local toughs make for good fights in **Kito's Kave** (on Sing Lee Alley, 907/772-3207). The nautically themed **Harbor Bar** (on Nordic Dr., 907/772-4526) is a good place to meet local fishermen over a beer.

RECREATION

Contact **Tongass Kayak Adventures** (907/772-4600, www.tongasskayak.com) for sea kayaking around the harbor and up Petersburg Creek. Four-hour trips with guide are $70. The company also runs multi-day kayaking tours to LeConte Glacier, the Stikine River, and Tebenkof Bay, and rents kayaks for do-it-yourselfers.

Stop by the **Forest Service district office** (reservations: 518/885-3639 or 877/444-6777, www.reserveusa.com, $35) at Nordic and Haugen for detailed maps of local hiking trails and 25 nearby cabins. A pleasant walk takes off from Nordic Drive, three miles from town and just beyond Sandy Beach, and continues down a mile-long boardwalk to **Frederick Point.** Along the way, you get a taste of muskeg, rainforest, and a creek that's packed with salmon in August. You can return to town along the beach.

A short in-town boardwalk leads through the muskeg from the top of Excel Street to the senior center on 12th Street. The center is crowded with flowers outside, along with a menagerie of ducks, rabbits, geese, turkeys, and chickens. Right across the street is the Forest Service's area office. In addition, the half-mile **Hungry Point Trail** traverses the muskeg from Hungry Point to the ball field.

Ravens Roost Cabin

Petersburg has one of the few Forest Service cabins in Southeast Alaska that can be reached by hiking from town. The Ravens Roost cabin lies 1,600 feet above sea level at the end of a four-mile trail that starts near the airport. The trail crosses muskeg for the first mile and becomes very steep (and often mucky) for the next mile through the forest before breaking into open muskeg again along a ridge. Here the trail is in better condition and you are treated to grand views of Devil's Thumb and the surrounding country. The path ends at a two-level Forest Service cabin with space for up to eight people. Allow three hours for the hike up and be sure to make advance reservations for the cabin through the Forest Service.

Three Lakes Recreation Area

Very popular with locals for picnicking, fishing, and berry picking is the beautiful Three Lakes Recreation Area along Forest Service Road 6235, 22 miles southeast of town. You can hitch there, but it's a long hike back to town if your thumb is numb. Each lake has a rowboat and picnic table and you may want to camp nearby at the old three-sided shelter built by the CCC along tiny **Shelter Lake.** An easy three-mile boardwalk loop trail connects the lakes, and a boardwalk trail continues from Sand Lake to nearby Ideal Cove, a mile and a half away. The three main lakes (Sand, Hill, and Crane) are named after the sandhill cranes that announce each spring.

Kupreanof Trails and Cabins

On nearby Kupreanof Island, the Petersburg Mountain and Petersburg Lake trails provide good hiking and great views. Both paths begin at Bayou Point directly across Wrangell Narrows. Contact **Petersburg Creek Charters** (907/772-2425, www.alaska.net/~psgcreek) for a water taxi from town. A number of Forest Service cabins are available on Kupreanof.

For **Petersburg Mountain Trail,** walk north (right) up the road 1.5 miles to the trail marker. Be prepared for a very steep, muddy, and brushy path, rising 3,000 feet in a distance

of only 2.5 miles. From the top, however, you'll be rewarded with outstanding views of the entire Petersburg area.

Petersburg Lake Trail provides an easy 6.5-mile hike to a Forest Service cabin on Petersburg Lake within the 46,777-acre **Petersburg Creek-Duncan Salt Chuck Wilderness.** Check with the Forest Service for current conditions on both of these trails. From Petersburg Lake it's possible to continue another 10.5 miles along a primitive trail to the Forest Service's Salt Chuck East Cabin. The trail is nearly level the entire distance and offers spectacular views of Portage Mountain.

On the south end of Kupreanof Island is **Kah Sheets Lake,** where the Forest Service has a very popular A-frame cabin. It's a 30-minute flight from Petersburg. A three-mile trail leads from the lake to Kah Sheets Bay, where you can fish for coho and sockeye salmon. A second Forest Service cabin sits along the bay.

West Point Cabin, in Portage Bay on the north end of Kupreanof Island, is a great spot to watch for whales, and the beach makes for good hiking.

Thomas Bay Area

Several of the most popular local Forest Service cabins are in the country around Thomas Bay, on the mainland approximately 20 miles from Petersburg. Spectacular Baird and Patterson Glaciers feed into this bay. Reserve months ahead to ensure a spot. **Cascade Creek Cabin** is on the saltwater and is accessible by either air or charter boat. Backpackers will love **Cascade Creek Trail,** one of the best (and steepest) paths in the Southeast. This three-mile path climbs 3,000 feet from the cabin to Falls Lake, passing cascading water much of the way. A three-sided shelter (free) sits along the shore of Falls Lake, and there's good fishing for rainbow trout. Hikers can continue two more miles up the trail beyond Falls Lake to Swan Lake. **Swan Lake Cabin** is on the opposite end of the lake from the trailhead and offers great views of the rocky mountain country. Contact the Petersburg Forest Service office for details on trail conditions and access.

ACCOMMODATIONS

For a complete list of local lodging choices, see the Petersburg Chamber of Commerce website (www.petersburg.org) or try www.petersburgalaska.com.

The best deal in town is **Alaska Island Hostel** (805 Gjoa St., 907/772-3632 or 877/772-3632, www.alaskaislandhostel.com, $25 per person) where Ryn Schneider makes everyone welcome. There are separate men's and women's dorms (four bunks per room), along with a kitchen, laundry, and free Internet access. No children under six, and check-in is 5–8 P.M. Reservations required for winter stays.

Petersburg's largest lodging place, **Tides Inn** (307 N. 1st., 907/772-4288 or 800/665-8433, www.tidesinnalaska.com, $90 s, $105 d) has clean and well-maintained rooms, Wi-Fi, a guest computer, and very friendly owners. Some rooms include fridges and microwaves.

Scandia House (110 Nordic Dr., 907/772-4281 or 800/722-5006, www.scandiahouse hotel.com) is a modern building with 33 brightly furnished rooms. Standard rooms (some with kitchenettes) go for $90–110 s or $100–110 d. Full suites with in-room hot tubs and king beds cost $185 d. A courtesy van and Wi-Fi are available.

The Lucky Loon (907/772-2345, www.the luckyloon.com) is a private beach house three miles south of town. It sleeps up to five for $190 a day with a three-day minimum.

A number of fishing lodges line the Wrangell Narrows, offering multi-night stays, but the nicest is **Rocky Point Resort** (907/772-4420, www.rockyptresort.com), midway along the channel.

Bed-and-Breakfasts

Water's Edge B&B (705 Sandy Beach Rd., 907/772-3736 or 800/868-4373, www .petersburglodgingandtours.com, $100–110 d) is a fine place if you want peace and quiet, with a beachfront room facing Frederick Sound. The two guest rooms have private baths, and a light breakfast is served. Bikes, free Wi-Fi, and courtesy transport are available for guests,

and the owners (30-year residents) also run Kaleidoscope Cruises.

One of Petersburg's older homes (built in the 1920s), **Broom Hus B&B** (411 S. Nordic, 907/772-3459, www.broomhus.com, closed Feb.–April, $90 d) has a downstairs apartment and a kitchen stocked for a make-it-yourself breakfast.

Das Hagedorn Haus—The Hawthorne House (400 2nd St., 907/772-3775 http://home.gci.net/~dhh, $90 d)—is similar, with an attractive basement apartment. The owners prepare a full breakfast and provide a guest computer and free Wi-Fi.

Nordic House B&B (1106 Nordic Dr., 907/772-3620, www.nordichouse.net, $75–95 s, $85–95 d) is a comfortable and attractive home with a glassed-in deck overlooking the harbor. Six guest rooms have private or shared baths, and a light breakfast is served. A separate apartment costs $115.

Waterfront B&B (1004 S. Nordic Dr., 907/772-9300, www.waterfrontbedand breakfast.com, $95–115 d) stands on pilings along the shore just north of the ferry terminal. Five guest rooms have private baths and share a sitting room and large waterside deck; full breakfast and free Wi-Fi included.

Other places to check out include **Feathered Nest B&B** (907/772-3090, www.feathered nestbandb.com), **Heather & Rose Guest Hus** (907/772-4675, www.alaska.net/~hrosehus), and **A Lille Hus B&B** (907/772-4810).

CAMPING

Those with a vehicle or willing to try hitching should head south 22 miles to the Forest Service's **Ohmer Creek Campground** ($6). This is a quiet place in a flower-filled meadow along Blind Slough, with tap water available. Not far away is the quarter-mile-long, wheelchair-accessible Ohmer Creek Trail, complete with interpretive signs. This is a beautiful old-growth rainforest walk, with steelhead fishing in the spring.

Le Conte RV Park (4th and Haugen, 907/772-4680) has tent and RV spaces in town. Out-of-town options are **Twin Creek**

RV Park (7 miles south, 907/772-3244, www.twincreekrv.com, $25 RVs, $10 tents), and **The Trees RV Park** (10 miles south, 907/772-2502, $30 RVs).

FOOD

Open seasonally, **Tina's Kitchen** (907/772-2090) occupies a little downtown stand next to Scandia House with chicken teriyaki, halibut tacos, burritos, and even Philly steak sandwiches for $7–9. The local latte joint, **Java Hus** (907/772-2626) is next door. Get sandwiches, soups, and salads, plus ice cream and shakes from **Helse Café** (13 Sing Lee Alley, 907/772-3444).

Given the importance of fishing in the local economy, it comes as no surprise that Petersburg has a number of places offering fresh seafood. **Coastal Cold Storage Fish Market** (306 N. Nordic Dr., 907/772-4177) serves tasty halibut beer bits, shrimp baskets, reubens, wraps, and other lunch fare, plus Ole and Lena omelets for a Norwegian breakfast. You can also buy fresh fish, scallops, crab (cooked if you like), and other seafood—including, of course, lutefisk.

rockfish at Tonka Seafoods

© DON PITCHER

Tonka Seafoods (907/772-3662 or 888/560-3662, www.tonkaseafoods.com) specializes in premium smoked, canned, or fresh salmon, rockfish, and halibut. The retail store, across from the Sons of Norway Hall on Sing Lee Alley, is open weekdays, with hour-long tours ($5) at 1:30 P.M.

A small shop across from the ferry terminal, **Papa Bear's Pizzeria** (907/772-3727) serves pizzas (whole or by the slice), sandwiches, wraps, and ice cream.

Open three meals a day, **Rooney's Northern Lights Restaurant** (203 Sing Lee Alley, 907/772-2900) has windows facing the harbor and dependably good meals. Located inside Kito's Kave on Sing Lee Alley, **La Fonda** (907/772-3207) is worth a visit for fast Mexican lunches.

Prices for food and other items are higher in Petersburg than in other Southeast towns. Two local grocers have all the supplies: **Hammer & Wikan** (1300 Howkan Dr., 907/772-4246, www.hammerandwikan.com), with a full deli and bakery, and the downtown **Trading Union** (907/772-3881).

INFORMATION AND SERVICES

The **Petersburg Visitors Information Center** (corner of 1st and Fram Sts., 907/772-4636 or 866/484-4700 message only, www.petersburg .org) has travel brochures. Hours are Sunday noon–4 P.M., Monday–Saturday 9 A.M.–5 P.M., May–September; and Monday–Friday 10 A.M.–2 P.M. the rest of the year.

The Forest Service (907/772-3871) publishes a map of the Petersburg area, *Mitkof Island Road Guide,* available from the visitor center or its office on Main Street. The map is a must if you're planning to ride a mountain bike around the island.

Get cash 24 hours a day from ATMs at First Bank and Wells Fargo. The post office (907/772-3121) is out near the airport on Haugen Drive, and the **Petersburg Library** (907/772-3349, www.ci.petersburg.ak.us) is upstairs in the municipal building on Nordic Drive. Stop by here to check your email. For additional Internet access, plug into **System Overload** (110 Harbor Way, 907/772-2343).

Coin-op showers are downtown at the harbormaster's office, and at **Glacier Laundry** on Nordic Drive. For a better deal, paddle over to the Petersburg High School swimming pool (907/772-3304). A fine community gym is nearby, complete with weight room and racquetball courts. **Petersburg Medical Center** (on 2nd and Fram Sts., 907/772-4299) is the local hospital.

Shopping

Sing Lee Alley Books (907/772-4440), next to the Sons of Norway Hall, has an excellent collection of Alaskan books and other choice reading material. **CubbyHole** (102 S. 2nd St., 907/772-2717) sells Norwegian-style handicrafts decorated with *rosemaling* designs.

Petersburg has two notable galleries: **The Framers Loft Gallery** (on Sing Lee Alley, 907/772-2471) and **Seaport Gallery & Gifts** (on Main St., 907/772-3015). Get beautiful Norwegian and Icelandic sweaters at **Lee's Clothing** (207 Nordic Dr., 907/772-4229).

GETTING THERE AND AROUND

Petersburg is strung out along Wrangell Narrows, with the **ferry terminal** (907/772-3855) a mile south of the town center. During the summer, ferries run almost daily both northbound and southbound from Petersburg. They usually stop for an hour or two, long enough to walk into town or at least check out the nearby harbor. The ferry terminal opens two hours before ship arrivals and generally stays open a half-hour after it departs. For reservations and schedules, contact the **Alaska Marine Highway** (907/465-3941 or 800/642-0066, www.ferryalaska.com).

Metro Cab (907/772-2700) and **Midnight Rides** (907/772-2222) charge $5 for transport from the state ferry to town.

The **Inter-Island Ferry Authority's** (907/826-4848 or 866/308-4848, www.interislandferry.com) M/V *Stikine* provides summer-only service Thursday–Sunday between the south end of Mitkof Island and Wrangell, continuing south to Prince of Wales Island. The ferry dock is 28 miles south of Petersburg. If you have a vehicle, this is the fastest way to travel between Wrangell and Petersburg since the *Stikine* takes just two hours for the shorter route, versus four hours for the state ferry. Of course, this route requires a 45-minute paved-and-gravel drive to Petersburg, and the ferry doesn't go through scenic Wrangell Narrows. **Viking Travel** (907/772-3818 or 800/327-2571, www.alaskaferry.com) has a shuttle van to Petersburg for $23 one-way, but call ahead for reservations.

Rent cars from **Allstar Rent-A-Car** (907/772-4281 or 800/722-5006, www.scandiahousehotel.com) at Scandia House or **Avis** (907/772-4716 or 800/331-1212, www.tidesinnalaska.com) in Tides Inn.

Petersburg Airport is a mile southeast of town on Haugen Drive. **Alaska Airlines** (907/772-4255 or 800/426-0333, www.alaskaair.com), has daily service to other Southeast towns and the Lower 48. **Pacific Wing** (907/772-9258, www.pacificwing.com), **Kupreanof Flying Service** (907/772-3396, www.kupreanof.com), and **Nordic Air** (907/772-3535) all provide air charter service to Forest Service cabins. **Temsco Helicopters** (907/772-4780 or 877/789-9501, www.temscoair.com) offers helicopter flightseeing. **Sunrise Aviation** (907/874-2319 or 800/874-2311, www.sunriseflights.com) often has seat fares to Wrangell.

KAKE

The small Tlingit village of Kake (pop. 700) lies along the northwest shore of Kupreanof Island, halfway between Petersburg and Sitka. Kake's claim to fame is the **world's tallest totem pole,** exhibited at the 1970 World's Fair in Osaka, Japan. This 132-foot pole is unique in that it contains figures representing all the Tlingit clans on a single pole. Kake is also the starting point for sea kayak trips into two large wilderness areas on nearby Kuiu Island. Also of interest is the quaint **Kake Presbyterian Church.** Built in 1929, it is the oldest public building in town.

History

During the 1800s the Kake tribe had a reputation as one of the fiercest in the Southeast. Richard Meade recorded the following incident: "In 1855 a party of Kakes, on a visit south to Puget Sound, became involved in some trouble there, which caused a United States vessel to open fire on them, and during the affair one of the Kake chiefs was killed. This took place over 800 miles from the Kake settlements on Kupreanof Island. The very next year the tribe sent a canoe-load of fighting men all the way from Clarence Straits in Russian America to Whidby's Island in Washington Territory, and attacked and beheaded an ex-collector—not of internal revenue, for that might have been pardonable—but of customs, and returned safely with his skull and scalp to their villages. Such people are, therefore, not to be despised, and are quite capable of giving much trouble in the future unless wisely and firmly governed." John Muir later described a visit to a Kake village where human bones were scattered all over the ground, reminders of previous battles: "Chief Yana Taowk seemed to take pleasure in kicking the Sitka bones that lay in his way, and neither old nor young showed the slightest trace of superstitious fear of the dead at any time." Needless to say, the people of Kake treat outsiders in a friendlier manner today.

Practicalities

Keex' Kwaan Lodge (907/785-3434, www.kakealaska.com, $85 s or $98 d) is a comfortable and modern lodge with a full-service restaurant and free Wi-Fi. If you're in search of a budget place where the basic older rooms have a down-the-hall bath, try **Nugget Inn** (907/785-6469, $40 d).

Get groceries from **SOS Value-Mart** (907/785-6444), a quarter-mile from the ferry. Kake has a java joint and liquor store, but no bank. Get local information from the **City of Kake** (907/785-3804).

Camping facilities are not available and much of the land around Kake is privately owned, but camping is permitted on Forest Service land, two miles south of town. Kake is one of the drier towns in the Southeast, with only 50 inches per year of precipitation. The town has a fish hatchery and cold-storage plant but no Forest Service office. Ask at the Forest Service office in Petersburg about the Cathedral Falls, Goose Lake, and Hamilton River Trails. **Big John Cabin** on Big John Bay is accessible via the road network from Kake.

The **Alaska Marine Highway** (800/642-0066, www.ferryalaska.com) ferry *LeConte* visits Kake twice a week, heading both east to Petersburg and west to Sitka. It docks a mile and a half from the center of town. There is a covered shelter area, but no phone. The ferry usually stops just long enough to load and unload cars (a half-hour or so).

L.A.B. Flying Service (907/785-6435, www.labflying.com) has daily service from Kake to Petersburg and Juneau.

Kuiu Island

If you have the time, equipment, and skill, nearby Kuiu Island (pronounced Q-U) provides excellent kayaking and canoeing opportunities. Two wilderness areas encompass the south and west sides of Kuiu Island; other parts have been heavily logged. Dozens of interesting islands, islets, and coves crowd the west side of Kuiu in the 67,000-acre **Tebenkof Bay Wilderness,** while the south end includes the 60,000-acre **Kuiu Wilderness.** The Forest Service publishes a detailed map of Kuiu Island, with descriptions of all portages and routes. Get a copy of *Kuiu Island/Tebenkof Bay Canoe/Kayak Routes* from Petersburg Ranger District (907/772-3871, www.fs.fed.us/r10/tongass).

Experienced kayakers will enjoy the paddle between Kake and Petersburg around the south end of Kupreanof Island. There is open water in places, but a good portion of the route is protected and the state ferry makes it easy to get between Kake and Petersburg. Contact Tongass Kayak Adventures (907/772-4600, www.tongasskayak.com) for sea kayak tours within Tebenkof Bay Wilderness.

Sitka

With its gemlike, island-dotted setting, Sitka (pop. 9,000) is everybody's favorite Southeast Alaska town. On a typical summer day you'll see fishing boats heading out to sea from the four harbors around Sitka Sound, and cruise ships steaming by, their decks crowded with tourists as they pass Mt. Edgecumbe, the Fuji-like snowcapped volcano that adorns Sitka's outer waters. Back in town, other visitors glance inside the Russian church that dominates Sitka's center, wander along totem-pole-lined paths in peaceful Sitka National Historical Park, and climb the sharply rising wooded peaks behind town. The people who make this their home are similarly diverse, ranging from beer-guzzling fishermen barely making ends meet, to wealthy retirees from California who are pushing housing prices into the stratosphere. The gorgeous setting makes Sitka a detour well worth the effort. Be fore-warned, however, to expect rain—the town soaks in 94 inches a year. By the way, Sitka lays claim to being the "biggest city in America"; its boundaries encircle Baranof Island, fully 4,710 square miles! (New York City covers only 301 square miles.)

Peril Strait

Located on the western shore of Baranof Island, "Sitka-by-the-Sea" is Southeast Alaska's most remote ferry stop, and the only major Inside Passage town to front on the Pacific Ocean. Getting to Sitka by ferry requires a long detour through the scenic but treacherous Peril Strait that separates Baranof and Chichagof Islands—a great place to watch for eagles perched on trees along the shore. During larger tides, fierce currents prevent ferries from going through, and the ships must time their passage to coincide with a high or low slack tide. The

© DON PITCHER

Sitka

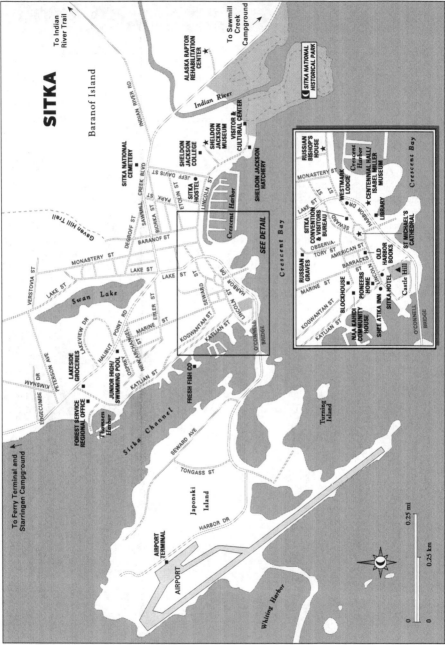

SITKA

Baranof Island

To Indian River Trail

To Sawmill Creek Campground

ALASKA RAPTOR REHABILITATION CENTER

SITKA NATIONAL HISTORICAL PARK

Indian River

INDIAN RIVER RD

Geavn Hill Trail

SITKA NATIONAL CEMETERY

SHELDON JACKSON COLLEGE

SHELDON JACKSON MUSEUM

VISITOR & CULTURAL CENTER

JEFF DAVIS ST

ETOLIN ST

LINCOLN ST

SITKA HOSTEL

SHELDON JACKSON HATCHERY

Crescent Harbor

SEE DETAIL

DEGROFF ST

SAWMILL CREEK BLVD

PARK ST

BIORKA ST

BARANOF ST

Crescent Bay

MONASTERY ST

LAKE ST

VERSTOVIA ST

LAKE ST

LAKE ST

Swan Lake

SEWARD

HARBOR DR

LINCOLN ST

LAKEVIEW DR

HALIBUT POINT RD

MARINE ST

NEW ARCHANGEL ST

ERLER ST

KOGWANTAN ST

KATLIAN ST

O'CONNELL BRIDGE

KIMSHAM ST

PETERSON AVE

EDGECUMBE DR

LAKESIDE GROCERIES

JUNIOR HIGH SWIMMING POOL

OSPREY ST

KATLIAN ST

FRESH FISH CO.

FOREST SERVICE REGIONAL OFFICE

Thomsen Harbor

Sitka Channel

SEWARD AVE

Turning Island

To Ferry Terminal and Starrigavan Campground

TONGASS ST

Japonski Island

HARBOR DR

AIRPORT TERMINAL

AIRPORT

Whiting Harbor

DETAIL:

RUSSIAN BISHOP'S HOUSE

MONASTERY ST

Crescent Harbor

WESTMARK LODGE

CENTENNIAL HALL/ ISABEL MILLER MUSEUM

LAKE ST

SEWARD

HARBOR DR

Crescent Bay

SITKA CONVENTION & VISITORS BUREAU

OBSERVA-TORY ST

AMERICAN ST

LIBRARY

RUSSIAN GRAVES

MARINE ST

BARRACKS

PIONEERS HOME

OLD HARBOR BOOKS

ST MICHAEL'S CATHEDRAL

KOGWANTAN ST

BLOCKHOUSE

LINCOLN ST

SITKA HOTEL

Castle Hill

KATLIAN ST

NAA KAHIDI COMMUNITY HOUSE

SHEE ATIKA INN

O'CONNELL BRIDGE

0   0.25 mi

0   0.25 km

© AVALON TRAVEL PUBLISHING, INC.

passage narrows to only 300 feet in one spot (24 ft. deep). When the tide is really cooking, the buoys are often bent far over by the wild currents. This has one side benefit: The ferry is forced to stay for three hours or so in Sitka, long enough for you to get a taste of this fascinating town. But to see this pretty place better, be sure to stay awhile.

HISTORY
Russian America

First established as a base for collecting sea otter pelts, Sitka has a long and compelling history. In 1799, Alexander Baranov—head of the Russian American Company—founded the settlement under a charter from the czar. Baranov (also spelled Baranof) built his original fort, Redoubt St. Michael, near the present Alaska ferry terminal, only to see it destroyed by a Tlingit attack in 1802. (There is evidence that the British, long enemies of the Russians, assisted the Tlingits in the fort's destruction.) Two years later, Baranov returned with 120 soldiers and 800 Aleuts in 300 *baidarkas,* defeating the Tlingits in what was to become the last major resistance by any Northwest Coast Indians. The Russians rebuilt the town, then called New Archangel, on the present site and constructed a stockade enclosing what is now downtown Sitka. New Archangel soon became the capital of Russian America and a vital center for the sea otter and fur seal trade with China. Although the Tlingits were invited back in 1821 (Native leaders say the Russians begged them to return), the groups coexisted uneasily. Tlingits built their houses just outside the stockade, facing a battery of eight Russian cannons.

Once labeled the "Paris of the North Pacific," New Archangel quickly became the Northwest's most cosmopolitan port. By 1840, it was already home to a library of several thousand volumes, a museum, a meteorological observatory, two schools, a hospital, an armory, two orphanages, and dozens of other buildings. The wealthier citizens lived in elaborate homes filled with crystal and fine lace, but as in czarist Russia itself, the opulence of Sitka did not extend beyond a select few. Slavelike working and living conditions were forced upon the Aleut sea otter hunters.

America Takes Over

An emotional ceremony at Sitka in 1867 marked the passage of Alaska from Russian to American hands, and most of the Russians returned to their motherland, including many third-generation Sitkans. Even today, there are locals who speak Russian. Although the town served as Alaska's first capital city for three decades, its importance declined rapidly under the Americans, and it was almost a ghost town by the turn of the century. The territorial government was moved to the then-booming mining town of Juneau in 1900.

During World War II, Sitka became a major link in the defense of Alaska against Japan. Hangars remain from the large amphibious air base just across the bridge on Japonski Island (Fort Ray), and the barracks that once housed 3,500 soldiers were turned into Mt. Edgecumbe High School, Alaska's only boarding high school for Natives. The boarding school is now fully integrated.

Sitka's largest employer until 1993 was a Japanese-owned pulp mill five miles east of town. The mill closed mainly because of the high cost of production and competition from mills elsewhere. Before it closed, the mill gained national attention for dumping large quantities of cancer-causing dioxin into nearby Silver Bay, and for being one of the primary forces behind the clear-cut logging of Tongass National Forest. Many Sitkans still work in the fishing and tourism industries, or for the government. The mill's closure did not have nearly the devastating effect the prophets of doom had predicted; in fact Sitka seems to be doing just fine, fueled by tourism and the arrival of retirees. Large cruise ships are in port most summer days, but things aren't nearly as bad (yet) as in Juneau, Ketchikan, or Skagway.

SIGHTS

One of the finest views of Sitka is from the walkway along the distinctive cable-stayed, girder-span bridge that connects Sitka with

Japonski Island. On a clear day, you'll have a hard time deciding which direction to look: The mountains of Baranof Island rise up behind the town, while the perfect volcanic cone of **Mt. Edgecumbe** (3,000 ft.) on Kruzof Island dominates the opposite vista. Beside the old post office on Lincoln Street a stairway leads up to **Castle Hill,** a tiny state park commemorating the spot where the ceremony transferring Alaska to the United States was held on October 18, 1867. The Kiksadi Indians inhabited this hill for many generations before the Russians' arrival. After defeating the Kiksadi, Alexander Baranov built his castlelike house here, but the building burned in 1894. The splendid view makes Castle Hill a must.

The most prominent downtown feature is the large yellow **Alaska Pioneers Home** (built in 1934), housing elderly Alaskans with 15 or more years of state residence. The *Prospector* statue out front was based upon William "Skagway Bill" Fonda, an Alaskan pioneer. Across the road is a **totem pole** bearing the Russian coat of arms, three old English anchors, and a couple of Indian petroglyphs. Adjacent to the Pioneers Home is **Sheet'Ka Kwaan Naa Kahidi Community House,** based upon traditional longhouse designs, offering Native dance performances in summer. Two tall housescreens dominate the interior.

Atop a small hill just west of the Pioneer Home stands a reconstructed **Russian blockhouse** from the stockade that kept the Indians restricted to the area along Katlian Street. It's open Sunday afternoons during the summer. **Kogwantan and Katlian streets,** directly below the blockhouse, are a picturesque mixture of docks, fish canneries, shops, and old houses, one with its exterior entirely covered in Tlingit designs. The main **Finnish Lutheran Cemetery** (400 graves dating from 1848) is behind the blockhouse at the end of Princess Street. The grave of the Russian **Princess Maksoutoff** is here, and nearby are more Russian graves, including that of Iahov Netsvetov, a Russian Orthodox saint. Cemetery buffs might also be interested in the small **Sitka National Cemetery,** accessible via Jeff Davis Street beside Sheldon Jackson College. It's the oldest national cemetery west of the Mississippi. Built in 1900, the **Geodetic Survey House** (210 Seward St., Tues.–Thurs. 9 A.M.–4 P.M.) houses displays on Mt. Edgecumbe and Tongass National Forest.

St. Michael's Cathedral

The most striking symbol of Russian influence in Sitka is St. Michael's Cathedral (907/747-8120), right in the center of town. Built in 1848, the building burned in 1966 but was replaced by a replica a decade later. The original Russian artifacts and icons, including the Sitka Madonna (purportedly a miraculous healer), were saved from the fire and have been returned to their original setting in this, the mother church for all of Alaska's 20,000 Russian Orthodox. During the summer, the church ($2) is open Monday–Friday 9 A.M.–4 P.M., or whenever a large cruise ship is in port. It's open by appointment at other times, but is not open to tourists during religious services.

Isabel Miller Museum

This small museum (330 Harbor Dr., 907/747-6455, www.sitkahistory.org, donation) is tucked away inside Centennial Hall. It's open daily 8 A.M.–5 P.M. in summer; Tuesday–Friday 11 A.M.–5 P.M. and Saturday 10 A.M.–4 P.M. in winter. The museum houses local artifacts and an interesting scale-model of Sitka in 1867 (the year Alaska became a U.S. territory). Out front is a 50-foot carved and painted replica of a **Tlingit war canoe.**

Russian Bishop's House

Administered by the National Park Service, the Russian Bishop's House (907/747-6281, www.nps.gov/sitk, daily 9 A.M.–5 P.M. in summer, by reservation the rest of the year) is Sitka's oldest building and one of just four Russian structures still standing in North America. Built in 1842, it was home to Ivan Veniaminov, bishop of Alaska and later head of the entire Russian Orthodox church hierarchy in Moscow. The first floor houses exhibits describing the building and its occupants, as well as the exploits of Russia's American colony. The second floor has been fully restored to its 1853 appearance and is filled with original furnishings and artifacts. Access to the second floor is part of a half-hour tour ($4) led by park interpreters.

Sheldon Jackson Museum

Farther along the waterfront is **Sheldon Jackson College,** with its distinctive brown and white buildings. Established in 1878 as a place to train Alaska's Natives, this is the oldest educational institution in the state. The outstanding Sheldon Jackson Museum (907/747-8981, www.museums.state.ak.us, daily 9 A.M.–5 P.M. mid-May–mid-Sept., Tues.–Sat. 10 A.M.–4 P.M. rest of year; $4, free for students) is the state's oldest museum. Dr. Sheldon Jackson (1834–1909) worked as both a Presbyterian missionary and as the first General Agent for Education in Alaska. His extensive travels throughout the territory between 1888 and 1898 allowed him to acquire thousands of Eskimo, Athabascan, Tlingit, Haida, and Aleut artifacts. To protect this priceless collection, a fireproof museum (the first concrete structure in Alaska) was built here in 1895. The museum houses a remarkable selection of kayaks, hunting tools, dogsleds, baskets, bentwood boxes, Eskimo masks, and other artifacts. Be sure to check out the drawers of artifacts beneath the display cases. Also here is a small gift shop selling quality Alaskan jewelry, crafts, and note cards. Native artisans are often at work inside the museum during the summer. Across the street is the **Sheldon Jackson College Aquarium and Hatchery** (907/747-5254, free) with an 800-gallon saltwater aquarium and three touch tanks to get up close to tidepool creatures.

◖ Sitka National Historical Park

For many, the highlight of a visit to Sitka is Sitka National Historical Park, at the mouth of Indian River where the Tlingits and Russians fought their final battle in 1804. The Indians kept the invaders at bay for a week, but with their ammunition exhausted and resup-

© DON PITCHER

Chilkat blanket weaving, Sitka National Historical Park

ply efforts thwarted, they abandoned the fortress and silently withdrew to Peril Strait. The visitors and Native cultural center (907/747-6281, www.nps.gov/sitk, daily 8 A.M.–5 P.M. in summer, and Mon.–Fri. 8 A.M.–5 P.M. the rest of the year, $4) includes an informative small museum of Tlingit culture. In summertime, Native craft workers can be seen producing bead blankets, jewelry, and woodcarving in the workshop. The 10-minute historical video, "Battle of Sitka," is very informative, and rangers offer daily historical walks in the summer.

Quite a few historical totems are housed in one large room, and outside are 15 more totems, most of which were carved for the 1904 St. Louis World's Fair. The totems line a one-mile trail through the lush second-growth spruce forest, with outstanding views of Sitka Sound along the way. You'll find spawning pink salmon in Indian River (near the 1804 battleground) late in the summer. The park is a peaceful place where mysterious in-the-trees totems, the strident calls of ravens and eagles, and the lapping of waves combine to enhance the beauty.

Alaska Raptor Center

Located off Sawmill Creek Road, this impressive facility (907/747-8662 or 800/643-9425, www.alaskaraptor.org, $12 adults, $6 kids under 12) has two dozen or so bald eagles and other birds of prey—including owls, hawks, falcons, and ravens—at any given time. Most are recovering from gunshots, car accidents, or encounters with power lines. Of the birds brought in, a third recover sufficiently to be released back into the wild. Most of the others end up in captive breeding or educational programs in the Lower 48. Get to the center by walking out of town along Sawmill Creek Road a couple hundred feet beyond the Indian River bridge. The access road takes off to your left a short distance beyond this. A more scenic route is to follow the trails through Sitka National Historical Park or along the Indian River behind Sheldon Jackson College. It's an easy 10-minute walk from Sitka National Historical Park, or 20 minutes from the center of town. The Community Ride Bus ($2) takes you within two blocks of the center.

A focal point is the 20,000-square-foot flight-training center that replicates the rainforest environment outside; visitors watch the eagles through one-way glass. Staff use the enclosure to teach eagles survival skills prior to their release. Out back is a deck overlooking a large enclosure (mew) where eagles unable to survive in the wild are kept. Additional mews with hawks, owls, and other birds are along a rain forest path. The gift shop sells all sorts of eagle paraphernalia.

Visitors get the chance to meet one of the birds up close, and are given a half-hour tour and video. The center is open daily 8 A.M.–4 P.M. May–September, and there's always someone on hand whenever a cruise ship is in town. No winter tours.

Whale Park

Six miles out Sawmill Creek Road is Whale Park, consisting of a roadside turnout with interpretive signs and a boardwalk to an overlook where there's a good chance of seeing whales during the fall and winter months. Offshore hydrophones broadcast the sounds of passing whales (if they are around).

ENTERTAINMENT AND EVENTS

Cultural Performances

When cruise ships are in town, Herrigan Centennial Hall auditorium comes alive with half-hour performances of traditional Russian, Ukrainian, Armenian, and Moldavian dance by the 35-member, all-female **New Archangel Dancers** (907/747-5516, www.newarchangeldancers.com, $8). The troupe has toured extensively, including visits to Japan, Russia, Canada, and Mexico.

For a very different form of dance, the **Sheet'Ka Kwaan Naa Kahidi Dancers** (907/747-7290, $7 adults, $5 kids) give Tlingit performances in full regalia through the summer months. These excellent half-hour productions are offered when cruise ships are in port. Most folks see them as part of a bus tour given by Tribal Tours. Performances take place in the imposing Sheet'Ka Kwaan Naa Kahidi Community House, next to the Pioneers Home on Katlian Street.

Nightlife

Fishermen and would-be crew members hang out at the sometimes-rowdy **Pioneer Bar** (on Katlian St., 907/747-3456). The P-Bar's walls are crowded with hundreds of photos of local fishing boats, and the blackboard often has "crew wanted" ads. Don't miss the **Sunday afternoon jam sessions** at Backdoor Café; it's an authentic taste of life in small-town Alaska.

Inside the Sitka Hotel, **Victoria's Pourhouse** (907/747-9301) has a gigantic TV, beer on draught, a smoke-free setting, and free Wi-Fi. **Ernie's Old Time Saloon** (907/747-3334) has live music most weekends and a couple of offbeat stuffed animals, including a "sidehill" salmon.

Events

For three weeks in June, the renowned **Sitka Summer Music Festival** (907/747-6774, www.sitkamusicfestival.org) attracts musicians from all over the world. Chamber music concerts are given several evenings a week in Centennial Hall, but the most fun is the annual BoatParty

Concert (reserve early). Concert tickets may be hard to come by, but you can always visit rehearsals for free. Another cultural event, the **Sitka Symposium** (http://home.gci.net/~island) in mid-July, attracts nationally known poets and writers.

In late May, visitors can join locals in the **Sitka Salmon Derby,** where the top fish is often a 60-pound-plus king salmon. **July 4th** features a parade, races, softball tournament, live music, dancing, and fireworks. On Labor Day weekend, the **Mudball Classic Softball Tournament** attracts teams from around the nation for fun in the muck.

As the town where Alaska was officially transferred from Russian to American hands, Sitka is also the place to be on **Alaska Day.** A celebration of "Seward's Folly" is held each October 18 with dances (including a remarkable performance by the New Archangel Dancers), traditional Russian costumes, a parade, and a reenactment of the brief transfer ceremony.

In early November, the **Sitka Whalefest** (907/747-7964, www.sitkawhalefest.org) attracts biologists and those who love whales and other marine mammals to a series of scientific seminars, whale-watching tours, concerts, crafts, and exhibits.

RECREATION

Sitka is a popular destination for **sportsfishing;** drop by the Sitka CVB office (www.sitka.org) for a handout listing more than 30 charter boats.

The protected waters near Sitka provide excellent kayak access to many Forest Service cabins and trails. **Sitka Sound Ocean Adventures** (907/747-6375, www.ssoceanadventures.com) guides kayak day trips (starting at $63 for 2 hrs.) and rents kayaks. **Esther G Sea Taxi** (907/747-6481, www.puffinsandwhales.com) provides kayaker and hiker drop-offs if you're heading out. **Island Fever Diving and Sports** (805 Halibut Point Rd., 907/747-7871, www.islandfeverdiving.com) sets up snorkeling excursions using dry suits.

Rent quality mountain bikes from **Yellow Jersey Cycle Shop** (329 Harbor Dr., 907/747-6317) downtown. Jeff Budd of **Sitka Bike & Hike** (907/747-4821 or 877/292-5325, www.sitkaadventures.com) leads biking and hiking tours, including trips to the summit Mt. Edgecumbe.

The Forest Service's **Sitka Ranger District Office** (204 Siginaka Way, 907/747-4220, www.fs.fed.us/r10/tongass) has up-to-date information on the more than 40 miles of local trails, ranging from gentle nature walks to treks that take you high up onto nearby peaks. Contact **Sitka Bike & Hike** (907/747-4821 or 877/292-5325, www.sitkaadventures.com) for guided treks.

Indian River Trail

One of the finest of Sitka's trails, this is an easy valley hike within walking distance of town. The route follows a clear salmon stream through the rainforest, with a chance to see brown bear and deer. Begin by heading out Sawmill Creek Road and turning left onto Indian River Road. Continue past the gate about a half-mile to the city water pumphouse. The gentle trail leads from here up along the Indian River and a tributary to the right as far as a lovely 80-foot waterfall in a V-shaped valley. The last mile of the trail is not well maintained. Allow six hours round-trip to cover the 5.5-mile trail.

Gavan Hill Trail

This "stairway to heaven" walkway starts at the end of Baranof Street and climbs three miles to the top of 2,650-foot Gavan Hill. (Bear right at the junction with Cross Trail just under a mile up.) Gavan Hill Trail then switchbacks to a long ridge that opens onto subalpine meadows before a steep final climb up the last 200 feet of elevation. From here, it's relatively easy to follow rock cairns on through the alpine, connecting to the Harbor Mountain Trail. This makes an outstanding loop hike with impressive vistas of Sitka Sound.

Harbor Mountain Trail

One of the easiest and most scenic ways to get into the alpine is via Harbor Mountain Trail. Built by the Army during World War II, the road originally provided access to a lookout post for invading Japanese ships and submarines (none were ever seen, though a whale was once mistakenly bombed). Head four miles out Halibut Point Road and turn right onto Harbor Mountain Road. The gravel road climbs five miles up the mountain to an elevation of 2,000 feet. Snow blocks the road until June, but you can park at the gate and walk up if you don't mind hiking atop snow. On sunny days the view over Sitka Sound is breathtaking. Those without a car or mountain bike should be able to hitch a ride up with locals.

A trail begins at the parking area on top and switchbacks up a side hill before leveling out in the subalpine meadows. A spur trail heads to an overlook here, but the main trail turns right and continues past the ruins of wartime lookout buildings. Beyond this, rock cairns follow the ridge, and the path eventually connects with the Gavan Hill Trail back to town. A small hut provides a camping place approximately three miles in.

Mt. Verstovia Trail

On a clear day get spectacular views of Sitka Sound and Mt. Edgecumbe from the Mt. Verstovia Trail, a strenuous climb to this pointy peak overlooking Sitka. The steep 2.5-mile trail begins on the west side of the Kiksadi Club, two miles east of town on Sawmill Creek Road. The trail is brushy and poorly maintained, and inexperienced hikers have gotten lost. You'll pass some old Russian charcoal pits (signposted) only a quarter-mile from the trailhead. The route switchbacks to a ridge, which you follow to the shoulder of Mt. Verstovia. The true summit is farther northeast along the ridge. Allow four hours for the return trip as far as the "shoulder" (2,000 ft.), six hours round-trip to the top (2,550 ft.).

Beaver Lake Trail

This family friendly mile-long trail begins at the bridge in Sawmill Creek Campground seven miles east of town. The path gains 250 feet in elevation as it climbs through the forest

Sitka Sound and Mt. Edgecumbe

© DON PITCHER

and out onto a boardwalk over the muskeg to Beaver Lake. The lake has been stocked with grayling and is one of the only places to catch these fish in the Southeast. There are fishing platforms along the lakeshore.

Mt. Edgecumbe

Mt. Edgecumbe, a 3,000-foot volcanic cone that looks like Mt. Fuji, can be climbed via a 6.5-mile trail that starts on the southeast shore of Kruzof Island. The last mile is above tree line through red volcanic ash. The island is 10 miles west of Sitka and can be reached by kayak (beware of ocean swells) or by arranging for a skiff drop-off. Stay in Fred's Creek Cabin at the trailhead or in the free three-sided shelter halfway up. Panoramic views can be had from atop this dormant volcano.

Cabins

The Forest Service has 24 cabins (reservations: 518/885-3639 or 877/444-6777, www.reserveusa.com, $35) in the Sitka area, most accessed by floatplane or water taxi from Sitka.

Redoubt Lake Cabin is at the end of a six-mile trail that starts in Silver Bay (10 miles southeast of Sitka). The cabin is also accessible by sea kayak from town, and a short portage takes you to Redoubt Lake.

The wheelchair-accessible **Lake Eva Cabin** is 27 miles northeast of Sitka on Baranof Island. **Plotnikof Lake Cabin** sits in the heart of the spectacularly rugged South Baranof Wilderness Area, a 45-minute flight from Sitka.

Baranof Lake Cabin looks across this blue-green lake to a waterfall. A trail at the end of the lake leads a half-mile to the little settlement of **Baranof Warm Springs**, where privately owned hot springs are available.

Brent's Beach Cabin is on the eastern shore of Kruzof Island, 15 miles northwest of Sitka. There's a white-sand beach out front (rare in the Southeast), and interesting caves and lava domes just up the shore.

The **Allan Point Cabin,** 16 miles north of Sitka, is an impressive, two-story log cabin that commands a fine view across Nakwasina Sound from its location on the northeast end of Halleck Island. The equally spacious **Samsing Cove Cabin** sleeps 10 folks comfortably and is just six miles south of Sitka.

ACCOMMODATIONS

The Sitka Convention & Visitors Bureau produces a pamphlet and website that detail hotels, motels, B&Bs, fishing lodges, wilderness lodges, private apartments, and houses.

Hostel

After many years of operating out of a church basement, the **Sitka Youth Hostel** (109 Jeff Davis Rd., 907/747-8661, open June–Aug., $24 per person) moved into a historic building next to Sheldon Jackson College in 2007. Inside are two dorms, a kitchen, and commons area. The hostel is open 6 P.M.–9:30 A.M., with an 11 P.M. curfew. If you're arriving by ferry, the shuttle bus will drop you at the door, but call ahead for reservations.

Hotels and Motels

Built in 1939, **Sitka Hotel** (118 Lincoln St., 907/747-3288, www.sitkahotel.com) has been restored to a Victorian splendor that it probably never had before. Rooms with private baths are a reasonable $85 s or $90 d, and most of these have small fridges. Those with a bath down the hall are a bargain: $65 s or $70 d, but these are small rooms with basic furnishings. The hotel isn't to everyone's liking, but is fine if you are looking for authenticity, with free Wi-Fi.

Cascade Inn (2035 Halibut Point Rd., 907/747-6804 or 800/532-0908, www.cascadeinnsitka.com) has standard rooms for $115–125 d, and kitchenettes for $140 d. The building is two miles out of town, and all rooms include private balconies facing the water. Guests also have access to a sauna. A convenience store is downstairs.

Westmark Lodge (330 Seward St., 907/747-6241 or 800/544-0970, www.westmarkhotels.com, $159 d, $199–249 for suites) is Sitka's largest lodging place, with a big lobby accented by a Tlingit screen, a lounge and restaurant, plus free Wi-Fi.

The newly renovated **Shee Atika Totem**

Square Inn (201 Katlian St., 907/747-3693 or 866/300-1343, www.totemsquare.com, $139–149 d) features a harborside setting, continental breakfast, exercise room, and Wi-Fi.

Sitka's most distinctive lodging option is **❰ Rockwell Lighthouse** (907/747-3056), a three-bedroom home built in the shape of a lighthouse on an island less than a mile from town. Access is by skiff (transport provided). With its nautical decor, curving interior staircase up into the lighthouse, and picture-perfect setting, you'll be signing up for lighthouse duty after a night or two here. The entire house rents for $150 d or $200 for four people. This place fills up fast in the summer, so call a year ahead for reservations in mid-summer. No credit cards, and a two-night minimum is required (but you will want more time).

Bed-and-Breakfasts

The Sitka Convention and Visitors Bureau website (www.sitka.org) has links to local B&Bs.

Ann's Gavan Hill B&B (415 Arrowhead St., 907/747-8023, www.annsgavanhill.com, $75 s, $85 d) features six guest rooms with shared baths, a hot tub on the covered side deck, filling homemade breakfasts, and a relaxed Alaskan atmosphere. One room is handicap accessible.

Helga's B&B (www.sitkaalaskalodging.com, 907/747-5497, $100–130 d) is a large beachside home three miles out Halibut Point Road. The four guest rooms have private baths, and a continental breakfast is available. The pricier rooms face the water, and a two-bedroom unit sleeps four for $190.

Alaska Ocean View B&B (1101 Edgecumbe Dr., 907/747-8310 or 888/811-6870, www.sitka-alaska-lodging.com, $109–189 s, $129–209 d) is a lovely home with fabulous Sitka Sound vistas. Two guest rooms and a suite have private baths, and include a big breakfast. Other amenities include in-room fireplaces, free Wi-Fi, and a hot tub on the patio.

Other B&Bs worth a look include **Annahootz B&B** (907/747-6498 or 800/746-6498, www.sitka.org/annahootz, $110 d), **Baranof Island B&B** (907/747-8306, www.baranofislandbandb.com, $85 d), **Biorka**

B&B (907/747-3111, $65–85 d), **Finn Alley B&B** (907/747-3655, www.finnalleybedand breakfast.com, $115 d), and **Sitka Woodside Lodging** (907/747-8287, http://home.gci.net/~sdenherder, $85–100 d).

Vacation Rentals and Lodges

Sitka has a number of homes, apartments, and cabins that are rented out to travelers, including **An Abode** (407 Degroff St., 907/747-4932, $85–150 d), **Frank & Gloria's Place** (907/747-8711, www.sitkadream.com, $125 d), **Chocolate Moose** (907/747-5159, $90–125), and **Baranov's Rest** (907/747-8368, www.baranovsrest.com, $250). Visit www.sitka.org for links to other rentals.

A number of Sitka-area lodges provide all-inclusive fishing, meals, and lodging packages. These include **Baranof Wilderness Lodge** (530/579-3394 or 800/613-6551, www.flyfishalaska.com), **Dove Island Lodge** (907/747-5660 or 888/318-3474, www.aksitkasport fishing.com), **Quest Alaska Lodges** (605/229-8685, www.questalaskalodges.com), and **Wild Strawberry Lodge** (907/747-8883 or 800/770-2628, www.wildstrawberrylodge.com).

Sitka Sound Ocean Adventures (907/747-6375, www.ssoceanadventures.com) has a floathouse ($175 for up to six) at Coogan Bay south of Sitka that makes a good base for soft-adventure kayaking or fishing. It sleeps six for $175, and includes a kayak. Access is by skiff (rentals available), and a two-night minimum is required.

CAMPING

No campgrounds are near downtown Sitka, but the Forest Service provides camping at each end of the road. The outstanding **Starrigavan Campground** ($12–30, reservations $9 extra) is seven miles northwest of town and three-quarters of a mile beyond the ferry terminal. Open all year, but no services October–April. All sites are wheelchair accessible. Campsites to the left of the road face onto a rocky beach, while those to the right border Starrigavan Creek, where you can watch spawning coho salmon in late summer. Starrigavan fills up with RVs in

July and August, but there are six walk-in sites on the ocean side of the campground. Starrigavan also has an **artesian well** with wonderfully fresh spring water. Sitkans often drive out to fill big bottles for themselves.

The 0.25-mile boardwalk **Estuary Life Trail** (wheelchair accessible) leads along the edge of the marsh from the campground, and connects with a 0.75-mile **Forest and Muskeg Trail.** Placards describe points along this easy trail. On the road between the ferry and campground are interpretive display signs marking the site of **Old Sitka**—burned by the Tlingits in 1802.

The quiet and little-used **Sawmill Creek Campground** (free, but no water) is up Blue Lake Road, six miles east of town. The campground is a bit remote, making it hard to reach on foot, and the rough road is not recommended for RVs.

Park RVs at the city-run **Sealing Cove RV Park** (907/747-3439, $21, open April–Sept.) on Japonski Island, with hookups. **Sitka Sportsman's RV Park** (907/747-6033, $20 RVs) is adjacent to the ferry terminal.

FOOD
Breakfast and Lunch

A delightful place to spend time is **Backdoor Café** (907/747-8856), an espresso shop behind Old Harbor Books on Lincoln Street. The Backdoor is the literary/greenie hangout, and also serves tasty bagels, soups, calzones, and pastries. This is the definitive Sitka meeting place.

Victoria's (118 Lincoln St., 907/747-9301), in the Sitka Hotel, is a decent breakfast and lunch spot but also serves a full dinner menu. Pop open your laptop for free Wi-Fi. A few doors up the street is a pharmacy that houses **Harry's Soda Shop** (907/747-8006) for malts, shakes, and banana splits and homemade ice cream.

All-American

Popular with tourists and families, **Bayview Restaurant** (407 Lincoln St., 907/747-5440), upstairs in Bayview Trading, is open 5 A.M.– 8 P.M. daily with every possible type of burger (16 at last count), plus Wednesday- and Friday-night prime rib. Big windows provide a view of the harbor.

Get burgers, milk shakes, and other fast food—plus hearty breakfasts—at **Lane 7 Snack Bar** (236 Katlian St., 907/747-6310). **Subway** probably has the cheapest meal-deal in town; it's behind the Westmark on Seward Street. Of course, there's always the **McDonald's** a mile out on Halibut Point Road for industrial-strength junk food. With the harbor-and-mountains view, this McD's certainly has one of the most impressive vistas in the entire corporate chain.

While waiting for your flight, stop by the airport's **Nugget Restaurant** (907/966-2480) for a slice of their locally famous pies.

International

Pizza Express (236 Lincoln St., 907/966-2428) serves surprisingly authentic Mexican food and decent pizzas. They're directly across from the Russian Orthodox church.

If you like Japanese food in an unpretentious setting, **Little Tokyo** (907/747-5699) is one of the best deals in town. In addition to fresh sushi, they offer a filling bento box dinner (miso soup, potstickers, sushi, salad, and teriyaki chicken) for just $11.

Fine Dining

Van Winkle & Sons (205 Harbor Dr., 907/747-7652), near the bridge, has seafood, pasta, prime rib, and pizzas, but is best known for halibut fish and chips. This is the real thing, Alaskan style. The upstairs setting is quiet and romantic.

Sitka's culinary gem, **C Ludvig's Bistro** (256 Katlian St., 907/966-3663, www .ludvigsbistro.com, closed Sun. and Mon.), ranks among the top cafés in Alaska. It's stylish and noisy, with a new Mediterranean-inspired menu every week. You'll always find Caesar salads, daily chowders, fresh seafood specials, and pasta. Ludvig's is two blocks down Katlian, which, fortunately, is too far for most of the cruise ship folks to walk. Dinner reservations are advised, but singles will usually find space at the wine bar. Entrées run $21–32, or you can choose a selection of small tapas dishes for

$15 each. The restaurant also has a soup cart on Lincoln Street in the summer if you're just looking for quick eats.

Groceries

Sea Mart (907/747-6266, www.seamart.com) two miles from town along Halibut Point Road, has a salad bar, deli, bakery, food court, and Sitka's most complete selection of groceries. Closer to town is **Lakeside Grocery** (705 Halibut Point Rd., 907/747-3317).

The **Fresh Fish Company** (907/747-5565 or 888/747-5565, www.sitkahookandline.com), behind Murray Pacific on Katlian Street, sells fresh local salmon, halibut, shrimp, snapper, and smoked salmon. They'll also smoke fish that you bring in.

INFORMATION AND SERVICES

The Centennial Building houses a small information desk and brochure rack, or stop by the **Sitka Convention & Visitors Bureau** (upstairs at 303 Lincoln St., 907/747-5940, www.sitka.org, Mon.–Fri. 8 A.M.–5 P.M.).

The Forest Service office (907/747-6671 or 907/747-6685 for recorded info) is in the orange-red building at 204 Siginaka Way.

Get showers at **Baranof Laundromat** (1211 Sawmill Creek Rd.) and **Sitka Laundry Center,** across from McDonald's on Halibut Point Road. A better deal is the public **swimming pool** (601 Halibut Point Rd., 907/747-8670) in Blatchley Middle School, where you can swim, sauna, and shower. The pool at Sheldon Jackson College is also open to the public daily.

Sitka's main post office is on Sawmill Creek Road, 1.5 miles south of town, but a substation is downtown at 338 Lincoln Street. For medical emergencies, head to **Sitka Community Hospital** (209 Moller Ave., 907/747-3241, www.sitkahospital.org).

Shopping

Sitka's specialty is Russian art, especially the colorful nesting eggs, painted icons, and other traditional works. Several shops sell Russian crafts downtown; walk around until you find something you like. More noteworthy is **Sitka**

Rose Gallery (907/747-3030 or 888/236-1536, www.sitkarosegallery.com) in a historic century-old home next to the Russian Bishop's House on Lincoln Street. Inside, find a mix of quality Native art and Alaskan paintings, sculpture, and jewelry. The same building houses **WinterSong Soap Company** (907/747-8949 or 888/819-8949, www.wintersongsoap.com), where colorful scented soaps are handcrafted on the premises.

Located five miles east of town, **Theobroma Chocolate Company** (907/966-2349 or 888/985-2345, www.theobromachocolate.com) manufactures gourmet chocolates in a building next to the old pulp mill. You can watch them creating and packaging the chocolates, or sample unusual varieties—try the Dark Midnight Espresso or one of the salmon and halibut-shaped chocolates.

Fairweather Gallery & Gifts (209 Lincoln St., 907/747-8677, www.fairweatherprints.com) is a good place to buy "wearable art" in the form of exquisite hand-painted dresses, tops, and scarves. It has the most unique T-shirts in town, plus a backroom art gallery. The Sheldon Jackson Museum sells Native crafts.

Books

Old Harbor Books (201 Lincoln St., 907/747-8808, www.oldharborbooks.com) has an outstanding collection of books on Alaska (and beyond), along with a pleasant coffee shop in the back.

The **Sitka public library** (907/747-8708, www.cityofsitka.com), next to Centennial Hall downtown, has a free paperback exchange with plenty of titles, plus a phone for free local calls. Check your email on the computers here, or borrow the binoculars to watch whales, seals, and porpoises from the library windows that overlook the bay. The curved benches out back make a pleasant lunch spot when it isn't raining.

GETTING THERE
Ferry

Alaska Marine Highway (907/465-3941 or 800/642-0066, www.ferryalaska.com) ferries reach Sitka several times a week during the summer, but the schedule is confusing with various ships plying different routes. When it's operational—and this can be frustratingly uncommon—the high speed *Fairweather* makes a quick 4.5-hour connection between Juneau and Sitka, but be sure to confirm the ferry departure time so you don't end up sitting in the ferry terminal. The terminal (907/747-8737) is open two hours before ship arrivals, and is seven miles north of town. **Sitka Tours shuttle buses** (907/747-8443) are available for $6 each way or $8 round-trip, and a taxi runs around $19 each way. Other options include tours and hitching—easy and often faster than the buses, both into and out of town.

Air

The airport is on Japonski Island, just under a mile from town by road. **Alaska Airlines** (907/966-2926 or 800/426-0333, www.alaskaair.com) flies to Juneau twice a day, plus non-stop to Seattle in the summer. Note that these flights can be canceled or delayed when the weather gets particularly adverse, a common winter experience. **Harris Aircraft Services** (907/966-3050 or 877/966-3050, www.harrisaircraft.com) has service several times a week to Angoon, Kake, Klawock, and Port Alexander, plus flightseeing and charters. **Hunter Air** (907/738-8098, www.hunterairak.com) also has flightseeing trips, and the plane features unusual windows that photographers love.

For transit into town, **Airport shuttles** (907/747-8443, $8 round trip) meet Alaska Airlines flights, or get a ride (around $9 one-way) with **Hank's Taxi & Tours** (907/747-8888) or **Sitka Cab** (907/747-5001).

GETTING AROUND

The city's **Community Ride Bus** (907/747-7103), has hourly service on weekdays, taking you from downtown out Halibut Point Road and Sawmill Creek Road for $2 one-way or $4 round-trip.

Transit Shuttle (907/747-7290, $10 day pass) buses cruise around Sitka, stopping at all the major sightseeing destinations. The bus operates weekdays and when cruise ships are in port.

Rent cars (starting at $60/day) at the airport from **North Star Rent-A-Car** (907/966-2552 or 800/722-6927) or **Avis** (907/966-2404 or 800/478-2847). Book ahead for the busy summer months.

Tours

The ferry terminal is seven miles from town, but despite the distance you'll have time for a quick "ferry stopover tour," even if you don't stay. Many folks ride the **Sitka Tours** buses (907/747-8443, round-trip $12 adults, $6 kids) that meet the ferries and stop at the cathedral and Sitka National Historical Park. They also offer guided historic and nature walks, but these are geared to cruise ship travelers.

Tribal Tours (907/747-3770 or 888/270-8687, www.sitkatours.com, $44 adults, $34 children), offers a Tlingit slant to tours of Sitka's sights. The 2.5-hour bus tours include a traditional dance performance at the Tribal Community House, plus visits to most local sights.

St. Lazaria Islands National Wildlife Refuge is a great place to see tufted puffins, storm petrels, auklets, whales, seals, and Steller sea lions. **Sitka's Secrets** (907/747-5089, www.sitkasecret.com) has three-hour cruises to the refuge and to other parts of Sitka Sound for $100 per person.

Allen Marine Tours (907/747-8100 or 888/289-0081, www.allenmarinetours.com) offers a two-hour "Wildlife Quest" ($59 adults, $39 children) Tuesday and Thursday evenings, plus three-hour tours ($79 adults, $49 kids) on Saturday and Sunday mornings. If sea conditions aren't too rough, these include time at St. Lazaria Island and Salisbury Sound. A naturalist is onboard.

For something completely different, **Sea Life Discovery Tours** (907/966-2301 or 877/966-2301, www.sealifediscoverytours.com, May–Sept., $84 adults, $63 kids) operates the only semi-submersible vessel in Alaska, with large underwater windows plus a camera for close-up views on the monitor as a diver heads to deeper water. This is a fun way to view kelp forests, fish, crab, sea urchins, anemones, starfish, and other creatures without getting wet.

Chichagof Island

HOONAH

The largest Tlingit village in the Southeast, Hoonah (pop. 900) nestles in Port Frederick, 20 miles south of Glacier Bay. Port Frederick has served as a home for the Tlingits since the last ice age drove them out of Glacier Bay and across Icy Strait to the north coast of Chichagof Island. There they found a protected bay they called Huna, meaning "place where the north wind doesn't blow." The Northwest Trading Company opened a store here in 1880 and missionaries added a church and school the following year. A cannery opened in 1912, operating until 1953. The attractively restored old cannery still stands a mile north of town on the entrance to Port Frederick, but the old village and many priceless Tlingit cultural items were destroyed by a fire in 1944. The people rebuilt their village on the ashes.

Today Hoonah is far from being the prettiest town in Alaska. The weathered clapboard houses are unpainted, and junk cars pile up in the yards. It's the sort of town where the eagle calls blend with the sounds of motorboats and mufflerless dump trucks. There are dogs in almost every house and children playing on every porch. Life in Hoonah follows a slow pace: Residents half-complain that they are unable to go anywhere without meeting someone who wants to talk the hours away. Hoonah's economy is a blend of commercial fishing, a bit of logging, and traditional activities such as deer hunting, fishing, and berry picking.

The impressive cliff faces of **Elephant Mountain** (2,775 ft.) guard the southern flank of Hoonah. Unfortunately, two Native corporations, Huna Totem and Sealaska, have logged much of their land near town, selling off their centuries-old heritage for short-term gain. Hoonah is now surrounded by a spider web of logging roads on both Native and Forest Service land, making this a good place to explore by mountain bike if you're ready for clearcuts.

In the last few years Hoonah has plunged into cruise ship tourism in a big way. The picturesque cannery building at Port Frederick (Icy Strait Point) has been restored, and cruise ship passengers get a look at the way canneries operated in the 1930s, along with cultural presentations, a salmon bake, Native crafts, whale- and bear-watching excursions, charter fishing, mountain biking, and other "soft" adventures. These are really for cruise passengers, but contact Huna Totem (907/789-8018, www.icystraitpoint.com) for access by independent travelers.

Recreation

The Hoonah area offers little in the way of developed trails or other recreation facilities for independent travelers. If you have a car, the quarter-mile **Bear Paw Lake Trail,** 18 miles south of town on Road 8508, leads to a good lake where you can catch trout or coho salmon. Kayakers and canoeists may want to paddle the 40 miles from Hoonah to Tenakee Springs. The route goes to the head of Port Frederick, where there is a 100-yard portage into Tenakee Inlet. Neka Estuary in Port Frederick is a good place to see bears. A Forest Service cabin is available at nearby **Salt Lake Bay,** but a considerable amount of logging has beaten you there. Ask at the **Forest Service Hoonah District Office** (907/945-3631, www.fs.fed.us/r10/tongass) for details on these and other possible kayak trips in the area, including to **Neka Hot Spring,** 16 miles west of Hoonah.

Accommodations and Food

Icy Strait Lodge (907/945-3636, www.icystraitlodge.com, $85 s or $95 d) is the main place in town, with 23 rooms, plus a full-service restaurant and bar. **Wind'N Sea Inn** (907/945-3438 or 877/945-3438, $75 s or $85 d) is a fine lodging choice, with seven guest rooms that share two baths and two kitchens, and include a self-serve breakfast.

Information and Services

The **Hoonah Cultural Center** (907/945-3545) has a few local artifacts. Hoonah has two small grocery stores, and a coin laundry with coin-operated showers. Showers are also available in the harbor building or at the **swimming pool** (907/945-9911) next to the high school. In addition, Hoonah has a bank, tavern, variety store, and liquor store. A few miles southwest of town is the only agricultural commune in Southeast, Mt. Bether Bible Center.

Getting There

Hoonah's **ferry terminal** (907/945-3293) is a half-mile from town. Across from the ferry terminal is a tiny but interesting old cemetery. Ferries arrive six days a week, stopping for approximately an hour, long enough for a quick jog into town and back. Make reservations through Alaska Marine Highway (907/465-3941 or 800/642-0066, www.ferryalaska.com).

Wings of Alaska (907/789-0790, www.wingsofalaska.com), **L.A.B. Flying Service** (907/945-3661, www.labflying.com), **Air Excursions** (907/697-2375 or 800/354-2479, www.airexcursions.com) all have frequent flights between Juneau and Hoonah.

PELICAN AND VICINITY

If you're looking for a place to get away from it all, it's hard to get more remote than the tiny, picturesque fishing village of Pelican (pop. 150) inside narrow Lisianski Inlet on the western shore of Chichagof Island. During the summer, Pelican's population doubles with the arrival of fishermen and cold-storage workers. The town received its name from *The Pelican,* a fishing boat owned by the town's founder; there are no pelicans in Alaska.

Locals drive 4-wheelers down the boardwalk connecting Pelican's restaurants, bars, general store, coin laundry, and cold-storage plant. Showers are available at the coin laundry, or try the steam baths at the liquor store (no joke). The **Pelican Visitors Association** (907/735-2460, www.pelican.net) has info on local businesses.

Tiny Pelican has achieved notoriety as a party town, particularly when festivities reach their peak at the **Boardwalk Boogie** (www.boardwalkboogie.com) in late May, with two days of live music (including a filthy-song contest) and some major-league partying. Lodging is in dorms at the old cannery, and Allen Marine makes a special boat run from Juneau for the event.

Practicalities

Situated in the heart of town, **Highliner Lodge** (907/735-2476, www.highlinerlodge.com) has a variety of lodging options, including simple sleeping rooms ($95 s or $120 d), and three large, nicely furnished units for $225–250 d, all with Wi-Fi and access to the sauna. Kayak and skiff rentals are available, along with fishing charters, kayak drop-offs, and meals at **Highliner Restaurant.**

Lisianski Inlet Lodge (907/735-2266 or 800/962-8441, www.pelicanalaskafishing.com, May–mid-Sept.), two miles west of Pelican, offers a pricey but idyllic setting for a splurge. Package trips are $2,350 per person for four nights, including lodging, meals, fishing, and guide service. Other lodging options include **Wheelwatch Lodge** (907/735-2252, www.wheelwatch.net) and **Salmon Way Inn** (907/735-2485).

Infamous **Rosie's Bar and Grill** (907/735-2288, www.rosesbarandgrill.com) is a good place for drinking and pub grub, including burgers, chicken dinners, oysters, and BLTs. The ceiling is plastered with signed dollar bills, but you may get a surprise when you put yours up.

Lisianski Inlet Café (907/735-2282) is open for delicious breakfasts and lunches in the summer, with big omelets, sandwiches, and a killer borscht. The bar is a hopping place.

Several local folks run fishing and sightseeing boat charters, and will be happy to run you and your kayak out to such local destinations as White Sulfur Springs.

Getting There

Ferry service to Pelican arrives only once or twice a month. The *LeConte* usually stays for two hours and then turns around for the return trip to Juneau. Get details from

Alaska Marine Highway (800/642-0066, www.ferryalaska.com).

Alaska Seaplane Service (907/735-2244 or 800/478-3360, www.akseaplanes.com) has daily flights to Pelican from Juneau.

West Chichagof-Yakobi Wilderness

On the northwestern shore of Chichagof Island is the wildly rugged 264,747-acre West Chichagof–Yakobi Wilderness. Brown bears, marten, and deer are common, with sea otters and Steller sea lions in the waters. The coast is deeply indented with many small bays, lagoons, and inlets. It also supports areas of distinctive open spruce forest with grassy glades. Except for White Sulfur Springs, this wilderness gets little recreational use because of its remoteness and the storms that frequently make it a dangerous place for small boats and kayaks.

One of the most popular Forest Service cabins in Southeast (make reservations well in advance) is at **White Sulfur Springs,** accessible by boat, sea kayak, helicopter, or floatplane. The springs are a 20-mile kayak trip from Pelican. Much of the trip is through the protected waters of Lisianski Inlet and Strait, but the last five miles are exposed to the open ocean and require great care. The cabin has a wonderful hot springs bathhouse overlooking Bertha Bay just 50 feet away. Note, however, that the springs are free and open to the public, so fishermen, kayakers, and others from nearby Pelican will probably disturb your solitude.

Elfin Cove

This tiny fishing settlement (pop. 50 year-round, but 200 in the summer) tops the north end of Chichagof Island and is considered one of Alaska's prettiest towns. The setting is hard to beat: right on the edge of the wild waters of Cross Sound, yet protected within a narrow harbor. Elfin Cove has two general stores, lodging facilities, plus showers and a sauna during the summer.

The waters of Cross Sound and Icy Strait separate Chichagof Island from Glacier Bay National Park. This is one of the best areas to see whales

in Southeast Alaska, especially near Point Adolphus. Charter boats offer day trips from Glacier Bay to Elfin Cove during the summer months. Also nearby is the 23,000-acre **Pleasant-Lemesurier-Inian Islands Wilderness.**

It's pretty easy to see what makes the village tick, with 10 fishing lodges in such a small place, including **Tanaku Lodge** (www.tanaku.com), **Elfin Cove Lodge** (www.elfincove.com), **Inner Harbor Lodge** (www.innerharborlodge.com), **The Cove Lodge** (www.covelodge.com), and **Eagle Charters & Lodge** (www.elfincoveeaglecharters.com). The last of these operates the only gift shop in town.

No state ferry service, but small cruise ships visit Elfin Cove several times a week in the summer, and **Alaska Seaplane Service** (907/789-3331 or 800/478-3360, www.akseaplanes.com) has scheduled flights from Juneau.

TENAKEE SPRINGS

Residents of the tiny hamlet of Tenakee Springs (pop. 100) include retirees, counterculture devotees, and a handful of fishermen. Many Juneau folks have second homes here. Tenakee's houses stand on stilts along the shoreline; some have "long-drop" outhouses over the water. The town has only one street, a dirt path barely wide enough for Tenakee's three vehicles (its oil truck, fire truck, and dump truck). Everyone else walks or uses four-wheelers and bicycles.

Tenakee is best known for its hot (106°F) **mineral springs,** housed in a building right beside the dock. The springs feed a small concrete pool with an adjacent changing room. There are separate hours for men (2–6 P.M. and 10 P.M.–9 A.M.) and women (6–10 P.M. and 9 A.M.–2 P.M.), but after midnight the rules tend to relax a bit. If the ferry is in town for more than a half-hour, be sure to take a quick dip in the pool.

Practicalities

You can pitch your tent two miles east of town along Indian River, but be sure to hang your food, since brown bears are sometimes a problem. Trails extend out of town for several miles in both directions along the shore. The trail south of town reaches eight miles to an old cannery and a homestead at Coffee Cove.

Beside the dock is **Snyder Mercantile Co.** (907/736-2205), a classic bush Alaska store with groceries, supplies, and the latest gossip. Great folks. The other main feature of town is the Shamrock building, which houses **Rosie's Blue Moon Café,** serving lunch and dinner daily: cheeseburgers (with freshly cut fries), chicken, and steaks, plus the **Artist Co-op,** displaying pieces by local artists. A coin laundry is in the back, and next door is **The Bakery** (907/736-2262) for pastries, coffee, light breakfasts, and lunches. There are local fishing charter boats, a small library, a grade school, and two bars, but only one place to stay: **Tenakee Hot Springs Lodge** (907/736-2400 or 9097/364-3640, $90 s or $150 d) on the edge of town. Five guest rooms share three baths.

Getting There

Tenakee is a popular weekend vacation spot for both Juneauites and travelers. The ferry *LeConte* arrives in Tenakee four times a week with a schedule that makes it possible to stop over for a Friday night before returning to Juneau the following evening. There is no ferry terminal and cars cannot be offloaded. The ferry usually stays in town briefly, sometimes not even long enough to get off the boat for a walk around. Get details from Alaska Marine Highway (800/642-0066, www.ferryalaska.com).

Both **Wings of Alaska** (907/789-0790, www.wingsofalaska.com) and **Alaska Seaplane Service** (907/789-3331 or 800/478-3360, www.akseaplanes.com) have flights most days between Tenakee Springs and Juneau.

Juneau

America's most beautiful state capital, Juneau (pop. 30,000) is a thriving slice of civilization surrounded by rugged Inside Passage scenery. The city perches on a thin strip of land at the mouth of Gold Creek, and behind it rise the precipitous summits of Mt. Juneau and Mt. Roberts. Out front, Gastineau Channel separates it from Douglas Island and the town of Douglas. The city abounds with cultural and artistic attractions, and the adjacent wild country provides a broad sampling of Southeast Alaska, from glacially capped mountains to protected coves where sea kayakers relax.

Juneau is the only state capital with no roads leading in or out. A government town, nearly half the local jobs are at state, federal, or city agencies. Tourism provides another mainstay for the local economy, fed by an annual influx of more than 700,000 visitors, primarily aboard luxury cruise ships. On summer days, up to five different ships tie up simultaneously, disgorging thousands of passengers. (To avoid the worst of the rush, get here before July or after August.) Juneau has a small fishing fleet and provides workers for a silver mine on nearby Admiralty Island.

Juneau may be small in population, but its boundaries extend to the Canadian border, covering 3,100 square miles. Less than half of Juneau's population actually lives downtown. The rest are spread into Douglas (across the channel), Mendenhall Valley (10 miles northwest), and other surrounding areas. As might be expected, these areas exhibit diverse personalities. Even the weather varies, with an average of 92 inches of rain each year downtown, but only 55 inches in Mendenhall Valley.

Downtown Juneau is marked by a mix of modern government offices and older wooden structures, many dating from the early 1900s. Across the bridge is Douglas Island and its bedroom community of Douglas. The town now consists of a few shops, but at its peak in 1915, when the Treadwell Gold Mine was operating, Douglas housed 15,000 miners. The road north from downtown Juneau is the Southeast's only divided highway. Heading north, you first reach Mendenhall Valley, Juneau's version of

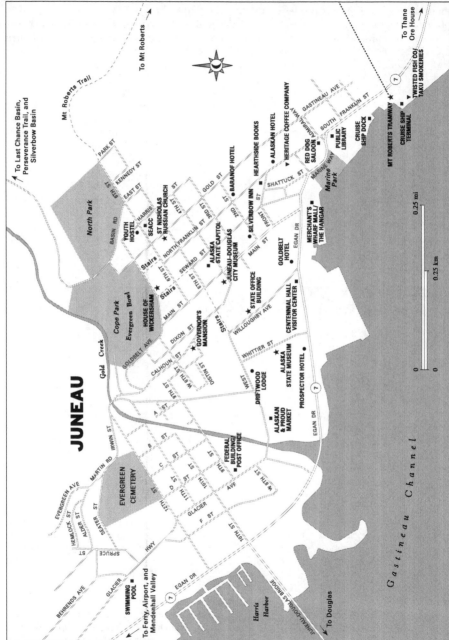

JUNEAU

Gastineau Channel

To Thane
Ore House

TWISTED FISH CO/
TAKU SMOKERIES

CRUISE SHIP
TERMINAL

CRUISE
SHIP DOCK

MT ROBERTS TRAMWAY

PUBLIC
LIBRARY

SOUTH FRANKLIN ST
GASTINEAU AVE

ADMIRAL WAY

RED DOG
SALOON

Marine
Park

Marine Way
Park

HERITAGE COFFEE COMPANY

HEARTHSIDE BOOKS

ALASKAN HOTEL

SILVERBOW INN

BARANOF HOTEL

MERCHANT'S
WHARF MALL/
THE HANGAR

GOLDBELT
HOTEL

SHATTUCK ST

ST NICHOLAS
RUSSIAN CHURCH

EGAN DR

FRONT ST

MAIN ST

2ND ST

3RD ST

GOLD ST

4TH ST

NORTH FRANKLIN ST

SEWARD ST

5TH ST

6TH ST

7TH ST

ALASKA
STATE CAPITOL

JUNEAU-DOUGLAS
CITY MUSEUM

STATE OFFICE
BUILDING

CENTENNIAL HALL
VISITOR CENTER

WILLOUGHBY AVE

WHITTIER ST

ALASKA
STATE MUSEUM

PROSPECTOR HOTEL

DRIFTWOOD
LODGE

WEST ST

DIXON ST

CALHOUN ST

DISTIN ST

GOVERNOR'S
MANSION

Stairs

Stairs

HOUSE OF
WICKERSHAM

Evergreen Bowl

Cope Park

GOLDBELT AVE

Gold Creek

Gold Creek

North Park

BASIN RD

PARK ST

KENNEDY ST

EAST ST

HARRIS ST

YOUTH
HOSTEL

SEACC

Stairs

MAIN ST

To Mt Roberts

Mt Roberts Trail

To Mt Roberts

To Last Chance Basin,
Perseverance Trail, and
Silverbow Basin

ALASKAN
& PROUD
MARKET

FEDERAL
BUILDING/
POST OFFICE

EGAN DR

A ST

B ST

C ST

D ST

F ST

9TH ST

10TH ST

11TH ST

12TH ST

GLACIER AVE

W 8TH ST

W 9TH ST

W 12TH ST

GLACIER HWY

EVERGREEN
CEMETERY

EVERGREEN AVE

MARTIN RD

IRWIN ST

HEMLOCK ST

ALDER ST

SEATER ST

SPRUCE ST

BEHRENDS AVE

GLACIER AVE

SWIMMING
POOL

To Ferry, Airport, and
Mendenhall Valley

Harris Harbor

JUNEAU-DOUGLAS BRIDGE

To Douglas

EGAN DR

0   0.25 mi

0   0.25 km

© AVALON TRAVEL PUBLISHING, INC.

suburbia: three shopping malls, a slew of fast fooderies, and hundreds of pseudo-rustic, split-level homes and condos. But you can also see something most suburbs don't have: a drive-up glacier spilling out from the massive Juneau Icefield. The road continues north from Mendenhall Valley for another 30 miles, passing Auke Lake, the ferry terminal, and scattered homes along the way, ending at scenic Echo Cove.

HISTORY
Gold in the Hills

In October 1880, two prospectors –Joe Juneau and Richard Harris—arrived at what would later be called Gold Creek. Along its banks was a small Tlingit fishing camp of the Auke tribe. Chief Kowee showed the prospectors gold flakes in the creek, and the resulting discovery turned out to be one of the largest gold deposits ever found. Harris and Juneau quickly staked a 160-acre town site. The first boatloads of prospectors arrived the next month, and almost overnight a town sprouted along the shores of Gastineau Channel. Three giant hard-rock gold mines were developed in the area, eventually producing some seven million ounces of gold, worth *$4 billion* at today's prices! Compare that to the $7.2 million the United States paid Russia for Alaska only 13 years before the discovery.

The **Alaska Juneau (AJ) Mine** proved the most successful, operating for more than 50 years. Built in Last Chance Basin behind Juneau, its three tunnels connected the ore source to the crushing and recovery mill site on Gastineau Channel. Inside the mine itself was a maze of tunnels that eventually reached over 100 miles in length. Because the ore was low grade—it could take 28 tons of ore to yield one ounce of gold—enormous quantities of rock had to be removed. At its peak, the mill (still visible just south of town) employed 1,000 men to process 12,000 tons of ore a day. Tailings from the mill were used as the fill upon which much of downtown Juneau was constructed. (Franklin St. was originally built on pilings along the shore.) The AJ closed down in 1944 because of wartime labor shortages and never reopened.

gold panning on Gold Creek

© DON PITCHER

The **Perseverance Mine** operated between 1885 and 1921, with a two-mile tunnel carrying ore from Gold Creek to the mill four miles south of Juneau. It eventually ran into low-grade ore and was forced to close.

The best known Juneau-area mine was the **Treadwell,** on Douglas Island. The Treadwell Complex consisted of four mines and five stamping mills to process the ore. It employed some 2,000 men who were paid $100 a month, some of the highest wages anywhere in the world at the time. The men enjoyed such amenities as a swimming pool, Turkish baths, tennis courts, bowling alley, gymnasium, and 15,000-volume library. The giant Treadwell stamping mills where the ore was pulverized made so much noise that people in downtown Douglas had to shout to be heard. Everything changed on April 21, 1917, when the ground atop the mines suddenly began to collapse, swallowing first the gymnasium and swimming pool, then the fire hall. Sea water rushed in, filling the tunnels as the miners ran for their lives. Amazingly, all apparently escaped alive. (The

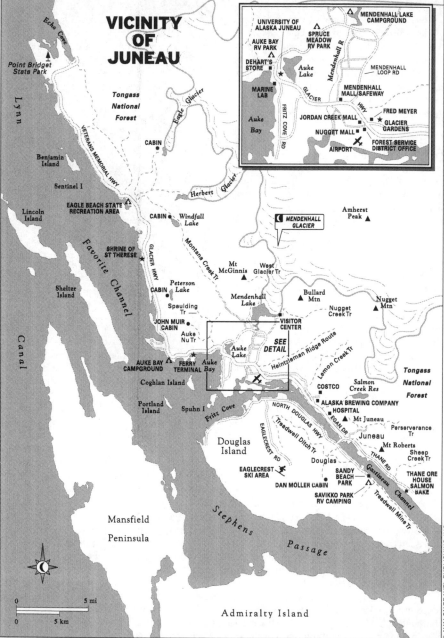

VICINITY OF JUNEAU

Echo Cove

Point Bridget State Park

Tongass National Forest

Lynn Canal

Benjamin Island

Sentinel I

Lincoln Island

Shelter Island

Favorite Channel

Eagle Glacier

CABIN

EAGLE BEACH STATE RECREATION AREA

VETERANS MEMORIAL HWY

SHRINE OF ST THERESE

GLACIER HWY

CABIN Windfall Lake

Peterson Lake

CABIN

Spaulding Tr

JOHN MUIR CABIN

Auke Nu Tr

AUKE BAY CAMPGROUND

FERRY TERMINAL Auke Bay

Coghlan Island

Portland Island

Spuhn I

Herbert Glacier

Montana Creek Tr

Mt McGinnis West Glacier Tr

Mendenhall Lake

Auke Lake

SEE DETAIL

Fritz Cove

Amherst Peak

☾ MENDENHALL GLACIER

VISITOR CENTER

Bullard Mtn

Nugget Creek Tr

Heintzleman Ridge Route

Lemon Creek Tr

COSTCO

ALASKA BREWING COMPANY

HOSPITAL

Mt Juneau

Nugget Mtn

Salmon Creek Res

Tongass National Forest

NORTH DOUGLAS HWY

Treadwell Ditch Tr

EAGLECREST RD

EGAN DR

Juneau

Perserverance Tr

Mt Roberts

Sheep Creek Tr

THANE RD

Douglas Island

EAGLECREST SKI AREA

DAN MÖLLER CABIN

Douglas

SANDY BEACH PARK

SAVIKKO PARK RV CAMPING

Gastineau Channel

Treadwell Mine Tr

THANE ORE HOUSE SALMON BAKE

Mansfield Peninsula

Stephens Passage

Admiralty Island

0   5 mi

0   5 km

Detail (inset):

UNIVERSITY OF ALASKA JUNEAU

AUKE BAY RV PARK

DEHART'S STORE

MARINE LAB

Auke Bay

SPRUCE MEADOW RV PARK

Auke Lake

Mendenhall R

Mendenhall Glacier

MENDENHALL LAKE CAMPGROUND

MENDENHALL LOOP RD

FRITZ COVE RD

GLACIER HWY

MENDENHALL MALL/SAFEWAY

JORDAN CREEK MALL

NUGGET MALL

AIRPORT

MENDENHALL HWY

FRED MEYER

GLACIER GARDENS

FOREST SERVICE DISTRICT OFFICE

© AVALON TRAVEL PUBLISHING, INC.

only missing miner was reportedly later seen in a nearby tavern before he skipped town.) Only one of the four mines was not destroyed in the collapse, and that one closed five years later.

Later Years

Juneau became the capital of Alaska in 1906 as a result of its rapid growth and the simultaneous decline of Sitka. Several attempts have been made to move the capital closer to the state's present power center, Anchorage. In 1976, Alaskan voters approved a new site just north of Anchorage, but six years later, when expectations for petro-billions had subsided into reality, voters thought better of the move and refused to fund it. Juneauites breathed a sigh of relief and went on a building spree that only ended with the sudden drop in state oil revenue from the 1986 oil-price plummet. Recent years have seen ever-increasing cruise ship tourism. Locals are starting to tire of the influx and its impact on the town; in 1999 they slapped a head tax on every cruise passenger who steps off in Juneau. By the way, Fridays are usually a light day for cruise ship traffic, so time your downtown visits accordingly.

SIGHTS

Juneau is jam-packed with things to see and do, from glaciers to salmon bakes and tram rides. It's the sort of place that travelers love. Many interesting places are right downtown—including two museums, numerous historic buildings, unusual shops, and even a library-with-a-view. Farther afield are dozens of hiking trails, several easily accessible glaciers, and such attractions as an informative fish hatchery, a brewery, old mining buildings, a stone church, and much more. Even on a rainy day, you'll find something fun in Juneau.

Alaska State Museum

Anyone new to town should not miss the Alaska State Museum (395 Whittier St., 907/465-2901, www.museums.state.ak.us, $3, free for under 18). Inside, you'll find an impressive collection of Native artifacts (including wildly creative Yup'ik Eskimo spirit masks) and exhibits relating to the Russian-American period and other aspects of Alaskan history. The museum also houses a gallery of contemporary fine arts, and brings in special exhibits each summer. But the highlight is the circular stairwell, which houses a full-size bald eagle nest and other Alaskan wildlife. The museum is open daily 8:30 A.M.–5:30 P.M. mid-May–late September, and Tuesday–Saturday 10 A.M.–4 P.M. the rest of the year.

Juneau-Douglas City Museum

The fine Juneau–Douglas City Museum (4th and Main Sts., 907/586-3572, www.juneau.org/parksrec/museum, $4) houses an interesting collection of maps, artifacts, photos, and videos from Juneau's rich gold-mining history. Be sure to check out the three-dimensional model of Perseverance Mine with its intricate maze of tunnels. Other features include a 19th-century store, a hands-on history room that's popular with kids, and a small gift shop, as well as brochures describing **walking tours** of historic Juneau—60 remaining downtown buildings were built before 1904! The museum is open Monday–Friday 9 A.M.–5 P.M. and Saturday–Sunday 10 A.M.–5 P.M. mid-May–late September; Thursday–Saturday noon–4 P.M. the rest of the year.

Mt. Roberts Tramway

The Mt. Roberts Tramway (907/463-3412 or 888/461-8726, www.goldbelttours.com, daily 9 A.M.–9 P.M., May–Sept.) provides a fast way into the high country above Juneau. The tram starts at the cruise ship dock on the south end of town and climbs 1,800 feet up the mountain, providing panoramic views of the surrounding land and water. The six-minute ride ends at an observation deck surrounded by tall Sitka spruce trees. Facilities here include a nature center, restaurant, gift shops, and theater where you can watch an award-wining 20-minute film about Tlingit culture. The tram costs $24 adults, $13 for kids ages 7–12, and is free for children under seven. If you hike up (see *Climbing Mt. Roberts*), the ride down is only $5. Tickets are good all day, but the lines can

© DON PITCHER

Mt. Roberts Tramway, with Juneau and Gastineau Channel in the background

get very long in late afternoon as cruise ship passengers rush back down to avoid missing their ship departures.

Gastineau Guiding (907/586-2666, www.stepintoalaska.com) leads easy "tram and trek" hikes that include a short bus tour of town, a tram ride up Mt. Roberts, and a one-hour hike for $59 ($32 kids). Or you can save your cash and simply strike out on your own along scenic alpine trails. Be sure to look for several live spruce trees carved with traditional Tlingit designs.

State Office Building

Enter the State Office Building (SOB) from Willoughby Avenue and take the elevator up to the 8th floor. Here you'll discover a 1928 Kimball organ, a lovingly preserved totem pole from the 1880s, the Alaska State Library, and an incredible panoramic view from the big **observation deck** (great for bag lunches). The airy lobby is also a pleasant place to stay dry on a rainy day; Friday at noon you'll enjoy the added bonus of an organ recital.

Governor's Mansion

Just up Calhoun Avenue from the SOB is the large, white Governor's Mansion. Built in 1912 in the New England Colonial style, it overlooks much of Juneau from its hilltop location. The mansion is not open to the public. Out front is a **totem pole** carved in 1939–1940. Near its base are the figures of a mosquito and a man, representing the Tlingit tale of the cannibalistic giant, Guteel, and his capture by hunters in a pit. The hunters built a fire to kill him, but just before he died he warned, "Even though you kill me, I'll continue to bite you." His ashes swirled into the air, becoming the mosquitoes that fulfill Guteel's promise.

More than 20 other totems are scattered around downtown. Most are recent carvings, but some date to the 19th century. Pick up the "Totem Pole Walking Tour" brochure from the Juneau–Douglas City Museum to find them all.

State Capitol

Back on 4th Street is the marble Alaska State Capitol. Completed in 1931, it was originally the federal office building and post office. The building is not at all like a traditional state capitol, and from the outside it could easily be mistaken for an aging Midwestern bank, complete with wide steps and marble columns. Free tours (907/465-2479 for reservations) of the bank—oops, Capitol are every half-hour Monday–Friday 9 A.M.–4:30 P.M. and Saturday noon–4:30 P.M. June–mid-September. Historical photos line the 2nd floor. You may sit in on the legislature when it's in session January–May. The antics of the legislature are always a hoot, especially after the FBI raided their offices in 2006 and found T-shirts brazenly labeled "Corrupt Bastard's Club." Makes me proud to be an Alaskan.

Last Chance Mining Museum

Behind town, Basin Road climbs 1.5 miles to the old AJ Gold Mine. The former compressor building here has been turned into the Last Chance Mining Museum (907/586-5338, daily 9:30 A.M.–12:30 P.M. and 3:30–6:30 P.M. mid-

May–late Sept., $4, free for kids), which houses mining paraphernalia and a 3-D map of the ore body.

Historic Downtown

Dozens of historic buildings fill the heart of downtown Juneau. Get a brochure describing them from the Juneau–Douglas City Museum. One of Juneau's most photographed sights is the onion-domed **St. Nicholas Russian Orthodox Church** (5th and Gold Sts., 907/586-6790, Mon.–Fri. 9 A.M.–5 P.M. mid-May–Sept., $2), built in 1894. Inside are icons and artwork, some dating from the 1700s. For a more evocative experience, attend a service (Sat. 6 P.M., Sun. 10 A.M.).

Marine Park, along Shattuck Way, with its lively mix of people and picturesque views, is a good place to relax after your tour of downtown. Directly across the street a bright mural depicts the Haida creation legend.

Evergreen Cemetery, between 12th and Seater streets on the north side of town, has the graves of Juneau's founders, Joe Juneau and Richard Harris, along with a marker near the spot where Chief Kowee was cremated.

House of Wickersham

Built in 1889, the House of Wickersham (213 7th St., 907/586-9001, www.alaskastateparks.org, open daily except Wed. 10 A.M.–noon and 1–5 P.M. mid-May–Sept., $2) offers a good view of Juneau and the surrounding country, and visitors are provided a fine tour. This was the home of Judge James Wickersham (1857–1939), a man who had a major impact upon Alaskan history. As Alaska's longtime delegate to Congress he introduced the first statehood bill in 1916—43 years before it passed—and was instrumental in the establishment of the territorial legislature, McKinley National Park, the University of Alaska, and the Alaska Railroad. Be sure to take a gander at the Native ivory carvings that Judge Wickersham collected from around the state.

Macaulay Salmon Hatchery

The impressive Douglas Island Pink and Chum

Franklin Street in downtown Juneau
© DON PITCHER

(DIPAC) salmon hatchery (2697 Channel Dr., 907/463-4810 or 877/463-2486, www.dipac.net, $3.25 adults, $1.75 kids under 13) is three miles north of town. Here you can learn about salmon spawning and commercial fishing, watch fish moving up one of the state's largest fish ladders, and check out the saltwater aquariums and underwater viewing windows. The facility includes shops and a visitor center where tours are offered. It's a fascinating place, and well worth the entrance fee. Open Monday–Friday 10 A.M.–6 P.M. and Saturday–Sunday 10–5 P.M. May–September, or by appointment the rest of the year. The king, coho, and chum salmon return mid-June–September, and during that time you can try your hand at fishing out front.

Glacier Gardens   AHS?

This unique private botanical garden (7600 Glacier Hwy., 907/790-3377, www.glaciergardens.com, daily 9 A.M.–6 P.M. May–Sept., $20 adults, $17 ages 6–12, under 6 free) is eight miles north of downtown Juneau. The gardens are spread over 50 acres of hillside forest and include hiking trails, waterfalls, ponds, and "flower tower" cascades of blooms from upside down trees. Motorized carts (some set up to carry wheelchairs) transport visitors along four miles of paved paths to an overlook 500 feet up the mountainside, with views across the Mendenhall Wetlands. The city bus stops out front.

Alaskan Brewing Company

For something completely different, take the city bus to Anka Street in Lemon Creek and walk two blocks to Shaune Drive. Follow it a block to the Alaskan Brewing Company building (907/780-5866, www.alaskanbeer.com, tours every half-hour Mon.–Sat. 11 A.M.–4:30 P.M. May–Sept., free). You're given a sample of various beers at the end of the tour. The brewery has developed into one of America's finest, with its beers winning top prizes at national and international festivals. The brewery gift shop sells T-shirts, hats, and other items.

◀ Mendenhall Glacier

The Southeast's best-known drive-up ice cube, Mendenhall Glacier is without a doubt Juneau's most impressive sight. This moving river of ice pushes down from the 1,500-square-mile **Juneau Icefield** (fifth largest in North America) and is 12 miles long and up to 1.5 miles wide. Since 1750, the glacier has been receding, and is now several miles farther up Mendenhall Valley. It is retreating at about 150 feet each year, but still calving icebergs into Mendenhall Lake.

The **Mendenhall Glacier Visitor Center** (907/789-6640, www.fs.fed.us/r10/tongass, $3, free for kids) provides panoramic views of the glacier from the floor-to-ceiling windows. Use the spotting scopes to check the slopes of nearby Bullard Mountain for mountain goats. Walk through the interpretive exhibits, slip into the theater for an excellent 11-minute film on the glacier, or buy a couple of glacier postcards in the bookstore. The center is open daily 8 A.M.–7:30 P.M. May–mid-September, and Thursday–Sunday 10 A.M.–4 P.M. the rest of the year. Forest Service naturalists lead walks

on nearby trails and can answer your questions. Walk up at least one of these excellent paths if you want to come away with a deeper appreciation of Mendenhall Glacier.

Although it's 13 miles northwest of town, the glacier is easily accessible by city bus. Have the driver let you off when the bus turns left a mile up Mendenhall Loop Road. It's a one-mile walk up the road from here to the glacier. Buses run both directions around Mendenhall Loop Road. On the way back you can catch a bus heading either direction since both eventually drop you off downtown.

Mighty Great Trips (907/789-5460, www.mightygreattrips.com) provides transportation from downtown to the glacier for $12 round trip, and offers a 2.5-hour tour that includes time at the glacier for $22. Most other tour companies also offer tours to Mendenhall (see *Getting Around* for details).

University and Auke Lake

The campus of the University of Alaska Southeast (2,600 students) is a dozen miles northwest of Juneau on beautiful Auke Lake. The view across the lake to Mendenhall Glacier makes it one of the most attractive campuses anywhere. Also here is **Chapel by the Lake,** a popular place for weddings, with a dramatic backdrop of mountains and the Mendenhall Glacier. Across the highway, **Auke Bay Fisheries Lab** (Mon.–Fri. 8 A.M.–4:30 P.M.) has a small saltwater aquarium and fisheries displays.

Glacier Highway

If you have a vehicle, the 40-mile drive north from Juneau provides a wonderful escape. Twenty-three miles out is a quaint Catholic chapel built in 1939, the **Shrine of St. Therese** (907/780-6112, www.shrineofsainttherese .org). The cobblestone chapel is hidden away on a small, bucolic, wooded island connected to the mainland by a 400-foot causeway. Named for Alaska's patron saint, St. Therese of Lisieux, the chapel is open all the time, with Sunday service at 1 P.M. This is a nice, quiet place to soak up the scenery or to try your hand at fishing for salmon from the shore. The *[handwritten annotations: "Ferry from Juneau to Hoonah? Glacier Bay? Hop from town to town (Ketchikan, Wrangell etc.?)", "Fly out 2nd place", "cakutut"]*

trail to Peterson Lake is nearby, and cabins are available for rent.

Eagle Beach (at Mile 28, $5 parking) is a popular day-use area with picnic tables and panoramic vistas of the snowcapped Chilkat Range. Pull out your binoculars to look for whales in Lynn Canal. Stop at **Point Bridget State Park** (Mile 38) for a pleasant hike. The road ends at scenic **Echo Cove,** a launching point for boats and kayaks.

Taku Glacier Lodge

Historic Taku Glacier Lodge (907/586-6275, www.takuglacierlodge.com, early May–Sept.) sits just across Taku Inlet from the glacier of the same name. This classic log structure (no overnight visits) was built in 1923, and short nature trails lead into the surrounding country. Black bears and eagles are frequent visitors (the bears were Juneau garbage bears that would have been shot if they had not been brought here). Visits to the lodge cost $225 for adults or $185 for kids, and include a half-hour scenic flight over Taku Glacier, along with two hours at the lodge and a filling salmon lunch or dinner. Flights depart the Juneau waterfront up to five times a day between 9 A.M. and 5 P.M. The lodge is oriented to the cruise-ship crowd, so expect to see lots of other folks if you go on a day when several ships are docked.

ENTERTAINMENT AND EVENTS
Nightlife

Juneau has an active night life, with plenty of live music almost every evening. The famous **Red Dog Saloon** (on South Franklin St., 907/463-3658, www.reddogsaloon.cc) has sawdust on the floor and honky-tonk music in the air every day and night during the summer, starting at 2 P.M. Be sure to look for Wyatt Earp's gun; he checked it in when passing through on June 17, 1900, but his ship left for Nome before the Marshall's office reopened, so

© DON PITCHER

Red Dog Saloon

it remained unclaimed in Juneau. This is where cruise ship tourists and crewmembers drink.

A block up the street, inside the Alaskan Hotel, is the **Alaskan Bar** (167 S. Franklin, 907/586-1000), a quieter place with blues or folk music on weekends, and Thursday night jam sessions. It's always packed with locals, who head here in summer to escape the Red Dog crowds. The Alaskan has a Victorian decor and you can hear lawyers and lobbyists talk shop from any seat in the place during the legislative session.

Billiards aficionados fill the half-dozen tables upstairs at the **Viking Lounge** (218 Front St., 907/586-2159). Downstairs in the back is a classy disco with occasional live music and the best dance floor in Juneau. Across the street is **Imperial Bar** (907/586-1960), popular with the young crowd on weekends, when live bands perform. More music around the corner at the **Rendezvous** (184 S. Franklin, 907/586-1270); very loud rock and a lowlife crowd.

The Hangar (2 Marine Way, 907/586-5018, www.hangaronthewharf.com), on the wharf, has music to make you kick up your rain boots on Friday and Saturday nights, and is especially popular with state government workers on weeknights, with over 100 brews on tap or in bottles. Get here early for the window seats facing the water. **The Island Pub** (1102 2nd St., 907/364-1595, www.theislandpub.com) is a classy smoke-free bar in Douglas with live bands most Friday and Saturday nights.

Out near the airport, **The Sandbar** (2525 Industrial Blvd., 907/789-3411) has a large dance floor and rock or country music on weekends. Also out in Mendenhall Valley is **Marlintini's Lounge** (9121 Glacier Hwy., 907/789-0799), which mixes karaoke on weeknights with rock bands Thursday–Saturday nights.

Performing Arts and Music

On Friday evenings 7–8:30 P.M. in the summer, Marine Park in downtown Juneau comes alive with free **Concerts in the Park** (907/586-2787), ranging from classical to Middle Eastern folk. The **Juneau Symphony** (907/586-4676, www.juneausymphony.org) has monthly concerts October–April at vari-

ous local venues. **Perseverance Theatre** (907/364-2421, www.perseverancetheatre.org) is a respected Douglas-based group that puts on plays September–May.

Movies

Local movie houses are the **20th Century Twin Theatre** (222 Front St., 907/586-4055) downtown and **Glacier Cinemas** (9091 Cinema Dr., 907/789-9191) in Mendenhall Valley. **Silverbow Inn** (120 2nd St., 907/586-9866 or 800/586-4146, www.silverbowinn.com) screens free classic flicks Monday–Wednesday in the back room, or head to **Goldtown Nickelodeon** (174 S. Franklin St., 907/586-2875) for indy and art-house films.

Events

Call 907/586-5866 for a recording of upcoming events and activities in Juneau. If you're around in April, don't miss the free weeklong **Alaska Folk Festival** (907/463-3316, www.juneau.com/aff), which attracts musicians from Alaska and the Northwest. You can attend workshops and dance to some of the hottest folk and bluegrass bands. Lots of fun, and completely authentic.

In late May, culture comes to town with the **Juneau Jazz and Classics** (907/463-3378, www.jazzandclassics.org), a 10-day series of performances and workshops by local musicians and nationally acclaimed guest artists.

During even-numbered years (2008 and 2010) Juneau is home to a colorful **Native Celebration** (907/463-4844) that attracts hundreds of participants from throughout the state. This is primarily a conference, but there are also performances, crafts, and a grand procession. The celebration takes place on the first weekend of June.

As in most every Alaskan town, June 21, the **summer solstice** is a time for celebration in Juneau; there's always some sort of party that long day and short night. **July 4th** is Juneau's day to play. Parades and a big fireworks show (see them from Douglas Island for the most impressive backdrop) are joined by dog Frisbee-catching and watermelon-eating contests, along with a sand castle contest at Sandy Beach Park.

Those who like to fish should throw in their lines at the annual **Golden North Salmon Derby** in early August. A top prize of $15,000 in cash makes it *the* big summer event for locals.

SHOPPING

Most locals do their shopping out the road at Nugget Mall in Mendenhall Valley, Fred Meyer (near the airport), or at either Costco or Wal-Mart in Lemon Creek.

Foggy Mountain Shop (134 N. Franklin St., 907/586-6780, www.foggymountainshop.com) sells camping gear, topographic maps, and sports equipment. It also rents skis and inline skates. The best place for rugged raingear, boots, and outdoor clothes is **Nugget Alaskan Outfitter** (Nugget Mall, 907/789-9785 or 800/478-0770, www.outdoorhq.com). While there, check out the mall's nine-foot-tall stuffed brown bear.

Galleries

If you happen to be in town, be sure to check out the **First Friday Art Walk** the first Friday of each month, with art openings and snacks at local galleries. **Wm. Spear Designs** (174 S. Franklin St. upstairs, 907/586-2209, www.wmspear.com) has the complete collection of colorful enameled pins by this local artisan with an international reputation. A former lawyer, Spear's work covers the spectrum from UFOs to dinosaurs. Definitely worth a stop.

Rie Muñoz Gallery (2101 Jordan Ave., 907/789-7411, www.riemunoz.com), near the airport, features works by several of Alaska's best-known artists. Muñoz's works are famous for their bold colors and fanciful designs of Alaskans at work and play.

The cooperatively run **Juneau Artists Gallery** (175 S. Franklin St., 907/586-9891, www.juneauartistsgallery.com) features a wide range of artwork, including paintings, pottery, jewelry, and photography.

Annie Kaill's Fine Art and Craft Gallery (244 Front St., 907/586-2880, www.annieandcojuneau.com) is packed with whimsical gifts, pottery, jewelry, and fine art.

For Native and other fine Alaskan art—plus changing exhibits in the back rooms—visit **Alaska State Museum Gift Shop** (124 Seward St., 907/523-8431).

Native Arts

Juneau is a good place to purchase Native Alaskan artwork, and one of the best is downstairs at the airport: **Hummingbird Hollow Gift Shop** (907/789-4672, www.hummingbirdhollow. net). Fair prices and authentic Alaskan work, with a big choice of Tlingit, Haida, Yup'ik, and Eskimo pieces. **Raven's Journey** (439 S. Franklin St., 907/463-4686), across from the tram, is another reputable shop with authentic Native Alaskan and Canadian art.

Scads of other galleries and gift shops sell artwork and trinkets. The quality varies widely, but much of it is overpriced, particularly anything by a Native artisan. Unfortunately, the romanticized paintings, carvings, and sculpture depicting these original Alaskans hunting seals in kayaks or carving totem poles meets head-on a much sadder picture of inebriated Natives leaning against the windows of downtown Juneau bars.

The Literary Scene

Juneauites enjoy several fine public libraries. The award-winning **Juneau Main Library** (907/586-5249, www.juneau.lib.ak.us/library), is on the top floor of the parking garage on South Franklin Street. There's a wonderful view of all the activity in Gastineau Channel from the outside walkway. Visitors may want to stop by the freebie shelves near the entrance for a trashy novel to read. Located on the 8th floor of the State Office Building, the **Alaska State Library** (907/465-2921, www.library.state.ak.us), is a good place to track down historical documents and photos.

Hearthside Books (254 Front St., 907/586-1760 or 800/478-1000, www.hearthsidebooks .com) is a packed downtown bookshop; it also has a larger store (907/789-2750) in the Nugget Mall near the airport. **The Observatory** (235 2nd St., 907/586-9676, www.observatory books.com) sells used books—including the largest collection of out-of-print Alaskana—plus first editions and antiquarian maps. Also worthy of a visit is **Rainy Day Books** (113 Seward St., 907/463-2665, www.juneaubooks.com), with over 10,000 used and rare titles.

HIKING AND CABINS

The Juneau area has an amazing wealth of hiking paths leading into the surrounding mountains. For a complete listing, pick up a copy of *Juneau Trails* from the Centennial Hall Visitor Center (101 Egan Dr., 907/586-8751). This is also the place to go for hiking and cabin information in Juneau. Rubber boots are recommended for all these trails, though you could get by with leather boots on some of the paths when the weather is dry.

Guided Hikes

The **City Parks and Recreation Department** (907/586-5226 or 24-hour line 907/586-0428, www.juneau.lib.ak.us/parksrec) offers guided free day hikes into areas around Juneau every Wednesday (adults only) and Saturday all summer.

Gastineau Guiding (907/586-2666, www.stepintoalaska.com) leads hikes in the Juneau area, including a three-hour rainforest nature walk on Douglas Island ($64 adults, $39 kids), and a considerably more challenging four-hour "guide's choice" hike ($79 adults, $49 kids). Or you can join the blue-haired throngs for an easy "tram and trek" ($59 adults, $32 kids) that includes a 20-minute bus tour, a tram ride up Mt. Roberts, and a one-hour hike. The half-day "whales and trails" trip ($179 adults, $129 kids) combines a whale-watching boat tour and a Mendenhall Glacier hike, or join a photo safari ($169) for tips from a professional photographer on land and sea.

Mendenhall Glacier Trails

The Mendenhall area is laced with trails, including a couple of paved interpretive paths that swarm with visitors all summer. The relatively easy **East Glacier Loop Trail** (3.5 miles), also begins near the center and provides good views of the glacier. A more challenging hike splits off from this trail and follows Nugget

Creek uphill to an Adirondack shelter. Vegetation along the East Glacier Trail consists of brush and trees established since the glacier's recent retreat, while trees along the Nugget Creek Trail are much older.

My favorite Mendenhall trail is the **West Glacier Trail** (7 miles round-trip), which begins from the end of Montana Creek Road, just beyond the Mendenhall Lake Campground: incredible views of the glacier and icefalls en route. Experienced ice-climbers use the path to access the glacier itself. Finally, for the really ambitious there's a primitive route up 3,228-foot **Mt. McGinnis** from the end of the West Glacier Trail, an additional four miles (6 hrs.) round-trip. This trail is generally covered with snow until late summer, but offers panoramic vistas of the entire Juneau area—on clear days.

Up Gold Creek

Some of the finest hiking around Juneau is found in the old gold mining areas up beyond the end of Basin Road, a pleasant half-hour walk from town. The area is amazingly quiet and scenic, particularly given the proximity to hectic downtown Juneau. You'll hear birds singing, see waterfalls, and feel the land enveloping you. One could easily spend several days exploring this scenic area. In Last Chance Basin, 1.5 miles up Basin Road, are the fascinating remains of the **AJ Mine.** A number of paths lead around the compressor building (which houses the Last Chance Mining Museum), a locomotive repair shop, and a variety of remains from the heyday of gold mining. For more details of the area, pick up the "Last Chance Basin Walking Tour" brochure from the Juneau–Douglas City Museum.

Perseverance Trail leads past Last Chance Basin to Silverbow Basin, site of the Perseverance Mine, three miles away. The **Mt. Juneau Trail** branches off from Perseverance Trail a half-mile up. It's very steep and only suitable for experienced hikers, but offers unparalleled vistas across Gastineau Channel. Plan on seven hours round-trip. Directly across from the Mt. Juneau trailhead is a short path down to Ebner

Falls. Continue another mile out Perseverance Trail to the **Granite Creek Trail** (1.5 miles each way), which follows the creek up past several waterfalls into the alpine. Just before Silverbow Basin yet another side trail leads right to the Glory Hole, which is connected to the AJ Mine by a tunnel. Old mining ruins are at the end of the trail, but signs warn of potential hazards from toxic tailings at the mine site.

Douglas

The remains of the **Treadwell Mine,** destroyed by the collapse and flood of 1917, offer a fascinating peek into the past. Pick up the "Treadwell Mine Historic Trail" brochure from the Juneau–Douglas City Museum for a description of the area. The trail starts from the south end of St. Ann's Avenue in Douglas and passes the crumbling remains of old buildings. Get there by catching the hourly Douglas bus ($1.50) in Juneau and riding it to the end of the line at Sandy Beach. Keep right on the main trail to reach the **Treadwell Glory Hole,** once the entrance to a network of shafts under Gastineau Channel, but now full of water and wrecked cars. A waterfall drops into the hole. Return to the fork in the trail and continue down to the shore to see remains of more buildings and pieces of old mining machinery. Mine tailings dumped into Gastineau Channel created an attractive sandy beach along the shore here (Sandy Beach Park). Just to the south is a steep-sided pit where the mine collapsed in 1917. Walk back along the beach and past the Small Boat Harbor to Douglas Post Office, where you can catch a bus back to Juneau.

Climbing Mt. Roberts

The most convenient way to get a panoramic view of Juneau and Gastineau Channel is by taking the tram ($24 round-trip) to the summit of Mt. Roberts, directly behind town. A more aerobic way is to take the 2.5-mile rainforest trail that begins at the east end of 6th Street. This enjoyable climb attracts many locals, especially on summer weekends, when you'll even encounter ironman-type joggers.

After a strenuous hike you're suddenly surrounded by hundreds of folks—some barely ambulatory—who have ridden the tram from their cruise ships to commune with nature in the gift shop, restaurant, espresso stand, and theater. It's a bit disconcerting, but that's the new *Alaskan Wilderness Experience,* made easy for everyone. Beyond the tram station, well-maintained trails climb uphill past Native-carved trees to spectacular viewpoints and a large wooden cross just above the tree line at 2,030 feet. There may be snow above this point until late July.

Once you get beyond the cross, the crowds quickly thin and then virtually disappear. The trail continues up to 3,666-foot **Gastineau Peak,** six miles from town, then on along the ridge to the summit of **Roberts Peak** (3,819 ft.), nine miles from your starting point. Experienced hikers with a map and compass may want to continue along the ridge, eventually connecting up with other trails in the area. Weather conditions change rapidly on these ridge tops, so be aware of incoming clouds and never hike into fog.

Point Bridget State Park

Point Bridget is a delightful park along the edge of Lynn Canal, 38 miles north of Juneau, and near Echo Cove. It's a great place to hike if you have the wheels to get there. Several paths lace this 2,850-acre park, including the **Point Bridget Trail** (7 miles round-trip) which takes hikers out to a fine vantage point across Lynn Canal to the Chilkat Mountains. Sea lions, harbor seals, and humpback whales are often seen from here. Before heading out, pick up a park map from the Department of Natural Resources (400 Willoughby Ave., 907/465-4563, www.alaskastateparks.org). Three cozy public-use cabins ($45) each sleep eight.

Cabins

The Juneau area has four popular Forest Service cabins that can be reached by hiking trails or on skis in winter. Some of these book up six months in advance. For more details on all Forest Service cabins in the area, contact the

Forest Service Information Center downtown or the district office near Nugget Mall.

Located on a scenic alpine ridge, the **John Muir Cabin** overlooks Auke Bay and the surrounding islands. Get there by following the **Spaulding Trail** a half-mile, turning left onto the **Auk Nu Trail,** and continuing another 2.5 miles to the cabin. The trail starts from a parking area on the right side of the road 12 miles northwest of town and just beyond the Auke Bay Post Office.

The **Peterson Lake Cabin** lies at the end of a 4.5-mile trail. Although it's mostly boardwalk, rubber boots are highly recommended. The trailhead is on the right, 24 miles northwest of town, and just beyond the Shrine of St. Therese. Experienced hikers or cross-country skiers with a map and compass may want to cross the alpine ridges from Peterson Lake to the John Muir Cabin (2.5 miles away), where they can head back along the Auke Nu and Spaulding Trails.

The **Dan Moller Cabin** on Douglas Island lies at the end of a three-mile trail. Get there by taking the Douglas bus to West Juneau. Get off the bus on Cordova Street and hike three blocks up the street. Turn left onto Pioneer Avenue; the trail begins from a small parking lot next to 3185 Pioneer Avenue. One of the most popular wintertime skiing trails in the area, it leads up to the beautiful alpine country of central Douglas Island.

Eagle Glacier Cabin faces this magnificent glacier, and is accessed via the **Amalga (Eagle Glacier) Trail** that begins 28 miles north of town. The path is relatively easy to hike, passes the cabin at the 5.5-mile point, and ends at the Eagle Glacier, 7.5 miles from the trailhead. The cabin faces across a lake to the glacier, offering some of the most dramatic vistas anywhere. Wear rubber boots for the oft-muddy trail.

Windfall Lake Cabin is a modern cabin with a gorgeous setting on this lake north of Juneau. It's accessible via a three-mile trail from Herbert River Road.

Two trail-accessible cabins (reservations: 907/465-4563, www.alaskastateparks.org, $45) are in Point Bridget State Park, at Mile

39 of Glacier Highway. The 12-person **Cowee Meadows Cabin,** is a three-mile hike (or wintertime ski) from the road, and the **Blue Mussel Beach Cabin** is four miles with a wonderful bay vista.

In addition to these hike-in cabins, there are five other Forest Service cabins on the mainland around Juneau, plus another 15 on nearby Admiralty Island. Access to these cabins is by floatplane or sometimes by sea kayak. The **Berners Bay Cabin** is just eight kayak miles from the north end of Glacier Highway. The location is grand, with fine vistas across the bay, good fishing, a beautiful waterfall, and lots to explore on the two-mile-wide river delta just north of here. But book early for this cabin.

Two close and extremely popular cabins (they fill up several months in advance) are on **Turner Lake,** 20 miles east of Juneau. Great fishing for cutthroat trout and incredible waterfall-draped rock faces on all sides. The flight in takes you near the enormous Taku Glacier, an added bonus.

RECREATION

Rent mountain bikes from **Driftwood Lodge** (435 W. Willoughby Ave., 907/586-2280 or 800/544-2239, www.driftwoodalaska.com). **Cycle Alaska** (907/780-2253, www.cycleak.com) leads fun "bike & brew" tours through Mendenhall Valley, with a van ride to the Alaskan Brewing Co. for some sampling afterwards. Owner John McConnochie is one of the most experienced cyclists in the area.

The **Augustus Brown Swimming Pool** (1619 Glacier Ave., 907/586-5325) at the high school has a pool, co-ed sauna, and workout equipment.

Rock climbers will enjoy a visit to the **Rock Dump** (1310 Eastaugh Way, 907/586-4982, www.rockdump.com, $10 day pass), an indoor climbing facility south of Juneau off Thane Road.

Juneau Racquet Club/Alaska Club (2841 Riverside Dr., 907/789-2181, www.thealaskaclub.com) features exercise equipment, indoor racquetball and tennis courts, a sauna, and

[handwritten margin note: see saved website Need bedding]

a hot tub. A second downtown location (641 W. Willoughby Ave., 907/586-5773) has more limited facilities. Non-members pay $10 per day.

Golfers should head to **Mendenhall Golf Course** (907/789-1221), a nine-hole course near the airport, where $25 gets you the full package. Not quite up to Arizona standards, but where else would you have a glacier backdrop?

Sea Kayaking

For an adventurous intro to sea kayaking, join **Above & Beyond Alaska's** (907/364-2333, www.beyondak.com, $185 adults, $165 kids) five-hour trip that includes a bus to Auke Bay and two hours of kayaking followed by a boat-based whale-watching trip. The company also provides water taxi drop-offs for kayakers at local bays and cabins. **Alaska Travel Adventures** (907/789-0052 or 800/478-0052, www.alaskaadventures.com, $85) has kayak three-hour trips from the north end of Douglas Island, but these are mainly for the cruise ship crowd.

Rent kayaks from **Alaska Boat & Kayak Rental** (907/789-6886, www.juneaukayak .com) at Auke Bay boat harbor 12 miles north of Juneau. Guided trips and water taxi services are also available. **Auke Bay Landing Craft** (907/790-4591, www.aukebay landingcraft.com), operates a helpful kayak drop-off service to Oliver's Inlet and other points in the Juneau area, and **Adventure Bound Alaska** (907/463-2509 or 800/228-3875, www.adventureboundalaska.com) provides kayak drop-offs in Tracy Arm.

Floating Mendenhall River

Experienced rafters and canoeists sometimes float the Mendenhall River, but be sure to ask the Forest Service for the details. The river is not particularly treacherous, but a number of people have died in independent boating accidents. For a guided float, join the cruise ship folks on a raft from **Goldbelt Tours** (907/586-8687 or 800/820-2628, www.goldbelttours.com, $99 adults, $66 kids) or **Alaska Travel Adventures** (907/789-0052 or 800/478-

0052, www.alaskaadventures.com, $85 adults, $57 kids). These four-hour floats include lunch and transportation from downtown.

Fishing and Whale-Watching

The visitor center offers a listing of Juneau's many **charter boat** operators. All sorts of options are available, from half-day fishing and whale-watching ventures to two-week cruises around Southeast. If you want to do it on your own, rent a skiff and fishing gear from Alaska Boat & Kayak Rental at Auke Bay.

A half-dozen companies specialize in whale-watching day trips out of Juneau, including **Orca Enterprises** (907/789-6801 or 888/733-6722, www.alaskawhalewatching.com), **Dolphin Whale Watch Tours** (907/463-3422 or 800/719-3422, www.dolphintours.com), **Four Seasons Marine** (907/790-6671 or 877/774-8687, www.4seasonsmarine.com) and **Juneau Sportfishing & Sightseeing** (907/586-1887, www.juneausportfishing.com).

Skiing and Snowboarding

Come wintertime, the **Eaglecrest Ski Area** (907/790-2000, www.skijuneau.com, Thurs.–Mon. early Dec.–March) on Douglas Island provides excellent skiing opportunities—when the weather cooperates. Thirty ski trails are available, with a vertical drop of 1,400 feet. Adult lift tickets cost $34, and cross-country skiers can get a special two-ride pass for $10 that takes them into the alpine meadows, or you can play on the tubing hill for $10. Call 907/586-5330 for current snow conditions. A bus provides weekend-only transport to Eaglecrest for $5 each way. Just downhill from the ski area are 5 kilometers of groomed cross-country trails (free).

The City Parks and Recreation Department (907/586-5226, www.juneau.lib.ak.us/parksrec) leads **guided cross-country ski tours** in the winter if there's enough snow. These take place every Wednesday (adults only) and Saturday.

Flightseeing and Glacier Landings

Flightseeing and charter flights are available from **Ward Air** (907/789-9150 or 800/478-9150, www.wardair.com), a long-established company with a good safety record. Glacier Bay flightseeing can also be booked, but they're expensive due to the distance. Wait until you visit Haines, Skagway, or Gustavus where the cost and flying time to the park are less.

Several companies offer helicopter glacier tours to the spectacular Juneau Icefield, with landings on crevasse-free portions of the glaciers. These flights remain controversial in Juneau, primarily because of the constant din they create in Mendenhall Valley. Flights operate May–September, but trips that include dog-sledding start later and end earlier due to snow conditions. All prices are per person.

Era Helicopters (907/586-2030 or 800/843-1947, www.flightseeingtours.com) lands on Norris or Taku Glacier. A one-hour trip with a 15-minute walk is $244. It also offers a longer two-hour trip ($425) that includes a dogsled ride.

Temsco Helicopters (907/789-9501 or 877/789-9501, www.temscoair.com) has a one-hour flight ($199) that spends 25 minutes on Mendenhall Glacier. Other flight options include a "pilot's choice" 90-minute flight ($339) with two glacier landings, and a 1.5-hour trip ($419) that includes a 25-minute dogsled ride.

Coastal Helicopters (907/789-5600 or 800/789-5610, www.coastalhelicopters.com) charges $192 for a 60-minute trip, or $315 for a 90-minute trip; both include 15 minutes on a glacier. Also popular are dogsled tours on Herbert Glacier. These include an hour on the ice with the dogs and 30 minutes of flying time for $395.

Northstar Trekking (907/790-4530, www.glaciertrekking.com) specializes in Mendenhall Glacier hikes of varying lengths, starting with a flight plus one-hour hike for $295, up to a trek that includes more technical climbing and four hours on the ice for $459. Clients are fully outfitted with mountaineering gear and crampons for these adventures.

All four of these companies include transportation from downtown to their landing pads and also provide chartered flights to the glaciers for

heli-hiking or skiing. Warning: Helicopters can be dangerous, and a number of fatal crashes have taken place around Juneau. Be sure to ask about safety procedures before stepping onboard.

Glacier Hikes

Travelers looking for something more challenging than a helicopter glacier tour should check out **Above & Beyond Alaska** (907/364-2333, www.beyondak.com). Their six-hour Mendenhall Glacier trek ($185) involves a hike to the west side of the glacier and time on the ice exploring its features, including the ice caves; crampons, helmet, and ice axe are provided. Another trek ($185) teaches basic ice climbing skills. Recommended, but you need to be in good physical condition.

Ziplines

Juneau is home to two high-adventure (literally) ziplines. The locally owned **Alaska Zipline Adventures** (907/790-2547, www.alaskazip.com) operates at Eaglecrest Ski Area on north Douglas Island, with access via a road to a high suspension skybridge and seven ziplines that drop through the forest and along a beautiful creek. The cost is $115 for a fun three-hour adventure. They also have a "zip and feast" trip that includes the zipline and a cooking demonstration.

A second company, **Alaska Canopy Adventures** (907/523-2920, www.alaska canopyadventures.com), operates on the site of the old Treadwell Gold Mine on Douglas Island. Participants take a short boat ride over from Juneau and then hop on an off-road vehicle to climb to the starting point in a platform high up a tree. A series of nine ziplines (one 800 ft. long) take you through the forest and eventually over the "glory hole" 200 feet below. Two suspension bridges link other sections, providing treetop views of the rainforest. The cost is $169 per person for a three-hour tour.

ACCOMMODATIONS

A full range of options is available to travelers staying in Juneau, but you should make reservations well in advance for arrivals in July and

August, when everything in town is sometimes booked. See the Juneau Convention and Visitors Bureau website (www.traveljuneau.com) for links to many local hotels, motels, B&Bs, lodges, and resorts. If you aren't bringing a vehicle up on the ferry, be sure to ask about if your lodging place offers a free pickup; it could save you the $30 taxi fare.

Hostel

Alaska's finest hostel, **Juneau International Hostel** (614 Harris St., 907/586-9559, www.juneauhostel.org) is in a lovely old home just a few blocks uphill from downtown. In addition to dorm space for 46 people, the hostel has a comfortable community room with guest computer, kitchen facilities, washer, and dryer. It does not have a TV. The hostel is open year-round, but is closed daily 9 A.M.–5 P.M. The doors are locked at midnight, putting a damper on your nightlife. Lodging costs just $10, with a maximum stay of three nights. Rooms are clean and the managers are friendly, but things are often crowded. Reserve ahead in summer, or get here early to be certain of a place.

Hotels and Motels

In-Town: The **Alaskan Hotel** (167 S. Franklin St., 907/586-1000 or 800/327-9347, www.thealaskanhotel.com) has reasonably priced downtown Juneau lodging in a historic setting. Built in 1913, this is Juneau's oldest lodging place, with 45 small, but surprisingly charming rooms. Bare-bones units with a shared bath and no TV cost $60 s or d; nicer ones with private baths and TVs are $80 s or d, and some of these include fridges and microwaves. Larger kitchenette units sleep four for $90. Try to get a room away from the bar and not on the second floor since these can get noisy when bands are playing. During the Folk Festival each April the Alaskan is the heart of the music scene, with impromptu jams in the halls and downstairs at all hours. The Alaskan is a classic—and rustic—place, so it may not please people expecting the latest in accouterments. Wi-Fi is available in the lobby and bar.

Driftwood Lodge (435 W. Willoughby Ave., 907/586-2280 or 800/544-2239, www.driftwoodalaska.com), is convenient to town, with dated rooms (some with kitchenettes) for $94 d; one-bedroom units with kitchens for $102 d, and two-bedroom units that sleep four for $125. The Driftwood provides a courtesy van to the airport or ferry terminal, and a guest computer.

Prospector Hotel (375 Whittier St., 907/586-3737 or 800/331-2711, www.prospectorhotel.com), has spacious in town rooms, most of which contain kitchenettes. Rates are $159 d in standard rooms, up to $179 d in two-room kitchenette suites. Amenities include a restaurant, courtesy van to the airport or ferry terminal, and Wi-Fi.

Baranof Hotel (127 N. Franklin St., 907/586-2660 or 800/544-0970, www.westmarkhotels.com) is a nine-story downtown classic with a dark lobby and a romantic restaurant. It's a favorite haunt of state legislators and lobbyists in the winter, and 20 of the rooms have kitchenettes ($209 d). Several smaller and older rooms have twin beds for just $109 d, but nicer rooms (ask for a remodeled unit) are $169–194 d, and suites run $209–259 d. The lobby has Wi-Fi and a guest computer. The higher levels offer the best views and least street noise.

The seven-story **Goldbelt Hotel Juneau** (51 W. Egan Dr., 907/586-6900 or 888/478-6909, www.goldbelttours.com, $169–179 d) has a convenient downtown location, modern rooms, Wi-Fi, a restaurant (The Zen), and a free airport shuttle. Ask for a room facing the water.

Mendenhall Valley/Airport: Most of Juneau's newest hotels are clustered around the airport in Mendenhall Valley. These lack the charm of the historic downtown places, and you will probably want a rental car to get around. Of course, they are also close to Mendenhall Glacier, and offer the predictability of corporate lodging.

Super 8 Motel (2295 Trout St., 907/789-4858 or 800/800-8000, www.super8.com, $111–120 s or d) has reasonable rates. Amenities include a continental breakfast, Wi-Fi, and courtesy shuttle. Some rooms have fridges and microwaves.

A good family place is **Frontier Suites Airport Hotel** (9400 Glacier Hwy., 907/790-6600 or 800/544-2250, www.frontiersuites.com, $130–160 d). It has a wide variety of rooms, all with full kitchens (including dishes), and some with jetted tubs. Three family units contain bunks. Free shuttle to the airport and ferry.

Also near the airport is **Grandma's Feather Bed** (2358 Mendenhall Loop Rd., 907/789-5566 or 888/781-5005, www.grand masfeatherbed.com, $160 d) a 14-unit motel with spacious rooms, whirlpool tubs, and a hot breakfast. Nearby (same owners) is **Best Western Country Lane Inn** (9300 Glacier Hwy., 907/789-5005 or 888/781-5005, www.countrylaneinn.com, $130–140 d) with standard motel rooms and a continental breakfast. Both places have guest computers, Wi-Fi, and a courtesy shuttle to downtown, the ferry, or the airport.

Extended Stay Deluxe (1800 Shell Simmons Dr., 907/790-6435 or 888/559-9846, www.extendedstaydeluxe.com)—just a block away from the airport and nine miles from downtown—has all the amenities travelers have come to expect, including an indoor swimming pool, hot tub, exercise room, kitchenettes in all rooms, continental breakfast, Wi-Fi, guest computers, and free shuttle service to town and the ferry. Most rooms go for $159 d and have either two queens or a king bed, but a few rooms ($179 d) also feature private whirlpool tubs.

Lighthouses and Cabins

For something really different, spend a night or two at **Sentinel Island Lighthouse** (907/586-5338, $50 per person) a few miles north of Juneau. Built in 1935, the art deco tower has bunks (bring sleeping bags), and guests can also stay in the keeper's house which contains a kitchen. Get to Sentinel Island by kayak, skiff, or helicopter. The island has two active eagle nests and sits right across from a Steller sea lion haulout.

Two other lighthouses currently being restored may be open to the public in the next few years: **Point Retreat Lighthouse** (907/364-2410, www.aklighthouse.org), on the northern tip of Admiralty Island west of Juneau, and **Five Fingers Lighthouse** (907/364-3632, www.5fingerlighthouse.com), 75 miles south of Juneau.

Located 23 miles north of Juneau, the **Shrine of St. Therese** (907/780-6112, www.shrine ofsainttherese.org) has a delightful collection of cabins for rent. A rustic cabin with wood stove is just $20 s or $25 d; no kitchen, and you'll need to use the nearby bathrooms. A historic 1938 log cabin has two bedrooms, plus a kitchenette and private bath for $35 s or $45 d. Three larger places are available, including a lodge that can sleep 22 guests! You don't have to attend Catholic mass, but guests must abide by the contemplative spirit of this unique and peaceful place.

Bed-and-Breakfasts

Couples may want to spend the extra money to stay at one of more than 40 Juneau B&Bs. Accommodations run the gamut from old miner's cabins to gorgeous log hillside homes. Pick up the *Juneau Visitors Guide* brochure at the visitor center for a listing of local places, or check its rack for flyers from many B&Bs. Two good Web resources for Juneau B&Bs are the Juneau Convention and Visitors Bureau (www.traveljuneau.com) and the B&B Association of Alaska INNside Passage Chapter (www.accommodations-alaska.com).

Downtown B&Bs: Gold Street Inn B&B (907/586-9863, www.juneauinn.com, open May–mid-Sept.) has unpretentious but clean accommodations in a historic downtown rooming house. The four rooms ($95–125 d) have private entrances and baths, and include a continental breakfast and Wi-Fi. A two-bedroom suite ($155 for four) has a kitchenette.

Best known for its bagels and other baked goods, **Silverbow Inn** (120 2nd St., 907/586-4146 or 800/586-4146, www.silverbowinn.com, $100–175 d) also has 11 bright guest rooms, each with private bath, phone, TV, and Wi-Fi. The least expensive rooms are small, while two more spacious new units have Jacuzzi tubs. Add $20 to access the rooftop deck with a hot tub, sauna, and fine views. Guests are served a tasty breakfast each morning, along with evening cheese and wine. A two-night minimum is required in mid-summer.

Built in 1906, and beautifully restored to its foursquare glory, **❰ Alaska's Capital Inn** (113 W. 5th St., 907/586-6507 or 888/588-6507, www.alaskacapitalinn.com) offers sumptuous heart-of-Juneau lodging with commanding views of the city. Four guest rooms ($179–239 d) are filled with period antiques—including an 1879 pump organ and maplewood floors from a 1920s YMCA—and the entire top level has been transformed into a very private suite ($275 d) with a gas fireplace, jetted tub, and king-size sleigh bed. Two smaller gardenside rooms ($149–179 d) are more contemporary, with private entrances—making them popular with families. All rooms have private baths, and most also feature clawfoot tubs. Amenities include a flower-filled yard with a gazebo-enclosed hot tub, free Wi-Fi and guest computer, a wonderful Alaskan breakfast, plus evening wine and treats. Two-night minimum in the summer.

Farther Afield B&Bs: Located on a cove near Auke Bay, **Serenity Inn** (907/789-2330 or 800/877-5369, www.alaskaserenityinn.com, $189 d, $239 for four) has an apartment suite that features a full kitchen (make-your-own breakfast fixings included), hot tub on the deck, and extraordinary views across Lynn Canal from the deck. Two-night minimum.

Pearson's Pond Luxury Inn and Garden Spa (907/789-3772 or 888/658-6328, www.pearsonspond.com, $249–349 s, $299–399 d) is a comfortable home with two hot tubs, a three-level deck, five guest rooms, guest computers, Wi-Fi, and Mendenhall Glacier vistas. The premium rooms include large spa tubs and canopy beds. Borrow a bike to ride around, paddle a kayak around the small pond, or just enjoy the beautiful gardens. Breakfast is a make-it-yourself affair. Two-night minimum.

On the north end of Douglas Island, six miles from Juneau and close to the Eaglecrest Ski Area, **Fireweed House B&B** (907/586-3885 or 800/586- 3885, www.fireweedhouse.com) has a scenic and very peaceful setting. Accommo-dations (all with private baths and jetted tubs) include two rooms in the main house ($189 d) and an apartment with kitchen ($229 d). A separate two-bedroom guesthouse ($399 for four; three-night minimum) sits on a quiet two-acre site away from the other buildings, and has its own hot tub. Delicious breakfasts are a real attraction, and kids are welcome. Wifi and guest computers are available.

A lovely waterside home on Douglas Island, **Gill's Horizon** (907/586-2829, www.gillshorizon.com) is eight miles from Juneau. Guests stay in the apartment suite ($169 d), and will appreciate the waterside hot tub, private beach, lush grounds, driving range, and even a pair of nesting eagles. Three-night minimum stay.

Auke Lake B&B (11595 Mendenhall Loop Rd., 907/790-3253, www.admiraltytours.com) occupies a prime piece of shoreline on this picturesque lake. The 5,000-square-foot home has a deck with a hot tub for relaxing, two suites ($145–165 d), and a rather small guest room ($125 d), all with private baths, fridges, and a light breakfast. Borrow the kayak for a paddle around the lake.

CAMPING

The Forest Service maintains two campgrounds (reservations: www.reserveusa.com) in the Juneau area, but neither is close to town, and both are only open in the summer. **Mendenhall Lake Campground** hugs the shore of Mendenhall Lake, with glacier views and access to several hiking trails. Here you will find backpacker units and vehicle sites ($10), along with RV sites with full hookups ($28). From the ferry terminal, turn right and go two miles to De Hart's Store, then left onto Loop Road. Follow it three miles to Montana Creek Road, then another three-quarters of a mile to the campground. From Juneau by foot, take the city bus to where Montana Creek Road intersects Mendenhall Loop Road. Walk up Montana Creek Road, bear right at the Y after a half-mile, then continue another half-mile to the campground (well marked).

Auke Village Campground ($8) is 16 miles north on Glacier Highway and another two miles out Point Louisa. The area is secluded, with a nice beach and views of nearby islands. If you lack a vehicle, the nearest city bus stop is four miles away.

Eagle Beach State Recreation Area (Mile 28, 907/465-4563, mid-May–mid-Sept., $10) has rustic campsites (no water). Nearby is a picnic area with all-encompassing views of the Chilkat Range.

RV Campgrounds

The city of Juneau has four RV spaces at **Savikko Park** (907/586-5255) on Douglas Island. Free, but no hookups, no tents, and stays are limited to three days.

Auke Bay RV Park (907/789-9467, open year-round, $24 with full hookups, no tent camping) is a mile and a half southeast of the ferry terminal. Reservations are recommended here.

Spruce Meadow RV Park (10200 Back Loop Rd., 907/789-1990, www.juneaurv.com, $27 RVs or $20 tents) is four miles from the ferry terminal. In addition, RVs can generally overnight at Nugget Mall near the airport for free, but no facilities, of course.

FOOD
Breakfast and Lunch

No other Alaskan restaurant is even remotely like **C Costa's Diner,** located in Merchant's Mall downtown. Owner, chef, and general rabble-rouser Costa Collette runs this free-form place where the board lists today's specials ($5–8), typically crepes, pancakes, and egg dishes. Write your order on a sticky note, pour your own coffee, dig out the dishes and silverware, open the fridge for condiments and salsa, and sit back to take in the chaos. Payment is on the honor system: just put your money in the bucket, along with a tip. Ask a local if you can't figure out the system at Costa's. At lunch, Costa's spot becomes **The Soup Queen,** with homemade soups for under $6.

Rainbow Foods (224 4th St., 907/586-6476, www.rainbow-foods.org) is the local natural foods market, but also has a buffet ($6.50/pound) with healthy hot meals to go; it's great for a fast lunch without a lot of fat.

For a Mendenhall Valley lunch, head to **Heritage Glacier Café** (9112 Mendenhall Mall Rd., 907/789-0692) where favorites include fajitas, burgers, and portobello wraps. Or just get today's soup with focaccia for $4. Well off the tourist path, and worth the side trip. They also have a breakfast menu and free Wi-Fi.

Coffee Shops and Bakeries

Three local spots are popular for coffee and light meals, and all three provide free Wi-Fi for customers. **Heritage Coffee** (174 S. Franklin St., 907/586-1087 or 800/478-5282, www.heritagecoffee.com) is easily the most popular and crowded Juneau espresso-and-pastries shop, and remains open until 11 most summer nights. It's a great place to meet tie-and-sportcoated politicians, ring-nosed teens, plaid-shirted fishermen, and Gore-Texed vacationers. Walk down the halls of this building to view over-sized historic photos of Juneau.

Valentine's Coffee House & Bakery (111 Seward, 907/463-5144, www.valentines coffeehouse.com) is smaller and away from the action, with a lunch menu of focaccia sandwiches, salads, and calzones.

Alaska's oldest bakery, **Silverbow Inn Bakery** (120 2nd St., 907/586-4146, www .silverbowinn.com) is great for a hot bagel (try one with cream cheese and lox), soup, or latte. The atmosphere is homespun and funky, and the side-street location keeps the crowds at bay. They're open till 8 P.M.

Get an ice cream to go at **Chilkat Cone Kitchen** (inside the Merchant's Wharf on Marine Way, 907/463-2663), where the waffle cones are decorated with traditional Native designs.

Local Favorites

The Hangar (2 Marine Way in Merchant's Wharf, 907/586-5018, www.hangaronthe wharf.com, $11–30) is an extremely popular waterfront pub with seafood, steaks, pasta, burgers, sandwiches, and salads, but I usually keep it simple with halibut fish and chips and a local beer. Historic photos line the walls, and you can head upstairs for a game of pool. It's a great place to watch the sun go down while enjoying one of its 24 brews on draught. Loud, energetic, and fun are the operative terms.

Farther afield is **Hot Bite** (907/790-2483) at Auke Bay Harbor. The menu includes charbroiled burgers (best in town), halibut and chips, grilled portobello mushroom sandwiches, milk shakes, and other tasty bites. Service can be slow since it's all made to order.

Pizza and Italian

Juneau's best-known pizza joint is **Bullwinkle's** (907/586-2400, www.bullwinklespizza.com), directly across from the State Office Building on Willoughby Avenue and also in Mendenhall Valley next to Super Bear Market. Daily lunch pizza specials start at $6, and the popcorn is always free. Good salad bar, too. You'll get better and more authentic pizza—including by the slice—from **Pizzeria Roma** (Merchant's Wharf, 907/463-5020).

Over in Douglas, **The Island Pub** (1102 2nd St., 907/364-1595, www.theislandpub.com) serves pizzas, sandwiches, and wraps in a great smoke-free setting with big windows facing Juneau.

International

In business since 1974, **Olivia's de Mexico** (222 Seward St. downstairs, 907/586-6870) serves traditional Mexican food, with fair prices and big portions.

Located across from the Auke Bay boat harbor, **◖ Chan's Thai Kitchen** (907/789-9777, lunch and dinner until 8:30 P.M., closed Sun. and Mon.) is popular with locals looking for a little spice in their lives. The food is dependably fine, but the place gets packed most nights so be ready to wait. The spring rolls, chicken coconut soup, and any of the curries are recommended. Delicious Thai ice tea too.

For surprisingly good Japanese sushi and Chinese head to the Korean-American owned **Seong's Sushi Bar** (740 W. 9th St., 907/586-4778, $7–9) across from the Federal Building. Lunches are the real attraction, with big plates of chicken sukiyaki, broccoli beef, or shrimp with veggies.

Another locals' favorite is **Dragon Inn** (5000 Glacier Hwy., 907/780-4616), three miles out in Lemon Creek, serving dim sum appetizers, seafood with pan-fried noodles, sautéed eggplant in garlic sauce, and more. Downtown, head to **Wild Spice Restaurant** (140 Seward St., 907/523-0344, www.thewildspice.com) for Mongolian BBQ–style meals; you select a bowl full of ingredients and spices, and watch the chefs do their wonders.

Out near the airport, **Sweet Dream** (8585 Old Dairy Rd., 907/789-4401, www.sweetdreamteas.com) is certainly the most unexpected Juneau establishment. The shop rents Japanese anime videos (and screens them on Saturday nights), and serves bubble tea—an iced Asian tea smoothie with tapioca balls—along with pho or udon soups. It's also a Wi-Fi hotspot.

Pel' Meni (on Marine Way in Merchant's Wharf, 907/463-2630) is a tiny Russian eatery, where the house specialty is dumplings made with sirloin steak and topped with a spicy curry and cilantro sauce. This late-night hangout is popular with teens.

Seafood

Juneau has two excellent salmon bakes with all-you-can-eat dinners and free bus transport from town. Both are open May–September. Housed in a rustic waterside building four miles south of town, **◖ Thane Ore House Salmon Bake** (907/586-3442, www.thaneorehouse.com), charges adults $22 and kids $11 for a big dinner of king or sockeye salmon, beer-battered halibut, BBQ ribs, baked beans, cornbread, and unusual salads. Outside tables are perfect for those rare sunny days.

Gold Creek Salmon Bake (907/789-0052 or 800/323-5757, www.alaskadventures.com, $32 adults, $21 kids) has a similar menu north of town near the hospital.

Get high-quality, freshly smoked salmon at **Taku Smokeries** (550 S. Franklin St., 907/463-3474 or 800/582-5122, www.takusmokeries.com), a few blocks south of town.

Drop by for a sample or to watch through the windows as they process the fish.

On the water side of the Taku Smokeries building is **Twisted Fish Co.** (907/463-5033, May–Sept., $16–26), where the decor is playful and the food is contemporary. Big windows face Gastineau Channel, where floatplanes and cruise ships create a busy scene all summer. Watch the crew in the open kitchen as they prepare grilled halibut burgers, halibut tacos, eight-inch pizzas, cedar plank salmon, and a tasty clam chowder. It's a noisy and fun spot. (The owners also operate the equally popular Hangar.)

Groceries

You'll find no-frills grocery shopping at the big **Fred Meyer** (907/789-6503), nine miles northwest of town along Glacier Highway. Other grocers out in Mendenhall Valley are **Safeway** (3033 Vintage Blvd., 907/790-5500) and **Super Bear Supermarket** (in Mendenhall Mall, 907/789-0173).

In town, head to friendly **Alaskan & Proud Market** (615 Willoughby Ave., 907/586-3101 or 800/478-2118)—better known as A&P, but not to be confused with the East Coast chain—for a complete selection of fresh produce and meats. Safeway, A&P, and Fred Meyer are all open 24 hours a day. You might also try the somewhat-downsized **Costco** (5225 Commercial Way, 907/780-6740) in Lemon Creek, though most visitors won't find much need for cases of tuna fish or 50-pound bags of charcoal.

The local natural foods market downtown, **Rainbow Foods** (224 4th St., 907/586-6476, www.rainbow-foods.org) has a healthy and tasty lunchtime buffet with salads, veggie dishes, and pizza slices.

INFORMATION AND SERVICES

Juneau's info spot is the **Centennial Hall Visitor Center** (101 Egan Dr., 907/586-2201 or 888/581-2201, www.traveljuneau.com). Hours are Monday–Friday 8:30 A.M.–5 P.M. and Saturday–Sunday 9 A.M.–5 P.M. May–September, Monday–Friday 9 A.M.–4 P.M. the rest of the year. Ask for the "Juneau Walking Tour" map on a nice day, or pick out a video for a rainy-day diversion. You can make ferry reservations here, and there's usually a Forest Service volunteer available to answer your questions.

Three other information kiosks in Juneau have brochures and may be staffed in the summer. Find them at Marine Park, the airport, and the Cruise Ship Terminal on South Franklin Street. Other useful online info sources for Juneau include www.juneaualaska.com, www.juneau.com, and the city site www.juneau.org.

Services

The main post office is in the downtown Federal Building at 9th Street and Willoughby Avenue, and a branch post office at 225 Front Street. **Bartlett Regional Hospital** (907/796-8900, www.bartletthospital.org), halfway between Juneau and Mendenhall Valley, is the largest medical facility in Southeast Alaska. For non-emergencies, contact **Juneau Urgent Care** (8505 Old Dairy Rd., 907/790-4111, www.juneauurgentcare.com).

A number of local places have computers where you can check your email. The Juneau Public Library has free computers and wireless Internet, or pay to view downtown at **Seaport Cyber Station** (170 S. Franklin St., 907/586-8676, www.seaportcyber.com).

Coin-operated showers can be found at **Harbor Washboard** (1114 Glacier Ave., 907/586-1133), **Zach Gordon Youth Center** (396 Whittier St., 907/586-2635), the **Alaskan Hotel** (167 S. Franklin St., 907/586-1000), and out of town at **Auke Bay Boat Harbor** (907/789-0819). A better deal is the high school **swimming pool** (1619 Glacier Ave., 907/586-5325), where your entrance buys access to a shower, pool, sauna, and weight-lifting equipment. Plus, you get to check out the pallid-skinned Juneauites. Coin laundries include Harbor Wash Board, along with **The Dungeon** (4th and Franklin Sts., 907/586-2805) and **Mendenhall Laundromat** (Mendenhall Mall, 907/789-9781).

SEACC

The Southeast Alaska Conservation Council, or SEACC (419 6th St., 907/586-6942, www.seacc.org), has material on regional environmental issues, plus activist T-shirts. This is the primary environmental group in the Southeast and has a reputation as a highly effective organization both locally and in Washington, D.C. Members receive a quarterly newsletter and periodic notices of important environmental issues. You can join for $25 per year.

GETTING THERE
Ferry

Juneau's Alaska Marine Highway **ferry terminal** (907/465-3940) is 14 miles northwest of town at Auke Bay. Ferries arrive and depart daily during the summer, headed north to both Haines and Skagway, southwest to Sitka, and south to other Alaskan towns. Arrivals are sometimes very late at night, so be ready to stumble off in a daze. Ferries generally stay one to two hours in Auke Bay. The *Fairweather* is a high-speed passenger and vehicle ferry with frequent service from Juneau to Sitka, Haines, and Skagway. Unfortunately, the ferry suffers from frequent breakdowns, so check ahead to make sure it's on schedule. The other state ferries are larger and slower. Several covered picnic tables are behind the terminal where you can crash if you have an early-morning departure. Make ferry reservations through Alaska Marine Highway (907/465-3941 or 800/642-0066, www.ferryalaska.com).

A cab ride to town will set you back $30, but hitching to town is relatively easy during the day. You can also walk the two miles from the ferry terminal to De Hart's Store, where hourly city buses will pick you up Monday–Saturday 7 A.M.–11:30 P.M.

Air

Juneau airport is nine miles northwest of downtown. Express **city buses** ($1.50) arrive hourly in front of the airport between 8 A.M.–5 P.M. On weekends or later hours (until 11:15 P.M.) you can catch the regular city bus behind Nug-

get Mall, a half-mile away. Taxis cost $20 to downtown.

Inside the terminal, take a look at the glass cases with various stuffed critters, including a huge polar bear (upstairs). The upstairs Glacier Restaurant offers impressive vistas out across Mendenhall Glacier, along with surprisingly good and reasonable meals; locals actually come here to eat!

A good place to see waterfowl and eagles is the **Mendenhall Wetlands** that surround the airport. An overlook provides a view from Egan Highway on the way into Juneau.

Alaska Airlines (800/426-0333, www.alaskaair.com) has daily flights into Juneau from Seattle, and on to Anchorage. Alaska's jets also connect Juneau with other Southeast towns and points south all the way to Mexico.

Options abound for small-plane service to communities around Juneau. **Wings of Alaska** (907/789-0790, www.wingsofalaska.com) has daily flights to Angoon, Gustavus, Haines, Hoonah, Skagway, and Tenakee Springs. **Alaska Seaplane Service** (907/789-3331 or 800/478-3360, www.akseaplanes.com) offers daily service to Angoon, Elfin Cove, Pelican, and Tenakee. **Skagway Air** (907/789-2006, www.skagwayair.com) flies to Haines and Skagway daily. **L.A.B. Flying Service** (907/789-9160, www.labflying.com) has daily service to Gustavus, Haines, Hoonah, Kake, and Skagway. **Air Excursions** (907/697-2375 or 800/354-2479, www.airexcursions.com) offers the cheapest flights to Gustavus from Juneau. Flightseeing and charter flights are also available from these companies.

GETTING AROUND
Tours

Mighty Great Trips (907/789-5460, www.mightygreattrips.com) runs 2.5-hour summertime tours that include Juneau and Mendenhall Glacier for $22. Other bus tour companies include **Gray Line of Alaska** (907/586-3773 or 800/544-2206, www.graylineofalaska.com), **Last Frontier Tours** (907/789-0742 or 888/396-8687, www.lastfrontiertours.com), and **Princess Tours** (907/463-3900 or

800/774-6237, www.princess.com). Princess operates excellent three-hour trips ($65 adults, $35 kids) to the historic AJ Mine south of town, with detailed tours inside the mine, plenty of historical info, and the chance to pan for gold.

For something different, hop onboard the **Juneau Steamboat Co.** (907/723-0372, www.juneausteamboat.com), a little wood-fired boat modeled after ones used a century ago. One-hour tours of Gastineau Channel depart the downtown dock and cost $30.

City Buses

Capital Transit buses (907/789-6901, www.juneau.org/capitaltransit, $1.50) operate daily, connecting Juneau, Douglas, and Mendenhall Valley. Buses to and from Mendenhall Valley run every half-hour 7 A.M.–10:30 P.M. (9 A.M.–5:30 P.M. on Sun.), with both regular and express service (weekdays only). Bus service to Douglas is hourly. Pick up route maps and schedules from the various visitor centers or at the ferry terminal or airport.

Trolley

The **Juneau Trolley Car Company** (907/586-7433, www.juneautrolley.com, daily May–Sept. 8 A.M.–6 P.M., day pass $19, $9 kids) covers most of downtown. This red trolley features a 30-minute narrated tour, and you can get on and off at various points along the way.

Taxis

The local taxi companies are **Alaska Taxi & Tours** (907/780-6400), **Capital Cab** (907/586-2772), **Juneau Taxi & Tours** (907/790-4511), and **Evergreen Taxi** (907/586-2121). From the airport to downtown the charge is typically around $20. A cab ride from downtown to the ferry terminal (14 miles) will cost upward of $30–35, but might be worth it if you get several people together. Taxi tours are $55 per hour.

Car Rentals

With nearly 100 miles of roads in the Juneau area, renting a car is a smart idea. Be sure to call two or three weeks ahead of mid-summer arrivals, or you may find every car already rented. Three national chains have offices at the airport: **Avis** (907/789-9450 or 800/478-2847), **Budget** (907/790-1086), **Hertz** (907/789-9494 or 800/654-3131), **Kipco Auto Rental** (907/796-2880, www.kipcoak.com), and **National** (907/789-9814 or 800/478-2847). The other companies are all within a few blocks, and will pick you up during business hours: **Rent-A-Wreck** (907/789-4111, www.juneaualaska.com/rent-a-wreck), **Mendenhall Auto Center** (907/789-1386 or 800/478-1386, www.mendenhallauto center.com; closed weekends), and **Evergreen Ford** (907/789-9386, www.evergreenmotors juneau.com). The best rates are typically with Mendenhall Auto or Kipco Auto Rental, starting around $50 per day for a compact. The Kipco and Rent-a-Wreck cars are older vehicles, so you might want to check them out first.

◖ TRACY ARM-FORDS TERROR WILDERNESS

Located 50 miles southeast of Juneau, the 653,000-acre Tracy Arm–Fords Terror Wilderness contains country that rivals Glacier Bay National Park, but costs half as much to reach. The wilderness consists of a broad bay that splits into two long glacially carved arms—Tracy Arm and Endicott Arm. (Fords Terror splits off as a separate channel halfway up Endicott Arm.) Within Tracy Arm, steep-walled granite canyons plummet 2,000 feet into incredibly deep and narrow fjords. We're talking rocks-to-the-waterline here. The fjords wind past waterfalls to massive glaciers, their icebergs dotted with hundreds of harbor seals. Humpback whales are a common sight, as are killer whales. Look closely on the mountain slopes and you're bound to see mountain goats, especially near North Sawyer Glacier. John Muir noted that the fjord was "shut in by sublime Yosemite cliffs, nobly sculptured, and adorned with waterfalls and fringes of trees, bushes, and patches of flowers, but amid so crowded a display of novel

© DON PITCHER

harbor seal on ice, Tracy Arm–Fords Terror Wilderness

beauty it was not easy to concentrate the attention long enough on any portion of it without giving more days and years than our lives can afford." Modern-day visitors come away equally impressed.

Two glaciers—Sawyer and South Sawyer—cap the end of Tracy Arm. Sawyer Glacier is retreating up-bay at 85 feet per year, while South Sawyer is losing over 300 feet per year. South Sawyer is larger and more interesting, but ice often blocks access. Other treats include get-wet visits to waterfalls and the chance to view seals lounging on the ice. Contact the Forest Service Information Center in Juneau (907/586-8751, www.fs.fed.us/r10/tongass) for details on Tracy Arm.

Boat Trips

Visitors to Tracy Arm have two all-day boat tour options. **Adventure Bound Alaska** (907/463-2509 or 800/228-3875; www.adventureboundalaska.com) is the original and best tour into Tracy Arm. Owner Steve

Weber has been doing this for many years and knows the best places to see mountain goats, seals, and whales. The boat typically spends at least an hour at the face of one of the glaciers, providing a great opportunity to witness the calving of icebergs. All-day cruises on the 56-foot boat are offered every summer day for $120 adults or $80 kids. Fresh sandwiches, drinks, and snacks are available onboard for a few bucks more, and kayak drop-offs are available. Highly recommended.

Goldbelt Tours (907/586-8687 or 800/820-2628, www.goldbelttours.com, $148 adults, $103 kids) offers a speedy 87-catamaran, and the higher price includes a light lunch. These run three days a week in the summer. No kayaker drop-offs, and the boat cannot approach the glaciers as closely as Adventure Bound trips. Goldbelt also makes occasional trips to Fords Terror and Dawes Glacier.

On Your Own

There are no trails in the Tracy Arm–Fords Terror

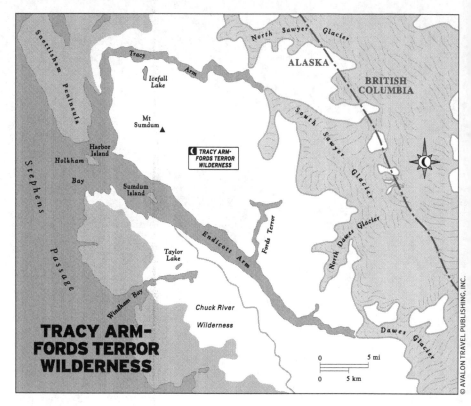

Wilderness, but experienced sea kayakers discover spectacular country to explore. Unfortunately, kayakers in Tracy Arm should be prepared for a constant parade of giant cruise ships, leaving large wakes and plenty of engine noise to contend with. (Sound travels a long way over the water. Wilderness rangers report being startled to suddenly hear loudspeakers announcing, "Margaritas will be served at 1630 in the aft lounge.") You can, however, escape the boats by hiking up the ravines into the high country, or by heading into the less-congested waters of Endicott Arm where the big cruise ships and powerboats rarely stray. Adventure Bound Alaska provides kayaker drop-offs.

If you plan to go into Tracy Arm in a kayak, check ahead with the Forest Service's Juneau Ranger District for the good campsites. As you

approach the glaciers at the upper end of Tracy, these become harder to find. Many boaters anchor in No Name Cove near the entrance to Tracy Arm. Kayakers will probably prefer to head to the middle part of the fjord and away from the motorboats. Ambitious folks (with a topo map) may want to try the steep half-mile cross-country climb up to **Icefall Lake** (1,469 ft. above sea level).

Massive **Dawes Glacier** jams the top of Endicott Arm with thousands of bergs of all sizes and shapes, making it tough to get close to the face of the glacier. **Fords Terror** is a turbulent but spectacular inlet that angles away from Endicott Arm. Tidal changes create wild water conditions near the entrance, so kayakers and boaters need to take special precautions. Only run the narrows at slack tides, when

© DON PITCHER

iceberg, Tracy Arm-Fords Terror Wilderness

the water is relatively calm. (The narrows are named for the terror felt by H.R. Ford, who rowed into the inlet one day in 1889 when the water was calm, but nearly died while fighting the currents, whirlpools, and icebergs on the way back out.) Fords Terror has no tidewater glaciers, but numerous hanging glaciers and craggy peaks are visible.

Chuck River Wilderness

Twelve miles south of Tracy Arm is **Windham Bay,** entrance to the Chuck River Wilderness. This small wild area receives very little use, but offers good fishing for salmon and a chance to explore the ruins of the Southeast's oldest mining community, Windham Bay. You can hike up the mile-long **Taylor Creek Trail** from Windham Bay to Taylor Lake.

Endicott River Wilderness

Although it encompasses 94,000 acres, this is one of the least-visited wilderness areas in America. Located some 60 miles northwest of Juneau, the wilderness borders on Glacier Bay National Park and includes the Endicott River watershed along the eastern slope of the Chilkat Range. The country is spruce and hemlock forests, mixed with alders. Trails are nonexistent, and access from Lynn Canal is virtually impossible. Visit the Forest Service's Juneau Ranger District office for more on this decidedly off-the-beaten-track area.

Admiralty Island

Just 20 miles west of Juneau lies the northern end of **Admiralty Island National Monument** (907/586-8800, www.fs.fed.us/r10/tongass) and the massive Kootznahoo Wilderness. At nearly a million acres, the wilderness covers 90 percent of Admiralty, making it the only large island in the Southeast that has not been extensively logged or developed. The Tlingit name for Admiralty is Kootznahoo (Bear Fortress). The island is aptly named: It has perhaps 1,500 brown bears, giving it one of the highest bear densities anywhere on earth. Eagles are extraordinarily abundant along the shoreline, and the cries of loons haunt Admiralty's lakes. This is truly one of the gemstones of Southeast Alaska.

ANGOON

Located along Admiralty's southwestern shore, the Tlingit village of Angoon (pop. 600) is the island's lone settlement. It sits astride a peninsula guarding the entrance to Kootznahoo Inlet, an incredible wonderland of small islands and saltwater passages. Locals have cable TVs and microwave ovens, but smokehouses sit in front of many homes and you'll hear older people speaking Tlingit. Angoon weather generally lives up to its reputation as Southeast Alaska's "Banana Belt"; yearly rainfall averages only 38 inches, compared to three times that in Sitka, only 40 miles away. By the way, the word *hootch* originated from the potent whiskey distilled by the "Hoosenoo" Indians of Admiralty in the 19th century. Today, Angoon is a dry town with a reputation as a place where traditional ways are encouraged.

History

The village of Angoon still commemorates an infamous incident that took place more than a century ago. While working for the Northwest Trading Company, a local shaman was killed in a seal-hunting accident. The villagers demanded 200 blankets as compensation and two days off to honor and bury the dead man. To ensure payment, they seized two hostages. Unaware of Tlingit traditions, the company manager fled to Sitka and persuaded a U.S. Navy boat to "punish them severely." On October 26, 1882, the town was shelled, destroying most of the houses. All the villagers' canoes were smashed and sunk, and all their winter supplies burned. Six children died from the smoke and the people nearly starved that winter. In a U.S. Congressional investigation two years later, the shelling was called "the greatest outrage ever committed in the United States upon any Indian tribe." Finally, in 1973, the government paid $90,000 in compensation for the shelling, but the Navy has never formally apologized.

Sights

Even if you don't stay overnight in Angoon, get off the ferry and walk across the road and down to the beach. From there you can look up to a small **cemetery** with old gravestones and fenced-in graves. Another interesting cemetery is near the end of the peninsula a half-mile behind the **Russian Orthodox church** in town. A number of rustic old houses line the shore, one with killer whales painted on the front. A hundred feet uphill from the post office are five memorial **totems** topped by representations of different local clans. Near Angoon Trading you get a great view of the narrow passage leading into **Kootznahoo Inlet,** where tides create dangerous rapids.

Accommodations and Food

Built in 1937, **Favorite Bay Inn B&B** (907/788-3123 or 800/423-3123, www.whalers covelodge.com, all year, $139 s, $209 d) is on the edge of town near the boat harbor. Five guest rooms share three baths; full breakfast included. The owners also run **Whaler's Cove Sportfishing Lodge** (open June–Sept.) with multi-day packages for anglers in search of salmon and halibut. Guests of Favorite Bay Inn can also eat other meals at Whaler's Cove, and canoe and skiff rentals may be available.

Angoon Trading (907/788-3111) sells a limited and rather expensive selection of groceries and supplies. Both Whaler's Cove Sportfishing Lodge and Favorite Bay Sportfishing Lodge serve meals during the summer, but you'll need to make reservations if you aren't a guest.

Getting There

The state ferry *LeConte* (800/642-0066, www.ferryalaska.com) visits Angoon six times a week, staying just long enough to unload and load vehicles. The dock (no ferry terminal) is 2.5 miles out of town, so you won't see Angoon up close unless you disembark, but "taxis" will run visitors into town.

Wings of Alaska (907/789-0790, www.wingsofalaska.com) and **Alaska Seaplane Service** (907/789-3331 or 800/478-3360, www.akseaplanes.com) have floatplane service between Angoon and Juneau.

PACK CREEK

Located a short flight from Juneau along the west side of Seymour Canal, Pack Creek is one of Alaska's premier brown bear–viewing areas. The creek fills with spawning humpback and chum salmon during July and August, and they attract the bears, which in turn attract the people. Most visitors arrive on day trips from Juneau on the local air taxis. Others come aboard kayaks and boats, or with commercially guided groups. Pack Creek is jointly managed and staffed by the U.S. Forest Service and the Alaska Department of Fish and Game. Special regulations apply to travel and camping in the area, and it's only open for visitation 9 A.M.–9 P.M.

Bear-Watching

The number of bears varies greatly through the summer, but most visitors see at least one bear, and often several. Plan to spend a full day—or longer—to increase your odds and to soak in the beauty of the area. Binoculars or a spotting scope are helpful, and photographers should be sure to bring plenty of film and long lenses. Rubber boots and raingear are highly recommended for anyone visiting Pack Creek. Food and drinks must be stowed in a special bear-resistant box, and neither is allowed in the viewing areas.

There are two primary bear-viewing areas along Pack Creek. The most accessible is a sandy spit of land right at the mouth of the creek and a short beach hike from where floatplanes land and boats tie up. A bit more challenging is a beautiful one-mile trail that leads through an old-growth rainforest to a viewing tower. The tower has room for eight people, and is an excellent place to watch bears as they pass directly below you.

Forest Service or Fish and Game rangers at Pack Creek will be happy to answer your questions, so it isn't necessary to come with a guide (unless you can't get in otherwise). They will not, however, accompany you to the observation tower.

Rules and Regulations

If you travel independently, you will need to obtain a permit and set up a charter with a local air taxi. Guided visitors are provided with transportation and permits, but the fee is much higher. Because of its popularity with both bears and people—and the potential for conflicts between the two—Pack Creek has stringent and rather confusing rules. Permits are required June 1–September 10, and only 24 people per day are allowed during the peak of the bear-viewing season (July 5–Aug. 25).

Reservations cost $50, and can be postmarked as early as February 20 for the following summer. Apply early to be sure of getting a permit for the peak season. Of the 24 permits, 4 are held for late arrivals, and are available three days in advance of your visit. These are in high demand, however, and are chosen by lottery from the applicants who show up. An unlimited number of shoulder-season permits (June 1–July 4 and August 26–September 10, $20) are available, but bear activity is lower. Get additional details from the Forest Service in Juneau (907/586-8800, www.fs.fed.us/r10/tongass).

Getting to Pack Creek

Most visitors to Pack Creek arrive by

floatplane on day trips from Juneau, landing next to the south sandspit. The following companies fly to Pack Creek: **Alaska Fly'N Fish Charters** (907/790-2120, www.alaskabyair.com), **Alaska Seaplane Service** (907/789-3331 or 800/478-3360, www.akseaplanes.com), **Ward Air** (907/789-9150, www.wardair.com), and **Wings of Alaska** (907/789-0790, www.wingsofalaska.com). The costs vary depending upon how many people are on the flight, but with three or more people in a group the price drops to around $155 per person round-trip (but you'll need to get your own permit).

Guided Trips

Several guide companies offer trips to Pack Creek, and are likely to have space available at the last minute. They're a good option if you can't get a permit—and if you have the cash. **Alaska Discovery** (510/594-6000 or 800/586-1911, www.akdiscovery.com) has $600 day trips to Pack Creek that include charter air service, an experienced guide, lunch, rubber boots, and raingear. They also have all-inclusive three-day kayak trips from Anchorage to Pack Creek for $1,090.

Alaska Fly'N Fish Charters (907/790-2120, www.alaskabyair.com) offers guided day trips to Pack Creek; $500 for a five-hour tour includes air transport from Juneau. Two companies have multi-day boat trips that include a day at Pack Creek: **All Aboard Yacht Charters** (360/898-7300 or 800/767-1024, www.alaskacharters.com) and **Dolphin Charters** (510/527-9622 or 800/472-9942, www.dolphincharters.com).

Camping

Camping is not allowed on Admiralty Island near the mouth of Pack Creek, but is permitted on Windfall Island, where you're far less likely to have encounters with the bears. The island is a quarter-mile from Pack Creek. Independent travelers can rent a sea kayak on Windfall from Alaska Discovery (advance reservation required) to reach Pack Creek or to explore the area.

Seymour Canal

The bear-viewing area along Pack Creek is only a tiny portion of Seymour Canal. This is a wonderful place to explore by sea kayak, with beautiful country, relatively protected waters, and the chance to see eagles, brown bears, and other wildlife. Many kayakers head south from Juneau, crossing the often-rough Stephens Passage and entering Oliver Inlet. **Auke Bay Landing Craft** (907/790-4591, www.aukebaylandingcraft.com) can deliver you to Oliver's Inlet, where an ingenious boat tramway makes it easy to bring kayaks across to upper Seymour Canal, a mile away. Alaska State Parks maintains the **Oliver Inlet Cabin** ($35) at the northern tip of Seymour Canal.

In Seymour you'll find many coves and islands to explore, and have a chance to observe bears that are protected from hunting. If you're adventurous, take a climb up the nearby peaks for fantastic views of the entire area. A three-sided shelter (free) is available in **Windfall Harbor**. Bears can be a real problem in Seymour Canal so be sure to select your camping spots very carefully (preferably on a small island) and hang all food.

Cross-Admiralty Canoe Route

Admiralty Island is ideally suited for people who enjoy canoeing or sea kayaking. Kootznahoo Inlet reaches back behind Angoon through a labyrinth of islands and narrow passages, before opening into expansive Mitchell Bay. From there you can continue to Salt Lake or Kanalku Bay, or begin the Cross-Admiralty Canoe Route—a chain of scenic lakes connected by portages, one of which is over three miles long. Using this 42-mile route you should reach Seymour Canal in four to six days (the record is 12 hours). Along the way are six Forest Service cabins ($35) and six Adirondack shelters (free), so you won't have to sleep out in the rain all the time. For more specific canoe-route information, contact the office of **Admiralty Island National Monument** (907/586-8790, www.fs.fed.us/r10/tongass) in Juneau.

Glacier Bay National Park and Preserve

America's national parks are this country's version of Mecca, places where hordes of pilgrims are drawn in search of a fulfillment that seems to come from experiencing these shrines of the natural world. Since Glacier Bay's discovery by John Muir in 1879, the spectacles of stark rocky walls, deep fjords, and giant rivers of ice calving massive icebergs into the sea have never ceased to inspire and humble visitors.

Established as a national park in 1925, Glacier Bay received major additions in the Alaska National Interest Lands Conservation Act of 1980. The park and preserve now cover more than 3.3 million acres and contain half a dozen glaciers that reach the ocean, making this one of the largest concentrations of tidewater glaciers on earth. These glaciers originate in the massive snowcapped Fairweather Range, sliding down the slopes and carving out giant troughs that become fjords when the glaciers retreat. **Mt. Fairweather,** rising 15,320 feet, is Southeast Alaska's tallest peak. On a clear day, it is prominently visible from park headquarters, 72 miles away. The vegetation of Glacier Bay varies from a 200-year-old spruce and hemlock forest at Bartlett Cove to freshly exposed moraine where tenacious plant life is just starting to take hold. Wildlife is abundant in the park: Humpback whales, harbor porpoises, harbor seals, and bird rookeries can be seen from the excursion boats and kayaks. Black bears are fairly common.

HISTORY

Glacier Bay has not always looked as it does today. When Captain George Vancouver sailed through Icy Strait in 1794, he found a wall of ice more than 4,000 feet thick and 20 miles wide. Less than 100 years later (1879) when Hoonah Indian guides led John Muir into the area, he discovered that the glaciers had retreated nearly 50 miles, creating a new land and a giant bay splitting into two deep fjords on its upper end. The bay was shrouded by low clouds, but Muir, anxious to see farther into the country, climbed a peak on its western shore:

> All the landscape was smothered in clouds and I began to fear that as far as wide views were concerned I had climbed in vain. But at length the clouds lifted a little, and beneath their gray fringes I saw the berg-filled expanse of the bay, and the feet of the mountains that stand about it, and the imposing fronts of five huge glaciers, the nearest being immediately beneath me. This was my first general view of Glacier Bay, a solitude of ice and snow and newborn rocks, dim, dreary, mysterious. I held the ground I had so dearly won for an hour or two, sheltering myself from the blast as best I could, while with benumbed fingers I sketched what I could see of the landscape, and wrote a few lines in my notebook. Then, breasting the snow again, crossing the shifting avalanche slopes and torrents, I reached camp about dark, wet and weary and glad.

Today's traveler is less likely to take such pains to see this grand place.

The rapid retreat of the glaciers over the last 200 years has caused the land to rebound, much like a sponge that has been squeezed and then re-forms. The process is astoundingly rapid by geological standards; around Bartlett Cove it is rising nearly two inches a year and even faster farther up the bay. Ask the park rangers to point out some of the changes in vegetation because of this rebound effect.

◖ VISITING GLACIER BAY

The vast majority of the over 350,000 visitors who come to Glacier Bay each year arrive aboard cruise ships, two of which are allowed in each day; they're given a talk by a Park Service naturalist as the ship heads up the west arm of the bay and never set foot on the land itself. Most other visitors stay

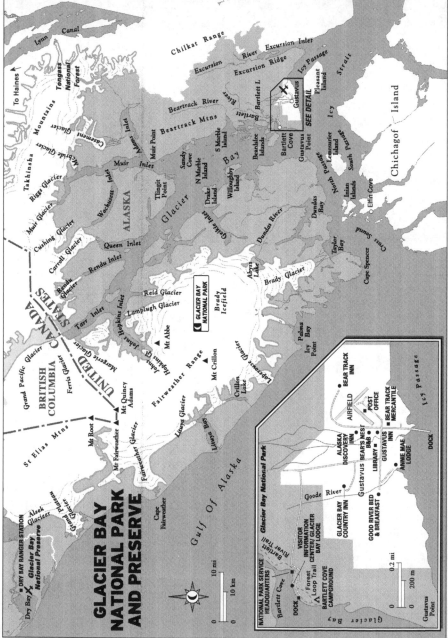

© DON PITCHER

Steller sea lions on South Marble Island

in Glacier Bay Lodge at Bartlett Cove or in nearby luxury lodges in the town of Gustavus, venturing out only to cruise past the glaciers on a tour boat. The tiny percentage who come to actually see and touch their national park—rather than view it in a naturalist's slide show—are often prevented from doing so by prohibitive costs. It is somewhat ironic that the park is most accessible to those who would rather look out on its glaciers from their stateroom windows.

The nearest tidewater glacier is 40 miles from park headquarters in Bartlett Cove. To see these glaciers, expect to spend at least $400 from Juneau for a fast two-day trip. A visit to Glacier Bay is a wonderful experience, but there are few options for the budget traveler, and you should probably make other plans if you're pinched for cash. (Consider a day trip from Juneau to Tracy Arm instead.)

The park concessionaire, **Glacier Bay Lodge & Tours/Aramark** (907/264-4600 or 888/229-8687, www.visitglacierbay.com) oper-

ates the ***Baranof Wind*** which heads up the west arm of Glacier Bay daily in the summer, departing at 7:30 A.M. and returning at 3:30 P.M. Tours on this high-speed catamaran cost $170 for adults or $85 for kids under 13. A light lunch is served, and a Park Service naturalist is on board to provide information on wildlife, geology, and cultural history along the route. The boat typically visits Margerie and Grand Pacific Glaciers before July, and heads up to Johns Hopkins Glacier later in the summer. Another *Baranof Wind* option is to pay $300 per person for a day-long trip that includes a flight from Juneau to Gustavus followed by a trip up the bay and another flight back to Juneau that evening.

Park Information

The Park Service maintains a visitor center upstairs in the Glacier Bay Lodge at Bartlett Cove, open daily 12:30–9 P.M. in the summer. A small museum here contains natural history and geology exhibits. Naturalists lead interpretive walks every day, and also put on evening talks and slide shows in the auditorium. The park's **backcountry office** is near the boat dock, a short hike from the lodge, and is open daily 8 A.M.–7 P.M. during the summer. Stop here before heading into the park on an overnight trip. For additional details, contact Glacier Bay National Park (907/697-2230, www.nps.gov/glba).

HIKING

There are several enjoyable walks in the Bartlett Cove area. The mile-long **Forest Loop Trail** connects the lodge, boat dock, and campground, providing an excellent introduction to the area. **Bartlett River Trail** (4 miles round-trip) leads from park headquarters to the mouth of the river, with opportunities to observe wildlife. Salmon can be seen moving up the river in August. For a satisfying beach walk, head south along the shore from the campground. If you're ambitious, it is possible to walk to **Point Gustavus** (six miles) or on to **Goode River** (13 miles). Follow the river upstream a mile to Gustavus, where you can walk or hitch back along the road. Beach walking is easiest at low tide; the backcountry office has tide charts. Note that none of these trails goes anywhere near the tidewater glaciers for which the park is famous, and there are no developed trails anywhere in the park's backcountry.

SEA KAYAKING
Guided Trips

Alaska Discovery (510/594-6000 or 800/586-1911, www.akdiscovery.com) has all-day ($130) and half-day ($90) guided kayak trips from the Bartlett Cove dock in the summer. These are a good way to learn the basics of sea kayaking, and include kayak and gear, guide, food, and boots. Alaska Discovery also offers several excellent but pricey longer trips into Glacier Bay National Park. Kayak trips up the bay cost $2,200 for a five-day trip, plus airfare from Juneau. The company also has nine-day trips to beautiful Icy Bay for $2,100. These trips are based out of Yakutat.

Spirit Walker Expeditions (907/697-2266 or 800/478-9255, www.seakayakalaska.com) runs excellent sea kayak tours, including overnight trips to nearby Pleasant Island. All sorts of longer voyages are available, all the way up to eight-day trips to remote islands off Chichagof Island. It does not tour within Glacier Bay National Park itself.

On Your Own

An increasingly popular way to visit Glacier Bay is by sea kayak. Some folks bring their own folding kayaks on the plane, but most people rent them from the friendly proprietors of **Glacier Bay Sea Kayaks** (907/697-2257, www.glacierbayseakayaks.com) in Bartlett Cove. Kayak rentals include a two-person boat, paddles, life vests, spray skirts, flotation bags, and a brief lesson. Reservations are a must during mid-summer. They also rent raingear and rubber boots, and will help set up your trip, including making the all-important boat reservations. In addition, you can rent kayaks in Gustavus from **Sea Otter Kayak** (907/697-3007, www.he.net/~seaotter).

Several focal points attract kayakers within Glacier Bay. The **Beardslee Islands,** in relatively protected waters near Bartlett Cove, make an excellent two- or three-day kayak trip and do not require any additional expenses. Beyond the Beardslees, Glacier Bay becomes much less protected and you should plan on spending at least a week up-bay if you paddle there. (It is 50 miles or more to the glaciers.) Rather than attempting to cross this open water, most kayakers opt for a drop-off. The locations change periodically, so ask at the backcountry office in Bartlett Cove for specifics.

Muir Inlet (the east arm of Glacier Bay) is preferred by many kayakers because it is a bit more protected and is not used by the cruise ships or most tour boats. The **West Arm** is more spectacular—especially iceberg-filled Johns Hopkins Inlet—but you'll have to put up with a constant stream of large and small cruise ships. If the boat operators have their way, even more ships can be expected in future years.

The *Baranof Wind* does camper and sea kayaker drop-offs in Glacier Bay ($190 round

© DON PITCHER

kayakers in Glacier Bay National Park

trip). For details, contact Glacier Bay Lodge & Tours (907/264-4600 or 888/229-8687, www.visitglacierbay.com).

Talk with Park Service personnel in Bartlett Cove before heading out on any hiking or kayaking trip. You'll need to be in Gustavus airport by 3 P.M. the day before to go through all the hoops (getting to Bartlett Cove, renting the kayak, going through the Park Service camping and bear safety session, and getting your kayak onboard the *Baranof Wind*). This means you cannot take the evening Alaska flight; it arrives too late in the day.

CAMPING

An excellent free campground at Bartlett Cove comes complete with bear-proof food storage caches, outhouses, and a three-sided shelter with a woodstove (great for drying your gear after a kayak trip up the bay). The campground is only a half-mile from Glacier Bay Lodge and usually has space. Running water is available next to the backcountry office. All cooking must be done below the high-tide line (where the odors are washed away every six hours) to reduce the chance of bear problems. You can store things for free in the shed next to the backcountry office.

Backcountry Camping

No trails exist anywhere in Glacier Bay's backcountry, but Park Service rangers can provide details on hiking and camping up the bay. Camping is allowed in most park areas. Exceptions are the Marble Islands—closed because of their importance for nesting seabirds—and a few other areas closed because of the potential for bear incidents. A gas stove is a necessity for camping, since wood is often unavailable.

Free permits (available at the backcountry office) are recommended before you head out. Park naturalists provide camper orientations each evening, including information on how and where to go, bear safety, and minimum-impact camping procedures. Bears have killed two people within the park in the past decade or so, and to lessen the chance of this happening, free bear-proof containers are loaned to all kayakers and hikers. A small storage shed beside the backcountry office is a good place to store unneeded gear while you're up the bay. Firearms are not allowed in Glacier Bay.

TATSHENSHINI AND ALSEK RIVERS

Along the western edge of Glacier Bay National Park flows the Tatshenshini River, considered one of the world's premier wilderness-rafting routes. Bears, moose, mountain goats, and Dall sheep are all visible along the way. The river rolls through Class III white water and spectacular canyons along its way to the juncture with the Alsek River. **Alaska Discovery/ Mountain Travel** (510/594-6000 or 800/586-1911, www.akdiscovery.com) has several trips each summer down this spectacular route, as well as down the more remote Alsek. A 12-day river-rafting trip isn't cheap at $3,700, but the price includes a van ride from Haines to the put-in point at Dalton Post in the Yukon, and a spectacular helicopter portage around the Class VI rapids of Turnback Canyon. One of the real treats of this trip is paddling past the seven-mile-wide Alsek Glacier. The trip begins in Haines and ends in Yakutat.

Other good companies offering Alsek and Tatshenshini trips include **Chilkat Guides** (907/766-2491 or 888/292-7789, www.raftalaska.com) and **Canadian River Expeditions** (867/668-3180 or 800/297-6927, www.canriver.com). Contact the park (907/697-2230, www.nps.gov/glba) for details on running the rivers.

GUSTAVUS AND VICINITY

There are two basic centers for visitors to Glacier Bay. **Bartlett Cove,** inside the park, has Park Service Headquarters, a campground, Glacier Bay Lodge (with bar, restaurant, and park service visitor center), and boat dock. Ten miles away (a $10 shuttle bus ride) and outside the park boundaries is the community of **Gustavus** (pop. 370). Here you will find the airport, main boat dock, a general store, B&Bs, and luxury lodges.

The town of Gustavus consists of equal parts park employees, fishermen, and folks dependent upon the tourism trade. It's one of the only places in Southeast Alaska that has enough flat country to raise cows, and the only Southeast town of any size without service from the state ferry system. Be sure to check out the historic—and still working—gas pumps decorated with the old Mobil flying horse at **Gustavus Dray** (907/697-2481), which also sells antiques and gifts. **Smokehouse Gallery** (907/697-2336) is a seasonal cooperative gallery along the river, with paintings, woodwork, drawings, watercolors, and pottery by local artisans. Gustavus is also home to the nine-hole **Mt. Fairweather Golf Course** (907/697-3080, www.gustavus.com/gdf.html).

The **Gustavus Visitors Association** (907/697-2454, www.gustavusak.com) has information and links to local lodging and other businesses; also try www.gustavus.com for info. Based in Gustavus, **Glacier Bay Travel Cruises and Tours** (907/697-2475, www.glacierbaytravel.com) can help you find local lodging and book trips into the park.

Fishing and Whale-Watching

Fishing, primarily for halibut and salmon, is a big attraction for many visitors, and most of the lodges offer package deals for anglers. Get a list of charter boat operators from the Park Service or at www.gustavusalaska.org. Most of these companies also run whale-watching trips, and some can carry sea kayaks onboard.

Flightseeing

Air Excursions (907/697-2375 or 800/354-2479, www.airexcursions.com) and **L.A.B. Flying Service** 907/789-9160, www.lab flying.com) both provide flightseeing trips over the park. Flightseeing over Glacier Bay are also available from Juneau, Haines, and Skagway, but prices are generally higher since you'll need to fly farther.

Accommodations

Located within Glacier Bay National Park is **Glacier Bay Lodge** (907/264-4600 or 888/229-8687, www.visitglacierbay.com, open late May–early Sept., $187–207 d). The shoreside lodge is surrounded by tall trees at Bartlett Cove (park headquarters), and has a restaurant, informal deck dining, a pleasant bar, plus a big stone fireplace that makes a cozy place to sit on a rainy evening—even if you're not a guest. Guests stay in plain-vanilla units with double or twin beds. Laundry facilities, coin-operated showers, and gear storage are available. The lodge rents a few mountain bikes and fishing poles. Many guests opt for a package that includes a night's lodging, an all-day tour of Glacier Bay, three meals, and transportation to and from Gustavus for $400 per person.

Glacier Bay Lodge provides the only in-park accommodations, but far nicer options are available in nearby Gustavus. Most of these provide free transport to and from the Gustavus airport or boat dock, along with clunker bikes to ride on the roads. All of these will also help set up tours, fishing, sea kayaking, and other activities within the park.

Honeymooners or others looking to splurge will love a visit to **(Gustavus Inn** (907/697-2254 or 800/649-5220, www.gustavusinn.com, open mid-May–mid-Sept.), the most famous local lodging place. Built in 1928 as the centerpiece for a homestead, the farmhouse was transformed into Gustavus Inn in 1965. Owners David and Jo Ann Lesh have created a delightful country place with a picturesque garden that provides fresh vegetables all summer. Gourmet meals are served family style. Lodging and meals cost $370 d per day, with private baths and Wi-Fi (a rarity in Gustavus).

Modern **Bear Track Inn** (907/697-3017 or 888/697-2284, www.beartrackinn.com, open mid-May–mid-Sept.) occupies a 57-acre spread six miles from Gustavus. This luxuriously furnished 15,000-square-foot log inn has a central lobby with fireplace, large windows fronting on Icy Strait, a big deck and grassy front lawn, plus 14 spacious guest rooms. A number of packages are available for stays of one ($990 d) to seven nights ($4,420 d), including transportation from Juneau, lodging, and sumptuous meals; activities are extra.

Glacier Bay Country Inn (907/697-2288 or 800/628-0912, www.glacierbayalaska.com,

open mid-May–mid-Sept.) combines a rambling log structure with modern amenities. Guests stay in five well-appointed cabins ($430 d) or the main lodge ($370 d) and are treated to three gourmet meals a day. Same owners for **Whalesong Lodge** (www.whalesonglodge.com, $75 s, $100 d) with five small and simple rooms, all with private bath. It's in "downtown" Gustavus. No phones, TVs, or meals, but you can eat dinners at the inn for $35.

Annie Mae Lodge (907/697-2346 or 800/478-2346, www.anniemae.com) is a quiet two-story lodge in a meadow-and-forest setting along the Goode River. The 11 guest rooms cost $80 s or $90 d with shared bath, and $90–100 s or $120–140 d with private bath, including three big meals and round-trip transportation from Juneau.

Bear's Nest B&B (907/697-2440, www.gustavus.com/bearsnest, $120–150 d) has a distinctive round cedar cabin, a cozy room over the café, and a simple A-frame cabin, all with private baths and full breakfasts. Package deals with three meals a day are also offered.

Good River Bed & Breakfast (907/697-2241, www.glacier-bay.us, open June–late Aug., $95–105 d) has four guest rooms (shared baths) in an attractive three-story log home, plus a private but rustic log cabin with outhouse. A full breakfast and free bikes are included.

Alaska Discovery Inn (907/780-6505 or 800/586-1911, www.akdiscovery.com, open June–Aug.) has five rooms for $125 d with a private bath. A full breakfast is served. They're often filled up by Alaska Discovery clients.

Food and Groceries

Bear's Nest Café (907/697-2440, www.gustavus.com/bearsnest) serves lunch and dinner in the summer, specializing in locally caught salmon, halibut, and crab, along with salads and daily specials. Save room for a slice of their rhubarb-strawberry pie. Saturday night brings a fun open-mic jam session with talented local musicians. The café is open daily in the summer.

Located six miles from town, **Bear Track Inn** (907/697-3017 or 888/697-2284, www.beartrackinn.com) has one of the finest local chefs; delicious four-course dinners are $40. Another outstanding dinner option is **Gustavus Inn** (907/697-2255 or 800/649-5220, www.gustavusinn.com, $35), where a few spots are held for those who aren't overnighting. Reservations required.

Glacier Bay Lodge (907/697-4000, $19–29 dinner entrées) in Bartlett Cove serves so-so meals; try the Dungeness crab or the sweet potato fries. A lighter bar menu is also available, and the outside deck is open for casual dining.

Open daily in the summer, the small grocery store at Gustavus, **Beartrack Mercantile** (907/697-2358), has a deli and sells essentials for a price, but it's cheaper to bring all your own food from Juneau. **Pep's Packing** (907/697-2295) sells locally caught salmon if you have access to a BBQ. Nobody in Gustavus sells alcohol, but Glacier Bay Lodge has a full bar, and Bear's Nest serves beer and wine.

Getting There

There is no ferry service to either Glacier Bay or Gustavus, and residents receive most of their supplies by barge every two weeks.

Many visitors fly by jet from Juneau to Gustavus on **Alaska Airlines** (800/426-0333, www.alaskaair.com); but book ahead to be sure of getting on these popular afternoon flights. The trip takes only 15 minutes in the air, so the flight attendants don't even have time to throw bags of pretzels at you.

More rewarding are flights by **Skagway Air** (907/789-2006, www.skagwayair.com), **Wings of Alaska** (907/789-0790, www.wingsofalaska.com), and **L.A.B. Flying Service** (907/789-9160, www.labflying.com). They offer more personal service and the small planes fly lower, providing excellent on-the-way sightseeing for around $165 round-trip. **Air Excursions** (907/697-2375 or 800/354-2479, www.airexcursions.com) doesn't have scheduled service, but usually fly to Juneau several times a day. L.A.B. also connects Gustavus with Skagway and Haines.

Note that it's illegal to transport white gas and other potentially explosive fuels in any commercial aircraft, so be sure your gas stove and fuel bottles are empty before you reach the airport. You can buy white gas in Bartlett Cove next to the visitor center or in Gustavus at Beartrack Mercantile. Also, you can't carry "bear mace" on the jets, though the floatplanes will sometimes carry it in their floats.

Getting Around

The airport in Gustavus is 10 miles from Bartlett Cove/Park Headquarters. A **shuttle bus** meets all Alaska Airlines flights, transporting you to Bartlett Cove for $10 each direction (free if you have a room reservation for Glacier Bay Lodge). Hitching eliminates this, but traffic can be downright scarce in tiny Gustavus. **TLC Taxi** (907/697-2239), provides passenger and kayak transport in the Gustavus area, and meets Alaska Airlines jets, air taxis.

Bud's Rent-A-Car (907/697-2403) has a dozen beater rental cars for $60 per day, and you don't even need to fill up the tank at the end. Of course, it's also pretty hard to put many miles on around here! Check out his nonexistent license plates; in their place it simply says "Bud's Rent-A-Car" in big red letters. Apparently the state doesn't require license plates in Gustavus because it's so difficult to get in or out of here. Most local lodging places have loaner bikes, and Glacier Bay Lodge in Bartlett Cove rents bikes.

Yakutat

The friendly town of Yakutat (pop. 800) is in a protected harbor on Yakutat Bay—halfway between Juneau and Cordova along the Gulf of Alaska. The name of this out-of-the-way settlement was derived from the Eyak name *Yak-tat* (lagoon behind the breakers). Behind Yakutat soars the pyramidal 18,008-foot summit of **Mt. St. Elias,** second-tallest in the United States. Across the bay is **Malaspina Glacier,** the largest piedmont glacier on the continent (it's bigger than Rhode Island). Both of these lie within mighty Wrangell–St. Elias National Park.

Yakutat is a famous fishing destination, particularly for steelhead on the Situk River, but also for king, silver, and sockeye salmon, plus halibut. But it isn't just fish that attracts visitors; in recent years Yakutat has drawn cold-water surfers who come to ride the big ones on the 70 miles of sandy beaches that stretch southeast from town. These beaches are also great places for bird-watching, beachcombing, or simply relaxing. Head out to **Ocean Cape** (just west of town) on a clear day for spectacular views of Mt. St. Elias and the Gulf of Alaska.

The weather in Yakutat can be summed up on one word: wet. Summers are rainy and winters are snowy. The town gets over 130 inches of precipitation annually, so visitors can plan on seeing their share of that. All this precipitation feeds the enormous glaciers and productive salmon and trout streams for which the area is famous.

HISTORY

The area around Yakutut served for centuries as a winter village for the Eyaks, a people with links to both the Tlingits to the east and Athabascans to the north. In 1805, the Russian-American Company built a fort at Yakutat, using it as a base for the harvesting of sea otters. The post was later destroyed by the Eyaks. Gold seekers came to the area in the 1860s, mining the black-sand beaches, followed by missionaries, loggers, and fishermen. During World War II, Yakutat was home to an aviation base, and the long paved runway that was developed now serves as the local airport. Quite a few military bunkers and other signs of the war are still visible. Today, commercial and sport-fishing provide most of the local jobs. More than half of the people who live in Yakutat are Native Alaskans.

SIGHTS
Surfing Safari

Yakutat is Alaska's surfing capital, with mile after mile of sandy beaches, virtually no competition for waves, and great swells rolling off the Gulf of Alaska. On a warm summer day you might see as many as 15 surfers—typically a mix of locals and wandering California beach bums—riding the waves at **Cannon Beach** (named for a World War II cannon here) and other spots. Because of all the rainfall, the ocean around Yakutut is less saline than in California or Hawaii, so the boards need to be thicker and more buoyant to keep surfers from sinking. Owned by local surfer Jack Endicott, **Icy Waves Surf Shop** (907/784-3253, www.icywaves.com) sells surfboards (the big ones), wetsuits, booties, hoods, and other gear, along with very popular T-shirts. No rentals, but you may be able to lease gear.

Russell Fiord Wilderness

This beautiful 348,701-acre wilderness is 15 miles northeast of Yakutat. It centers around Russell and Nanatak Fiords, where hanging glaciers fill the rugged mountains and valley glaciers pour icebergs into the water. The area made headlines in 1986 when the advancing **Hubbard Glacier** (the largest tidewater glacier in North America) temporarily dammed Russell Fiord, trapping sea mammals and threatening to change river courses as the water level rose 75 feet behind the ice dam. The ice gave way six months later, freeing the animals and reconnecting the fjord to the

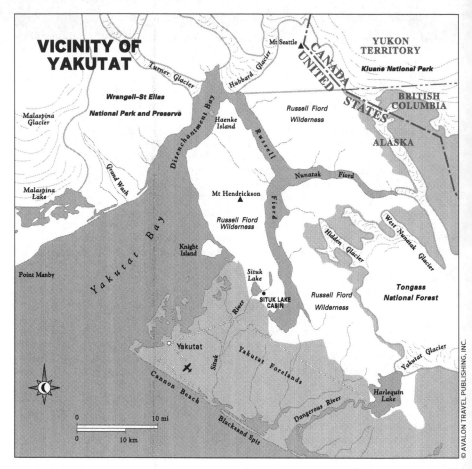

VICINITY OF YAKUTAT

Mt Seattle

YUKON TERRITORY

Kluane National Park

CANADA
UNITED STATES

Turner Glacier

Hubbard Glacier

Wrangell–St Elias

National Park and Preserve

Russell Fiord
Wilderness

BRITISH
COLUMBIA

Malaspina
Glacier

Disenchantment Bay

Haenke
Island

ALASKA

Grand Wash

Russell

Malaspina
Lake

Mt Hendrickson

Nunatak Fiord

Fiord

West Nunatak Glacier

Russell Fiord
Wilderness

Hidden Glacier

Yakutat Bay

Knight
Island

Point Manby

Situk
Lake

SITUK LAKE
CABIN

Russell Fiord
Wilderness

Tongass
National Forest

River

Yakutat

Situk

Yakutat Forelands

Yakutat Glacier

Cannon Beach

Dangerous River

Harlequin
Lake

Blacksand Spit

0   10 mi

0   10 km

© AVALON TRAVEL PUBLISHING, INC.

ocean. Because of all the icebergs from this glacier, access into Russell Fiord is difficult by boat, though floatplanes or wheeled planes fly into the area from Yakutat. The Hubbard Glacier is still an amazing sight, 6 miles wide by 70 miles long, and rising 400 feet out of the water at its snout. It is a prime stopping point for cruise ships heading between Southeast Alaska and Seward. Visit the U.S. Geological Survey website (http://ak.water.usgs.gov) for more on the Hubbard.

On the southeastern edge of the wilderness is the five-mile-long **Harlequin Lake,** dotted with ice from the enormous Yakutat Glacier. A 26-mile gravel road leads from Yakutat to just across the "bridge to nowhere" over the Dangerous River (which drains from the lake). A 0.75-mile trail leads to Harlequin Lake from here, and charter boats are available for trips to the face of the glacier.

The Forest Service's **Situk Lake Cabin** ($35) is inside the wilderness, and accessible by trail (often flooded) or floatplane. Eleven other cabins are scattered along the **Yakutat Forelands,** the relatively flat and forested area that stretches for 50 miles east of town. Especially popular with anglers are three cabins along the Situk River ($35).

ACCOMMODATIONS AND CAMPING

Leonard's Landing Lodge (907/784-3245 or 877/925-3474, www.leonardslanding.com, $165–175 s, $270–290 d) is a large fishing lodge with a seasonal restaurant. Package rates with meals and a fishing guide are available, along with boat rentals. **Yakutat Lodge** (907/784-3232 or 800/925-8828, www.yakutat-lodge.com) has a variety of all-inclusive fishing packages.

Mooring Lodge (907/784-3300 or 888/551-2836, www.mooringlodge.com, open all year) rents out six two-bedroom apartment units that can sleep six, with full kitchens, a sauna, and views across Monti Bay to the St. Elias Mountains. Rates are $350 for up to four people.

Red Roof B&B (907/784-3297, www.yakutatlodging.com, $85 s or $170 d) has three comfortable guest rooms with a full breakfast and private baths. **Blue Heron Inn B&B** (907/784-3287, www.johnlatham.com, $180 d) provides a hunting and fishing decor and two guest rooms, both with private entrances and baths. The home overlooks the bay, and rooms come with a full breakfast.

Camping

A couple of simple campsites are along Cannon Beach. In addition, much of the land surrounding Yakutat is within Tongass National Forest, and is open to camping. Above the tide line on Cannon Beach is a fun (but exposed) place to pitch a tent.

FOOD

Several places serve meals in Yakutat, but **Leonard's Landing Lodge** is your best bet, with good food three meals a day and a waterfront setting.

Get groceries and supplies from **Mallott's General Store** (907/784-3355). **Raven's Table Smokery** (907/784-3497 or 888/784-3497) sells freshly smoked fish. Yakutat's **Glass Door Bar** (907/784-3331) has a pool table and big-screen television for sports.

INFORMATION AND SERVICES

The **Yakutat Chamber of Commerce** (907/784-3933, www.yakutatalaska.com) will send you a brochure on the area, or call the **City of Yakutat** (907/784-3323, www.yakutatak.govoffice2.com) for additional information. The best local Internet site is www.yakutat.net, with links to local businesses. Alaska Pacific Bank has an ATM. A number of local folks run fishing charters; contact any of the lodging places for recommendations.

Wrangell-St. Elias National Park and Preserve has a district office (907/784-3295, www.nps.gov/wrst) in Yakutat, where you can get information on Malaspina Glacier and other incredible sights northeast of Yakutat. The office also exhibits Native artifacts, and the staff leads interpretive programs in the summer.

Stop by Tongass National Forest's **Yakutat Ranger District** (907/784-3359, www.fs.fed.us/r10/tongass) for details on the Russell Fiord Wilderness, public-use cabins, and other recreation opportunities. Looking for wildlife? Head out to the dump, where the brown bears often forage.

Fairweather Days each August at Cannon Beach is a good time to camp out and party with the surfers. There's live music, food, and local crafts.

GETTING THERE

Yakutat is the smallest community in the world served by year-round commercial jet service. **Alaska Airlines** (800/426-0333, www.alaskaair.com) connects Yakutat with the outside world, with two flights daily: one northbound flight to Cordova and Anchorage, and the other southbound to Juneau. **Yakutat Coastal Airlines** (907/784-3831, www.flyyca.com) provides air charters. **Leo's Vehicles** (907/784-3909) has pickups and Suburbans for $75/day.

The **Alaska Marine Highway** (907/465-3941 or 800/642-0066, www.ferryalaska.com) ferry *Kennicott* stops in Yakutat on its twice-a-month summertime sailings between Juneau and Whittier.

Haines

The pleasant and friendly town of Haines (pop. 1,400) provides a transition point between the lush greenery of the Southeast and the more rugged beauty of the Yukon and Alaska's Interior. As the ferry sails north to Haines on the Lynn Canal—at 1,600 feet deep it's the longest and deepest fjord in North America—the Inside Passage gets narrower, and you sense that this unique waterway, and your passage on it, are coming to an end. To the east, waterfalls tumble off the mountainsides, while to the west, glaciers lumber down from the icefields of the Chilkat Range. The long river of ice you see 40 minutes before Haines is **Davidson Glacier. Rainbow Glacier,** also on the left, hangs from a cliff just beyond. Both originate from the same icefield that forms part of Glacier Bay National Park.

Haines lies 90 miles north of Juneau, straddling a narrow peninsula between Chilkoot and Chilkat Inlets. Its mountain-ringed setting seems to define the word *spectacular:* From the ferry you catch a glimpse of the white Victorian buildings of Fort Seward in front of the 6,500-foot Cathedral Peaks. Haines has a wealth of outdoor experiences, almost as many for those without cash as for those with. Plenty of hiking trails run up surrounding peaks, camping is right next to town, and travelers will discover a pleasant mixture of working stiffs, fishermen, and artisans. It could serve as the poster child for what most folks expect in an Alaskan town: cozy, homespun, and earthy—the kind of place where the local radio station broadcasts birthday wishes, road updates for drivers heading over the pass, and bush messages for folks without a phone.

Unlike nearby Skagway where a tidal wave of tourists inundates the town daily, Haines only sees a few large cruise ships. Most Haines visitors arrive by ferry and head on up the highway (or vice versa), but Haines is also becoming a popular weekend getaway for Canadians from Whitehorse. With "only" 60 inches of precipitation a year, the weather here is decidedly drier than points farther south.

HISTORY

Long before the arrival of whites to the Haines area, the Tlingit people of the Chilkoot and Chilkat tribes established villages nearby. Fish were plentiful, as were game animals and berries. The area's "mother village" was Klukwan, 20 miles up the Chilkat River, but another large Chilkoot village nestled near Chilkoot Lake, and a summer camp squatted just northwest of present-day Haines. The Chilkat people were renowned for their beautiful blankets woven from mountain-goat wool and dyed with an inventive mixture of copper nuggets, urine, lichen, and spruce roots. The blankets were (and are) worn during dance ceremonies. Today they are also exceedingly valuable.

In 1879, the naturalist John Muir and the Presbyterian minister Samuel Hall Young reached the end of Lynn Canal. The Reverend Dr. Young was looking for potential mission sites to convert the Natives to Christianity. Muir was along for the canoe ride, wanting a

Portage Cove and the Coast Mountains

© DON PITCHER

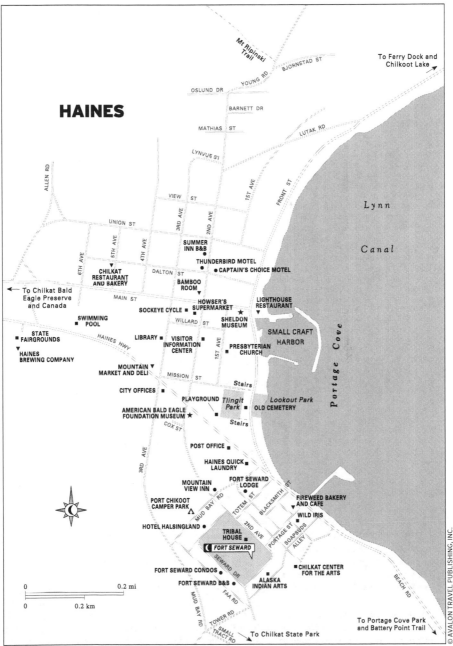

HAINES

To Ferry Dock and Chilkoot Lake

Mt Ripinski Trail

BJORNSTAD ST

YOUNG RD

OSLUND DR

BARNETT DR

MATHIAS ST

LUTAK RD

LYNVUE CT

ALLEN RD

1ST AVE

FRONT ST

VIEW ST

3RD AVE

2ND AVE

UNION ST

Lynn

Canal

5TH AVE

4TH AVE

6TH AVE

SUMMER INN B&B

THUNDERBIRD MOTEL

● CAPTAIN'S CHOICE MOTEL

CHILKAT RESTAURANT AND BAKERY

DALTON ST

BAMBOO ROOM

← To Chilkat Bald Eagle Preserve and Canada

MAIN ST

HOWSER'S SUPERMARKET ★

SOCKEYE CYCLE ■

LIGHTHOUSE RESTAURANT ▽

SWIMMING POOL ■

WILLARD ST

SHELDON MUSEUM

SMALL CRAFT HARBOR

Portage Cove

STATE FAIRGROUNDS ■

HAINES BREWING COMPANY ▽

HAINES HWY

LIBRARY ■

VISITOR INFORMATION CENTER ■

1ST AVE

PRESBYTERIAN CHURCH

MOUNTAIN MARKET AND DELI ▽

MISSION ST

CITY OFFICES ■

Stairs

PLAYGROUND ■ *Tlingit Park*

Lookout Park

AMERICAN BALD EAGLE FOUNDATION MUSEUM ★

OLD CEMETERY ■

Stairs

COX ST

3RD AVE

POST OFFICE ■

HAINES QUICK LAUNDRY ■

MOUNTAIN VIEW INN ●

FORT SEWARD LODGE ●

FORT SEWARD

MUD BAY RD

PORT CHIKOOT CAMPER PARK △

TOTEM ST

BLACKSMITH ST

FIREWEED BAKERY AND CAFE ■

WILD IRIS ■

HOTEL HALSINGLAND ●

TRIBAL HOUSE ■

2ND AVE

PORTAGE ST

SOAPSUDS ALLEY

◀ FORT SEWARD

SEWARD DR

CHILKAT CENTER FOR THE ARTS ■

FORT SEWARD CONDOS ●

FORT SEWARD B&B ●

ALASKA INDIAN ARTS ■

BEACH RD

0   0.2 mi

0   0.2 km

MUD BAY RD

FAA RD

TOWER RD

SMALL TRACT RD

To Chilkat State Park

To Portage Cove Park and Battery Point Trail

© AVALON TRAVEL PUBLISHING, INC.

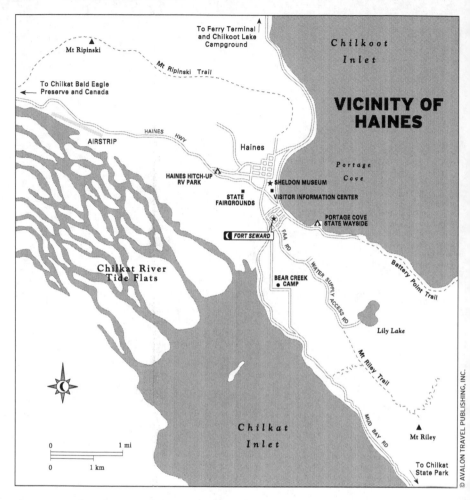

chance to explore this remote territory. While there, they met with members of the Chilkat tribe at a settlement called Yendestakyeh. Both men gave speeches before the people, but the Chilkats were considerably more interested in Muir's "brotherhood of man" message than Dr. Young's proselytizing. Muir wrote: "Later, when the sending of a missionary and teacher was being considered, the chief said they wanted me, and, as an inducement, promised that if I would come to them they would always do as I directed, follow my councils, give me as many

wives as I liked, build a church and school, and pick all the stones out of the paths and make them smooth for my feet." Two years later the mission was established by two Presbyterian missionaries (Muir had other plans) and the village was renamed Haines, in honor of Mrs. F. E. H. Haines of the Presbyterian Home Missions Board. She never visited her namesake.

During the Klondike gold rush, an adventurer and shrewd businessman named Jack Dalton developed a 305-mile toll road that began across the river from Haines and followed an old Indian trade route into the Yukon. He charged miners $150 each to use his Dalton Trail; armed men never failed to collect. To maintain order among the thousands of miners, the U.S. Army established Fort William H. Seward at Haines. Named for Alaska's "patron saint," it was built between 1900 and 1904 on 100 acres of land deeded to the government by the Haines mission. Renamed Chilkoot Barracks in 1923 (in commemoration of Chilkoot Pass), it was the only military base in all of Alaska until 1940.

In 1942–1943 the Army built the 150-mile Haines Highway from Haines to Haines Junction as an emergency evacuation route from Alaska in case of invasion by the Japanese. After World War II, the post was declared excess government property and sold to a veterans' group that hoped to form a business cooperative. The venture failed, but many stayed on, making homes in the stately old officers' quarters. The site became a National Historic Landmark in 1978 and its name was changed back to Fort Seward.

Today the town of Haines has a diversified economy that includes fishing (no canneries, however), tourism, and government jobs. Haines has also recently become something of a center for the arts, attracting artists and crafts workers of all types, from creators of stained glass to weavers of Chilkat blankets.

SIGHTS

Lookout Park (next to the harbor) is a great place to watch the fishing boats, eagles, and scenery. Bring a lunch. Behind it is a small cemetery with Tlingit graves dating from the 1880s. An old building, all that remains of **Yendestakyeh,** is just beyond the airport, 3.5 miles from town. The mission bell (1880) that once called the Tlingit people to worship now sits out front of the Presbyterian church on 2nd Avenue.

Tsirku Canning Company (5th and Main Sts., 907/766-3474, www.cannerytour.com, open mid-May–mid-Sept.) has re-created an old salmon-canning line with reconditioned antique equipment. The 45-minute tours, with a video, are $10, free for kids under 12. No fish guts here; for that you'll need to get a job at a salmon cannery to see how it's done today.

Walt Disney's *White Fang* was filmed next to Haines in 1990, and the **Dalton City** gold rush town created for the movie is at the Southeast Alaska State Fairgrounds. Wander around the buildings or poke your head inside Alaska's smallest brewery, **Haines Brewing Company** (907/766-3823), for a sample of Paul Wheeler's Lookout Stout, Eldred Rock Red, IPA, and seasonal beers. Haines bars have them on draught. Locals especially rave about the stout—at least until they taste the Bigger Hammer Barley Wine.

Museums

Located on Main Street in the center of town, the **Sheldon Museum** (907/766-2366, www.sheldonmuseum.org, $3 adults, under 13 free) houses a fine collection of items from the gold rush, such as Jack Dalton's sawed-off shotgun, and Tlingit artifacts—including Chilkat blankets, a gorgeous carved ceremonial hat from the Murrelet clan, and a model of a tribal house. Upstairs, you can watch the excellent Audubon Society video about the Chilkat Bald Eagle Preserve, or see a slide show about local history. The museum is open Monday–Friday 10 A.M.–5 P.M. and Saturday–Sunday 1–4 P.M. mid-May–mid-September, and whenever cruise ships are in port. Winter hours are Monday–Friday 1–4 P.M.

The strangest sight in Haines has to be the **Hammer Museum** (108 Main St., 907/766-2374, www.hammermuseum.org, Mon.–Fri. 10 A.M.–5 P.M. mid-May–mid-Sept., $3, under 13 free). Collector—and hammer expert—Dave Pahl displays some 1,500 types of hammers here, from cobbler's hammers to ones used by 19th-century bankers. The little museum is enough to make you break out in song: "If I had a hammer . . . ."

◖ Fort Seward

Circled around a grassy parade ground, the graceful buildings of historic Fort Seward are backdropped by snow-capped mountains.

Along the top of the hill is **"Officers' Row,"** the white century-old homes that once housed captains, lieutenants, and their families. Today, the buildings are used as private residences, bed and breakfasts, and the Hotel Halsingland.

A reconstructed **Tlingit tribal house**—decorated inside and out with colorful carvings—sits within the parade grounds, and the nonprofit **Alaska Indian Arts** (907/766-2160, www.alaskaindianarts.com, Monday–Friday 9 A.M.–5 P.M. year-round) operates from the old hospital building on the southeast side of Fort Seward. Inside you'll find master woodcarvers, silversmiths, blanket weavers, and other crafts workers, plus a gallery.

Stop by the Haines visitor bureau for a free, detailed historical guide and walking tour of Fort Seward.

American Bald Eagle Foundation

The Bald Eagle Foundation (907/766-3094, www.baldeagles.org, $3 adults, $1 ages 8–12, free for younger kids) sits at the intersection of Haines Highway and 2nd Avenue. Inside, you'll find a collection of stuffed animals and a video about eagles. Outside is a mew containing live bald eagles that could not survive in the wild. Don't miss talks by founder Dave Olerud, who provides an introduction to eagles and their role in the web of life. The facility is open Monday–Friday 9 A.M.–6 P.M., Saturday–Sunday 10 A.M.–4 P.M. May–August, with shortened hours the rest of September and during the Eagle Festival in early November; closed the rest of the year.

CHILKAT BALD EAGLE PRESERVE

Each fall, the Chilkat River north of Haines becomes home to the largest eagle gathering on earth. Throughout the summer, water flows into a massive underground reservoir created by gravel deposits at the confluence of the Tsirku, Klehini, and Chilkat Rivers north of Haines. When fall arrives this water percolates upward, keeping river temperatures above freezing. These warm waters attract an unusual late run of spawning chum

Fort Seward and the Chilkat Range

© DON PITCHER

and silver salmon. The dying salmon attract bears, wolves, gulls, magpies, ravens, and up to 3,500 bald eagles along a four-mile stretch of river just below the Tlingit village of **Klukwan** (pop. 140). Covering 48,000 acres, the Chilkat Bald Eagle Preserve (907/766-2292, www.dnr.state.ak.us) protects this unique gathering of eagles.

During the peak of the salmon run (Nov.–Jan.), black cottonwoods along the river are filled with hundreds of birds, and many more line the braided riverbanks. The area is very popular with photographers, but be sure to stay off the flats to avoid disturbing these majestic birds. During the summer, local eagle populations are much lower, but with 80 active nests and up to 400 resident eagles on the river, you're guaranteed to see some eagles.

A state campground ($10) is at **Mosquito Lake,** five miles north of Klukwan and three miles off the highway. Tours by van or boat go through the bald eagle preserve, and the Alaska

Bald Eagle Festival in mid-November brings more tours and educational workshops.

ENTERTAINMENT AND EVENTS
Entertainment
Chilkat Dancers' Storytelling Theater
(907/766-2540, www.tresham.com/show, Mon.–Fri. 4:30 P.M., $12 adults, $6 kids) brings four ancient Tlingit legends to life with theatrical performances, magnificent costumes, and masks. Hour-long shows take place in the tribal house at Fort Seward throughout the summer.

If you hit the bar at **Fort Seward Lodge** (907/766-2009), be sure to ask for a Road-kill, the flaming house drink that's guaranteed to set your innards on fire. Fishermen school up at two Front Street bars: **Harbor Bar** (907/766-2444) with occasional live bands and **Fogcutter Bar** (907/766-2555).

Events
The **Great Alaska Craftbeer & Homebrew Festival** in mid-May is a fine opportunity to taste regional microbrews.

Around the summer solstice in June, the **Kluane to Chilkat International Bike Relay** (www.kcibr.org) attracts more than 1,100 cyclists for an exciting 160-mile relay race that ends in Haines. Other solstice events include live music and dancing at the fairgrounds.

July 4th brings a parade, barbecue, pie-eating contest, soapbox derby races, a race up Mt. Ripinski, and other fun events.

Every year during the last week of July thousands of visitors from all over Alaska and the Yukon flock to Haines for the five-day-long **Southeast Alaska State Fair** (www.seakfair. org). Events include a logging show, farmers' market, parade, pig races, dog show, exhibits, and evening concerts by nationally known artists. Don't miss this one!

The **Alaska Bald Eagle Festival** (www .baldeaglefest.org) in early November—peak time for eagle viewing on the Chilkat Preserve—features scientific talks, workshops, and evening entertainment. The highlight comes with the dramatic release of formerly injured eagles back into the wild.

SHOPPING
Haines is an excellent place to buy arts and crafts. (For more about Alaska Indian Arts, see the *Fort Seward* section.) The best local gallery is **Wild Iris Shop** (on Portage St., 907/766-2300), run by Fred and Madeleine Shields, who act as a comedy tag-team. Fred (the mayor of Haines) will be happy to give you a dose of his "retail therapy," complete with a German accent stolen from old TV shows. Oh yes, the gallery is great too, with jewelry, trade beads, carved ivory, and photos. Find it a block up from the Port Chilkoot Dock and just down from the fort. The garden out front overflows with flowers all summer.

Extreme Dreams (907/766-2097, www.extremedreams.com) has the unusual watercolors, block prints, and textiles of John and Sharon Svenson, in a gorgeous setting, seven miles out Mud Bay Road. Another interesting Mud Bay Road gallery is nearby, **Catotti & Goldberg Studio** (907/766-2707, www.artstudioalaska.com), where you can see the paintings of Donna Catotti and Rob Goldberg. Although he isn't Native, Tresham Gregg makes distinctive woodcarvings and prints using Tlingit-inspired designs. Find them in his **Sea Wolf Gallery** (907/766-2540, www.tresham.com) near the center of Ft. Seward.

For quality outdoor gear, head to **Backcountry Outfitters** (210 Main St. upstairs, 907/766-2876, www.alaskanaturetours. net). Get Alaskan and other books from **The Babbling Book** (907/766-3356), on Main Street next to Howser's.

Haines is home to one of several birch syrup producers in Alaska—**Birch Boy Products** (907/767-5660, www.birchboy.com). The syrup is sold locally in gift shops. Don't expect the smoothness of maple syrup; birch syrup has a bit of a bite to it, but is quite good on ice cream and when blended with sugar syrup.

RECREATION

The Haines area has a number of excellent hikes, ranging from the easy (Battery Point) to the strenuous (Mt. Ripinski). For more details, pick up the *Haines is for Hikers* pamphlet from the visitor center.

Mt. Riley

Three trails lead to the top of 1,760-foot Mt. Riley, from which you get a panoramic view of Lynn Canal, Davidson and Rainbow Glaciers, the Chilkat River, Taiya Inlet, and 360 degrees of snowcapped peaks. The shortest and steepest route (2 miles) starts three miles southeast of Haines on Mud Bay Road. A small parking area is opposite the trailhead. You can also follow FAA Road from behind Fort Seward to another trail. This one is four miles long and follows the city water supply route for two miles before splitting off to join the more direct trail.

Battery Point

An easy and relatively level four-mile path starts from the end of the road at Portage Cove and follows the shore to a campsite at Kelgaya Point and across pebbly beaches to Battery Point.

Mt. Ripinski

The full-day hike up and down Mt. Ripinski (3,610 ft.) offers unparalleled views of mountains and inland waterways, but it's strenuous and long (10 miles round-trip). You may want to camp in the alpine country and make this a two-day hike. From Haines, take Young Road north until it intersects with a jeep road that follows a buried pipeline around the mountain. The trail begins about a mile along this dirt road and climbs through a spruce/hemlock forest to muskeg and finally alpine at 2,500 feet. You can continue along the ridge to the north summit (3,160 ft.), or on to the main peak. Return the same way, or via a steep path that takes you down to a saddle and then to the Haines Highway, seven miles northwest of Haines. Mt. Ripinski is covered with snow until mid-summer, so be prepared. Don't go in bad weather and do stay on the trail in the alpine areas.

Seduction Point

For a gentle, long, and very scenic beach walk, head to Chilkat State Park campground, seven miles southeast of Haines on Mud Bay Road. Seduction Point is on the end of the peninsula separating Chilkoot and Chilkat Inlets, a five-mile hike from the campground. The trail alternates between the forest and the beach, and it's a good idea to check the tides to make sure that you're able to hike the last beach stretch at low tide. This hike also makes a fine overnight camping trip.

ACCOMMODATIONS

The Haines Convention and Visitors Bureau website (www.haines.ak.us) has detailed info and links to local lodging places.

Hostel

The youth hostel in Haines, **Bear Creek Cabins and Hostel** (907/766-2259, www.bearcreek cabinsalaska.com, open May–mid-Nov.), is a mile and a half south of town on Small Tract Road. Dorm spaces are $18 and the six private cabins run $48 d. Bear Creek has kitchen facilities. The hostel is a clean and friendly place to stay, but reservations are advised in the summer. If it's full, pitch a tent out back for $12.

Hotels and Motels

◖ **Hotel Halsingland** (907/766-2000 or 800/542-6363, www.hotelhalsingland.com, open April–mid-Nov.) is a beautiful old Victorian hotel that originally served as the commanding officer's quarters at Fort Seward. In addition to the standard rooms ($109 d), it has a few small but inexpensive shared-bath rooms ($69 s or d). All rooms have been updated, but retain the original charm; it's like a step back in time to a quieter, more gracious era. Wi-Fi is available in the lobby, and the restaurant is one of the nicest in town.

Fort Seward Lodge (907/766-2009 or 800/478-7772, www.ftsewardlodge.com, open May–early Oct.) is located in another of the Fort Seward structures: This one once housed the fort's PX, bowling alley, and gym. Rooms are simple but clean; none have phones. Those with

Hotel Halsingland in Fort Seward

private baths are $70 s or $80 d. Tiny rooms with a bath down the hall and no television cost $50 s or $60 d. Also available are a couple of rooms with kitchenettes for $85 s or $95 d.

Head a mile out of town on Beach Road to **Beach Roadhouse** (907/766-3060 or 866/736-3060, www.beachroadhouse.com, $125 d), with a mix of kitchenette rooms (85 d) and small cabins ($125 d or $145 for four) with full kitchens and Lynn Canal vistas. A guest computer and Wi-Fi are available.

Mountain View Inn (Mud Bay Rd. near Ft. Seward, 907/766-2900 or 800/478-2902, www .mtviewinn.net, $78 s or $88 d) has nine large rooms, most with kitchenettes. Free Wi-Fi too.

Thunderbird Motel (216 Dalton St., 907/766-2131 or 800/327-2556, www.thunder bird-motel.com), has standard rooms with fridges and microwaves ($80 s or $90 d) and full kitchenettes ($118 for up to four).

On Haines Highway as you head out of town, **Eagle's Nest Motel** (907/766-2891 or 800/354-6009, www.alaskaeagletours.com, $79 s or $89–99 d) offers comfortable rooms and reasonable prices. Pets are $10 extra.

Housed within a historic officer's row building, **Fort Seward Condos** (907/766-2425, www.fortsewardcondos.com, $125–145 d) are one- and two-bedroom units with full kitchens; two-night minimum stay.

The nicest local motel, **Captain's Choice Motel** (108 2nd St., 907/766-3111 or 800/478-2345, www.capchoice.com) has standard rooms for $107–132 d, and suites (these sleep six comfortably) for $155. All rooms contain small fridges, and a courtesy van is available.

Bed-and-Breakfasts

Fort Seward B&B (907/766-2856 or 800/615-6676, www.fortsewardbnb.com, $89–135 d) is a beautifully maintained historic home that once housed the fort's chief surgeon. Four of the seven guest rooms have private baths, and two can be combined into a family suite for $239. Guests are served a filling sourdough pancake breakfast. Free Wi-Fi.

Built in 1912 by a member of Soapy Smith's gang, **Summer Inn B&B** (2nd and Main Sts., 907/766-2970, www.summerinnbnb.com, $75 s or $90 d) is a cozy five-bedroom home near the center of town. The five guest rooms share three baths, and a big breakfast is served each morning.

Other options include **Bear Lodge B&B** (907/957-1035, www.hainesbearlodge.com), **Chilkat Eagle B&B** (907/766-2763, www.eagle-bb.com), **A Sheltered Harbor B&B** (907/766-2741, www.geocities.com/asheltered), and **Tanani Bay B&B** (907/766-3936, www.tananibaybnb.com).

CAMPING

The best campsite near Haines is at **Portage Cove State Wayside** ($5), just three-quarters of a mile from town. Water and outhouses are available, but there is no overnight parking; the site is for hikers and cyclists only. The location is quiet and attractive, and eagles hang around nearby.

If you have a vehicle, stay at one of the two other excellent state-run campgrounds, both with drinking water, toilets, and picnic shelters. **Chilkat State Park** ($10), seven miles southeast of Haines, has a fine hiking trail to Seduction Point; and **Chilkoot Lake State Recreation Site** ($10), five miles northwest of the ferry, has good fishing and a lovely view over this turquoise-blue lake. More camping is at **Mosquito Lake State Park** ($10), 27 miles north of Haines.

RV Parks

Most local RV parks are open May–September. Located behind Hotel Halsingland, **Port Chilkoot Camper Park** (907/766-2000 or 800/542-6363, www.hotelhalsingland.com, $10–16 tents, $23 full hookups) has attractively wooded campsites, showers, and a coin laundry.

Salmon Run Adventures RV Campground (907/766-3240, www.salmonrunadventures.com, $14 for RVs or tents, no hookups), seven miles out Lutak Road, also offers showers for $2. **Haines Hitch-Up RV Park** (851 Main St., 907/766-2882, www.hitchuprv.com) is $27–32 with full hookups; no tents. RVers also park at the gravel lot on Main Street named **Oceanside RV Park** (907/766-2437). **Swan's Rest RV Park** (907/767-5662, May 30–Sept.

snow-covered cache near Haines

© DON PITCHER

15, $20 full hookups, $7 tents) is near Mosquito Lake, 27 miles north of Haines.

FOOD

For a town of this size, Haines has surprisingly good food, and the prices won't ruin your credit rating. Get filling meals, friendly service, and an unpretentious setting at the **Bamboo Room** (on 2nd Ave., 907/766-2800, www.bamboopioneer.net). Breakfasts are a standout, but the Bamboo also fills up at lunch and dinner when the menu features burgers, fried chicken, halibut fish and chips, and other greasy fare. Be sure to check the board for today's specials.

Chilkat Restaurant and Bakery (5th and Dalton Sts., 907/766-3653) bakes pastries, bagels, and croissants daily, and serves up tasty breakfasts and lunches (including homemade soups, burgers, and sandwiches) in a relaxing setting. The new owners are from Thailand, and they've added spicy Thai meals for lunch on Thursday and Saturday. The restaurant is open for breakfast and lunch most days, plus dinners (Thai and American food for $10–18) on Friday and Saturday nights.

When I'm in Haines on a chilly winter morning I bee-line it to the perpetually busy **Mountain Market & Deli** (3rd St. and Haines Hwy., 907/766-3340) for a steaming mocha and a scrambled egg croissant. Fresh baked goods fill the displays, and the lunch menu encompasses turkey club wraps, falafels, deli sandwiches, and smoothies. A natural foods market here sells organic produce and "Beware of the Crows" T-shirts.

New owners have transformed **Lighthouse Restaurant** (101 Front St., 907/766-2442) into an East-meets-West spot for harborside dining. They're open for dinner daily; try the ginger Alaskan sable fish with coconut wasabi sauce, the baked oyster appetizers, or the locally famous buttermilk pie.

Get groceries from **Howser's IGA Supermarket** (on Main St., 907/766-2040). Ask around the boat harbor to see who's selling fresh fish, crab, or prawns if you want to cook your own. A summertime **Farmers Market** takes place at the fairgrounds every other Saturday 9 A.M.–1 P.M.

Fort Seward Eateries

Housed in one of Fort Seward's historic buildings, ◖ **Fireweed Restaurant** (on Blacksmith Rd., 907/766-3838, $9–19, open May–mid-Nov. for dinner only; closed Sun. and Mon.) serves delicious meals in a classy setting. There's a wrap-around deck with a couple of tables outside, plus an earthy interior where the scents of freshly baked bread and the daily specials fill the air. The bar features local brews, and the menu encompasses salads, halibut burgers, eggplant parmesan heros, portabello mushroom ravioli alfredo, Caesar salads, pizzas with homemade sauce, and more. Highly recommended, but don't come here in a hurry. This is slow food that's worth the wait.

The restaurant at **Hotel Halsingland** (907/766-2000 or 800/542-6363, www.hotel halsingland.com, $19–28 entrées) is a pleasant place for an evening out, with a fine-dining menu that stars Caesar salads, braised lamb shank, pan-roasted duck, and butternut squash ravioli. The bar menu serves simpler meals.

Dejon Delights Smokery (on Portage Rd., 907/766-2505 or 800/539-3608, www .alaskasmokery.com) at Fort Seward has freshly smoked salmon for sale or will smoke fish that you catch.

Just downhill is **Local Catch** (907/766-3557, $4–9), a little hole-in-the-wall with a couple of tables out front and a morning menu (open weekdays 8 A.M.–3 P.M.) of breakfast burritos, eggwiches, fish tacos, curry spinach quesadillas, and lattes.

INFORMATION AND SERVICES

The **Haines Visitors Information Center** (907/766-2234 or 800/458-3579 message only, www.haines.ak.us) is on 2nd Avenue near Willard Street. Mid-May–mid-September, it's open Monday–Friday 8 A.M.–6 P.M., Saturday–Sunday 9 A.M.–6 P.M. The rest of the year, hours are Monday–Friday 8 A.M.–5 P.M. Packs can generally be left here while you walk around town. Stop here for a listing of local charter fishing boats if you want to catch salmon or halibut.

Check your email at **Northern Lights Internet Lounge** (715 Main St., 907/766-2337), or for free at the modern **Haines Public Library** (111 3rd Ave., 907/766-2545, www .haineslibrary.org). The post office is on Haines Highway near Fort Seward. Get cash from ATMs inside Howser's Supermarket and the First National Bank of Alaska. Buy topographic maps from **Chilkoot Gardens** (2nd Ave. and Main St.).

Showers are available at **Port Chilkoot Camper Park,** behind Hotel Halsingland, and **Haines Quick Laundry,** across from Fort Seward Lodge. Another option is the fine **swimming pool** (907/766-2666), next to the high school, where the entrance fee gets you a shower and swim.

The unique **Valley of the Eagles Golf Links** (907/766-2401, www.hainesgolf.com) is a mile north of town on tidelands that are occasionally covered by larger tides. The setting is dramatic, and you might even see the occasional moose or bear.

GETTING THERE
Ferry

The Haines **ferry terminal** (907/766-2111) is 3.5 miles north of town on Lutak Highway. Ferries arrive in Haines almost every day during the summer, heading both north to Skagway and south to Juneau. They generally stop for an hour and a half. Call Alaska Marine Highway for information (907/465-3941 or 800/642-0066, www.ferryalaska.com).

Alaska Fjordlines (907/766-3395 or 800/320-0146, www.alaskafjordlines.com) operates a high-speed catamaran with daily summertime runs from Skagway to Haines and then on to Auke Bay in Juneau. The boat leaves Haines at 9 A.M., arrives in Juneau at 11:30 A.M., and then heads back at 5 P.M., returning to Haines at 7:30 P.M. The cost is $139 round trip, including a bus to downtown Juneau. A light breakfast and dinner are included, and the skipper stops for wildlife and photo opportunities. One-way trips and overnight stays in Juneau are sometimes allowed; reservations recommended.

Chilkat Cruises (907/766-2100 or 888/766-2103, www.chilkatcruises.com, mid-May–mid-Sept., $51 round-trip, $25 kids) offers high-speed catamaran service between Skagway and Haines, with several departures a day. There is no bus service out of Haines.

Air

The airport is 3.5 miles west of town on the Haines Highway. The flight between Juneau and Haines is pretty spectacular; on clear days you'll be treated to views of glaciers along both sides of Lynn Canal. Several companies have scheduled daily service to Juneau and Skagway: **Wings of Alaska** (907/789-0790, www.wingsofalaska.com), **Skagway Air** (907/789-3233, www.skagwayair.com), and **L.A.B. Flying Service** (907/766-2222, www.labflying.com).

Mountain Flying Service (907/766-3007 or 800/766-4007, www.flyglacierbay.com), a few doors up from the visitor center, is a good company that offers charters and flightseeing trips over Glacier Bay starting at $139 per person for one hour. A longer trip ($279) includes two hours in the air and a beach landing within the park that gives you the chance to see bears and other wildlife. **Fly Drake** (907/723-9475, www.flydrake.com) and L.A.B. also offers Glacier Bay flightseeing trips and beach landings.

GETTING AROUND
Tours

The visitor center has a complete listing of local guide companies and charter boat operators. **Alaska Nature Tours** (210 Main St., 907/766-2876, www.alaskanaturetours.net) leads very educational three-hour bus-and-hiking trips to the eagle-viewing area along the Chilkat River and Chilkoot Lake for $65 ($50 kids). A four-hour tour with lunch is $77 ($62 kids); same price for a four-hour rainforest hike with lunch. Wintertime ski trips are also available, and their outdoor shop (Backcountry Outfitter) rents skis, snowboards, and snowshoes.

Keet Gooshi Tours (907/766-2168 or 877/776-2168, www.keetgooshi.com, $60) is a Native-owned company with 2.5-hour van tours that take in the Bald Eagle Preserve and the village of Klukwan, including an introduction to traditional culture.

Chilkat Cruises (907/766-2100 or 888/766-2103, www.chilkatcruises.com) leads half-day bus tours ($105) to a wildlife preserve run by well-known cinematographer Steve Kroschel (www.kroschelfilms.com). You'll see wolves, foxes, reindeer, wolverines, and more. Chilkat Cruises also offers sea kayak day trips and kayak rentals.

River Trips

Chilkat Guides (907/766-2491 or 888/292-7789, www.raftalaska.com, $79 adults, $62 kids) guides an excellent four-hour float trip down the Chilkat River. This is a leisurely raft trip (no white water) with good views of the Chilkat Mountains, glaciers, and roosting eagles. They also guide multi-night adventures around Alaska. **River**

Adventures (907/766-2050 or 800/478-9827, www.jetboatalaska.com) runs half-day jetboat tours up the Chilkat, and **Chilkoot Lake Tours** (907/766-2891, www.alaskaeagletours.com) has two-hour pontoon boat tours of this turquoise lake.

Glacier Valley Wilderness Adventures (907/767-5522, www.glaciervalleyadventures.net) offers a variety of trips that include a flight into a gold mine camp at the base of DeBlondeau Glacier followed by a rafting or jetboat trip down the Tsirku River, and then past the Chilkat Bald Eagle Preserve to Haines; $253 per person. Overnight accommodations are also available in a cabin or tent at the basecamp, and the company also has airboat trips and rafting floats.

Taxi and Car Rentals

Haines Shuttle & Tours (907/766-3138) charges a gut-wrenching $20 per person (!) to town from the ferry terminal or airport.

Rent cars from **Captain's Choice Motel** (907/766-3111 or 800/478-2345, www.capchoice.com), **Eagle's Nest Car Rental** (907/766-2891 or 800/354-6009, www.alaskaeagletours.com), or **Hotel Halsingland** (907/766-2000 or 800/542-6363, www.hotelhalsingland.com). Eagle's Nest has the cheapest rates, starting at $50 per day with 100 free miles.

Rent mountain bikes from **Sockeye Cycle** (907/766-2869, www.cyclealaska.com) at Fort Seward. A variety of bike tours are also offered.

Heading North

The paved highway north from Haines is the most direct route to Fairbanks (665 miles) and Anchorage (775 miles). For cyclists it's much easier than the Klondike Highway out of Skagway. If you're thinking of driving to Skagway from Haines, think again. It's only 15 water or air miles away, but 359 road miles. Take the ferry! There is no scheduled bus service from Haines.

Crossing the Border

The Canadian border is 42 miles north of Haines. Both Canadian and U.S. Customs are open 7 A.M.–11 P.M. Alaska Time (8 A.M.–midnight Pacific Time). Be prepared for lots of questions if you're traveling on the cheap. No handguns are allowed across the Canadian border.

Skagway

Occupying a narrow plain along the mouth of the Skagway River at the head of Lynn Canal, Skagway (year-round pop. 800; twice that in the summer) is a triangle-shaped town that seems to drive a wedge into the sheer slopes that lead to White Pass. The name of this northern terminus of the Inside Passage is derived from an Indian word meaning "home of the North Wind." During the Klondike gold rush, the town was the gateway to both the Chilkoot and White Pass Trails, a funnel through which thousands of frenzied fortune-seekers passed. Today, the boardwalks, frontier storefronts, restored interiors, gift shops, historic films and slide shows, and old-time cars and costumes all in the six-block town center give it the flavor for which it has been famous for nearly a century. Skagway survives on the thousands of visitors and adventurers who come each summer to continue on the trail that led to gold. This is the most popular cruise port in Alaska, and the Skagwegians are inundated with over 7,000 cruise ship visitors on a typical mid-summer day; up to five ships can dock at once. Today, 900,000 travelers spend time in Skagway each year, the vast majority stepping off these mega-ships.

Independent travelers often leave Skagway with mixed feelings, and some regard it as a schmaltzy shadow of its former self. To some extent this is true, but the town also has genuine charm, and when the cruise ships sail away each night, the locals come out to play. Skagway is compact enough to walk around easily, and is filled with all sorts of characters. Besides, if the downtown scene isn't to your taste, it's easy to escape into the surrounding mountains or to head up the Chilkoot Trail where only the hardy stray. One way to avoid most of the crowds is to get here before mid-May or after mid-September. Come in the winter and you'll have it almost to yourself!

Skagway's weather is considerably drier than other parts of the Southeast. It gets only 27 inches of precipitation a year, and alder, willow, and cottonwood carpet the adjacent hillsides. It is especially colorful in mid-September when the leaves are turning. The driest time is before July; after that rain is more likely.

HISTORY
Klondike Gold

An enormous amount of Alaskan history was compressed into the final decade of the 19th century at Skagway. In August 1896, on the day that George Carmack struck it rich on Bonanza Creek, Skagway consisted of a single cabin, constructed eight years previously by Captain William Moore, but only occupied sporadically by the transient pioneer. News of the Klondike strike hit Seattle in July 1897; within a month 4,000 people huddled in a haphazard tent city surrounding Moore's lone cabin, and "craft of every description, from ocean-going steamers to little more than floating coffins, were dumping into the makeshift village a crazily mixed mass of humanity." Almost immediately, Frank Reid surveyed and plotted the town site, and the stampeders grabbed 1,000 lots, many within Moore's homestead. There was no law to back up either claims or counterclaims, and reports from the time describe Skagway as "the most outrageously lawless quarter" on the globe.

Into this breach stepped Jefferson Randall "Soapy" Smith, Alaska's great bad man. A notorious con artist from Colorado, Soapy Smith oversaw a mind-bogglingly extensive system of fraud, theft, armed robbery, prostitution, gambling, and even murder. He had his own spy network, secret police, and army to enforce the strong-arm tactics. Finally, a vigilance committee held a meeting to oppose Soapy. Frank Reid, the surveyor, stood guard. Soapy approached. Guns blazed. Smith, shot in the chest, died instantly, at age 38. Of Soapy, the newspaper reported, "At 9:30 o'clock Friday night the checkered career of 'Soapy' Smith was brought to a sudden end by a 38 caliber bullet from a revolver in the unerring right

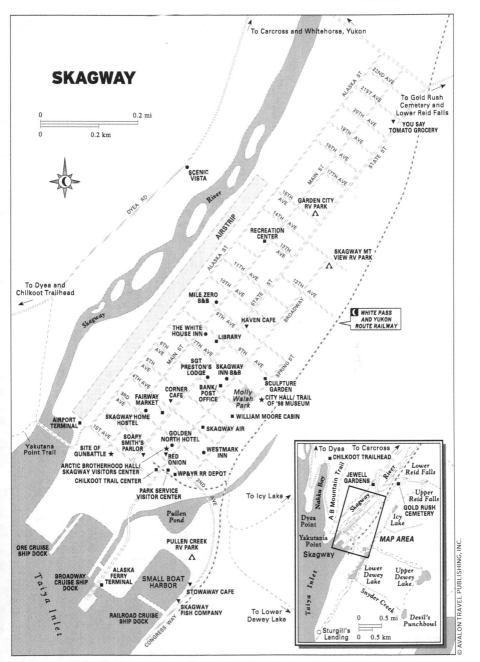

SKAGWAY

0 ——— 0.2 mi

0 ——— 0.2 km

To Carcross and Whitehorse, Yukon

To Gold Rush
Cemetery and
Lower Reid Falls

YOU SAY
TOMATO GROCERY

SCENIC
VISTA

River

22ND AVE
21ST AVE
ALASKA ST
20TH AVE
18TH AVE
18TH AVE
17TH AVE
STATE ST
MAIN ST
15TH AVE
14TH AVE
13TH AVE

AIRSTRIP

DYEA RD

GARDEN CITY
RV PARK

RECREATION
CENTER

SKAGWAY MT
VIEW RV PARK

ALASKA ST
11TH AVE
10TH AVE
STATE ST
12TH AVE
BROADWAY

MILE ZERO
B&B

9TH AVE

HAVEN CAFE

WHITE PASS
AND YUKON
ROUTE RAILWAY

THE WHITE
HOUSE INN

LIBRARY

8TH AVE
7TH AVE
MAIN ST
6TH AVE
5TH AVE
8TH AVE
SPRING ST

SGT
PRESTON'S
LODGE

SKAGWAY
INN B&B

SCULPTURE
GARDEN

CORNER
CAFE

BANK/
POST
OFFICE

Molly
Walsh
Park

CITY HALL/ TRAIL
OF '98 MUSEUM

4TH AVE
3RD AVE

FAIRWAY
MARKET

WILLIAM MOORE CABIN

SKAGWAY HOME
HOSTEL

SKAGWAY AIR

AIRPORT
TERMINAL

1ST AVE

SOAPY
SMITH'S
PARLOR

GOLDEN
NORTH HOTEL

Yakutana
Point Trail

SITE OF
GUNBATTLE

RED
ONION

WESTMARK
INN

ARCTIC BROTHERHOOD HALL/
SKAGWAY VISITORS CENTER

WP&YR RR DEPOT

CHILKOOT TRAIL CENTER

2ND AVE

PARK SERVICE
VISITOR CENTER

To Icy Lake

Skagway

To Dyea and
Chilkoot Trailhead

Pullen
Pond

ORE CRUISE
SHIP DOCK

PULLEN CREEK
RV PARK

BROADWAY
CRUISE SHIP
DOCK

ALASKA
FERRY TERMINAL

SMALL BOAT
HARBOR

Taiya Inlet

STOWAWAY CAFE

RAILROAD CRUISE
SHIP DOCK

SKAGWAY
FISH COMPANY

CONGRESS WAY

To Lower
Dewey Lake

Inset map

To Dyea   To Carcross

CHILKOOT TRAILHEAD

JEWELL
GARDENS

River

Lower
Reid Falls

Nahku Bay

A B Mountain Trail

Skagway

Upper
Reid Falls

GOLD RUSH
CEMETERY

Dyea
Point

Icy
Lake

Yakutania
Point

MAP AREA

Skagway

Lower
Dewey Lake

Upper
Dewey Lake

Taiya Inlet

Snyder Creek

Sturgill's
Landing

Devil's
Punchbowl

0 ——— 0.5 mi

0 ——— 0.5 km

hand of City surveyor Frank H. Reid . . . ." Reid was shot in the groin, and died in agony a week later. His gravestone reads, "He gave his life for the honor of Skagway." More recent evidence has been less kind to Frank Reid's reputation. It turns out that he had been a prime suspect in an Oregon murder, and as a surveyor for the railroad was deeply involved in the theft of William Moore's homestead lands. Some locals say both men got what they deserved.

Over the Top

Skagway was the jumping-off point for **White Pass,** which crossed the Coastal Range to Lake Bennett and the Yukon headwaters. This trail, billed as the "horse route," was the choice of prosperous prospectors who could afford pack animals to carry the requisite "ton of goods." But it was false advertising at best, and death-defying at worst. The mountains were so precipitous, the trail so narrow and rough, and the weather so wild, that the men turned merciless; all 3,000 horses and mules that stepped onto the trail in 1897–1898 were doomed to a proverbial fate worse than death. Indeed, men swore that horses leaped off the cliffs on purpose, committing suicide on the "Dead Horse Trail."

The famous **Chilkoot Trail,** which started in Dyea (die-EE), 15 miles from Skagway, was the "poor-man's route." Stampeders had to backpack their year's worth of supplies 33 miles to Lake Lindeman, which included 40 trips up and down the 45-degree "Golden Stairs" to the 3,550-foot pass. This scene, recorded in black and white, is one of the most dramatic and enduring photographs of the Days of 1898. At Lindeman, the men built wooden boats for the sometimes-treacherous journey to the gold fields at Dawson.

Building the Railroad

The late 19th century was a time when the railroad was king, and the sudden rush of men to the gold fields attracted entrepreneurs intent upon figuring a way to build a railroad from Skagway over White Pass. Into this breach stepped Michael J. Heney, an Irish-Canadian

contractor with a genius for vision, fund-raising, management, and commanding the loyalty of his workers. Heney punched through the 110-mile narrow-gauge White Pass & Yukon Route Railway to Lake Bennett by July of 1899, and then on to Whitehorse a year later. The route, so treacherous to pack animals, was no less malevolent to railroaders. They worked suspended from the steep slopes by ropes, often in 50-below temperatures and raging Arctic blizzards, for $3 a day. Completion of the railroad ensured the constant flow of passengers and freight to the gold fields—as well as Skagway's survival. For the next four decades, the railroad was virtually the only way into the Yukon.

During World War II, the White Pass & Yukon Route hauled much of the construction equipment and personnel to build the Alaska Highway. In the 1970s, the railroad shifted to hauling lead, zinc, and silver ore concentrate from a big mine in the Yukon. The concentrate was shipped from Skagway for processing in Asia. When metal prices plummeted in 1982, the mine closed and train traffic halted. (One legacy of this mine is the presence of lead and other toxins in the waters off Skagway.) But just as mining was ending, Alaska's current gold rush arrived in the form of cruise ships. The WP&YR reopened for excursion travel in 1988, and it is once again not only Skagway's favorite attraction, but one of the only operating narrow-gauge railroads in North America. Today, over 300,000 passengers ride the train each summer.

SIGHTS

Downtown Skagway is made up of seven blocks on Broadway, along which are most of the sights. The ferry terminal is at the bottom of Broadway: A three-minute hike and you're in the heart of beautiful downtown Skagway.

Corrington's Museum of Alaskan History (5th Ave. and Broadway, 907/983-2637 or 800/943-2637) is a combination gift shop and free scrimshaw museum. The collection includes 40 or so exquisitely carved pieces that tell the history of Alaska on walrus ivory. It's well worth a visit. The building is flanked by a colorful flower garden.

Be sure to poke your head into **Skagway Hardware Company** (Broadway at 4th Ave., 907/983-2233, www.skagwayhardware.com), one of the few old-time hardware stores left in Alaska. The wooden floors creak, and items of all types (even washers and dryers) are crammed into the shelves. A block away is the distinctive gold-colored cupola of the **Golden North Hotel.** Built in 1898, the hotel closed in 2002.

Skagway Sculpture Garden (8th Ave. at Spring St., 907/983-3311, www.skagway sculpturegarden.com, $7.50) features a flower garden filled with 37 bronze pieces by Austin Deuel, Sandy Scott, and other well-known artisans.

Broadway has more than its share of soak-the-tourists gift shops staffed by folks whose only connection to Skagway is a paycheck. The most egregious examples are the Caribbean, Colombian, British, and Swiss jewelry shops that barely make an effort to sell anything remotely connected with Alaska. Despite this, do step inside the Little Switzerland Store (Broadway and 5th Ave.), where you'll discover both the world's largest and smallest gold nugget watch chains. Local people do run many of the other shops in town.

◖ Klondike Gold Rush National Historical Park

More than a dozen historic downtown buildings are owned and managed by the National Park Service as Klondike Gold Rush National Historical Park in commemoration of the 1898 stampede of miners to Canada's Yukon. Most of the restored structures are leased to private businesses. (The park is actually split into two pieces, with one visitor center in Skagway, and another in Seattle, where nearly all the miners began their journey.)

The old White Pass & Yukon administration building houses the **Klondike Gold Rush National Historical Park Visitor Center** (907/983-2921, www.nps.gov/klgo). It's open daily 8 A.M.–6 P.M. early May–late September;

closed the rest of the year. Don't miss *Days of Adventure, Dreams of Gold,* a 30-minute film shown hourly. Ranger talks typically take place at 10 A.M. and 3 P.M., and 45-minute walking tours of old Skagway are offered five times a day—sign up early in the day to be sure of a space. Additional programs and daily tours to Dyea are also offered; see the event schedule for details. There's no charge for any of these talks. Personnel behind the desk have the latest weather and transportation information, and can probably answer that burning question you've been carrying around all day.

Across Broadway and next to the tracks, the historic Martin Itjen House contains the **Chilkoot Trail Center,** where rangers can provide details on hiking in the footsteps of the miners. This 32-mile trail starts from the old Dyea town site, nine miles from Skagway, and climbs over Chilkoot Pass (3,535 ft.) before dropping down to Bennett, British Columbia. (See *Chilkoot Trail* later in this chapter for the full story.)

Just up 2nd Street is **Soapy Smith's Parlor,** the saloon from which the infamous blackguard supervised his various nefarious offenses. The building is not open to the public.

The original **Captain William Moore cabin** (5th Ave. and Spring St., daily 10 A.M.–5 P.M., free), which was moved under pressure from the early stampeders to its present location, has been completely refurbished by the Park Service. Its interior walls are papered with newspapers from the 1880s.

Be sure to step inside another Park Service building, the old **Mascot Saloon** (3rd Ave. and Broadway, open daily in summer, free) with exhibits depicting the saloon and life in the days of '98.

◖ White Pass & Yukon Route Railroad

Adjacent to the Park Visitor Center is the **White Pass & Yukon Route Depot** (on 2nd St. 907/983-2217 or 800/343-7373, www.white passrailroad.com) built in the 1990s to closely resemble the town's many historic structures. Narrow gauge WP&YR trains depart from the depot several times a day from early May until late September; there is no winter service.

White Pass Summit Excursion trains leave Skagway at 8:15 A.M. and 1 P.M. and at 4:30 P.M. Monday through Thursday. These go to the summit of White Pass and back, a round-trip of 40 miles that takes three hours. The tracks follow along the east side of the Skagway River, with vistas that get better and better as the train climbs. Tour guides point out the sights and explain the railroad's history. Be sure to sit on the left side from Skagway (right side returning) for the best views. The diesel smoke is less toward the rear of the train. These excursions cost $98 for adults, $49 for ages 3–12, and are free for tots.

The WP&YR has two photogenic old **steam engines**—one built in 1920, the other from 1947—that huff and puff out of town most days, with video cameras rolling in all directions. For most runs the steam engine is replaced by a diesel engine on the edge of town to save it from wear and tear on the strenuous climb.

The railroad's special four-hour **Fraser Meadows Steam Excursions** ($125 adults, $63 kids) is a real treat for train lovers. Pulled by a steam engine, these trains leave at noon Saturday and Sunday and stop in the mountains just beyond the White Pass Summit to let passengers out for a chance to photograph as the engine rolls by with steam billowing before returning back down the mountain to Skagway at 4 P.M.

Also available is a **Skagway-Whitehorse rail-and-bus connection** that costs $106 for adults, $53 for kids, each way. Trains depart Skagway daily at 8 A.M., with passengers transferring to buses at Fraser, British Columbia, before continuing on to Whitehorse, arriving at noon. The buses leave Whitehorse daily at 12:30 P.M., connect with the train in Fraser, and reach Skagway at 4:30 P.M. You can also take the train one-way from Skagway to Fraser for $72 adults, $36 kids; several bus companies use this as part of a train-up, bus-back trip. Also available is a once-daily train service between Skagway and Carcross for $150 one-

way. Trains stop for a hot lunch (included) at Lake Bennett.

The **Chilkoot Trail Hikers Service** provides a shuttle Friday, Saturday, and Monday from late May to mid-September from Lake Bennett (the end of the trail) to Fraser ($50) or Skagway ($90).

Arctic Brotherhood Hall

You can't miss Arctic Brotherhood (AB) Hall between 2nd and 3rd streets—the only example of turn-of-the-century Alaska driftwood stick architecture, and probably the most-photographed building in Alaska. Thousands of pieces of wood—8,841 to be exact—decorate the exterior. The brotherhood was organized aboard the vessel *City of Seattle,* which waited out the winter of 1899 in Skagway Harbor. The order spread, and local chapters were established in most Alaskan towns, with dues paid solely in nuggets.

The AB Hall now houses the **Skagway Visitors Information Center** (907/983-2854 or 888/762-1898 message, www.skagway.com).

historic Arctic Brotherhood Hall

© DON PITCHER

It's open daily 8 A.M.–6 P.M. mid-May–mid-September, and Monday–Friday 8 A.M.–5 P.M. the rest of the year. It has the standard brochures, plus helpful walking tour and hiking maps. Stop in and take Buckwheat out to lunch, but be sure to ask about his travels with Martha Stewart. Tell him I sent you.

Skagway Museum

This excellent collection is housed in the beautifully restored City Hall (700 Spring St., 907/983-2420), a block off Broadway. It's open Monday–Friday 9 A.M.–5 P.M., Saturday 10 A.M.–5 P.M., and Sunday 10 A.M.–4 P.M. in the summer, with variable off-season hours. Check out the old gambling equipment, the "Moorish queen" from the Chicago World's Fair of 1893, the Native artifacts (including a 19th-century Tlingit canoe and an amazing seal-gut parka), the colorful duck-neck feather quilt, and Soapy Smith's derringer. Several videos are available if you want to know more about the characters in Skagway's past. Entrance costs $2 for adults, $1 for students, and free for under age 13.

North of Town

The historic Gold Rush Cemetery sits right beside the railroad tracks two miles north of town. The largest monument is Frank Reid's, while Soapy Smith only rates a wooden plank. While you're here, be sure to follow the short trail above the cemetery to scenic **Lower Reid Falls.** City-run SMART buses will take you as far as 23rd Avenue for $1.50 each way; from there it's an almost-level stroll to the cemetery.

Continue out the Klondike Highway and cross the bridge over Skagway River. On the left is **Jewell Gardens** (907/983-2111, www.jewellgardens.com, open early May–Sept.), with a very impressive collection of flowers and vegetables plus a garden railroad for model train enthusiasts. Tours cost $14, including round-trip transportation from downtown, or pay $9 for adults, $4 for kids, to just walk around on your own. The café serves nasturtium cucumber tea sandwiches and other garden treats.

Dyea

Located nine miles northwest of Skagway, the ghost town of Dyea is the starting point for the famed Chilkoot Trail. The old town site sits at the head of Taiya Inlet. During the Klondike gold rush of 1898, Dyea was where miners began the long trek into the Yukon Territory, and at its peak, the town provided a temporary home to some 10,000 people. Two factors caused Dyea to disappear: a devastating avalanche on Chilkoot Pass in April of 1898, and the completion of the White Pass & Yukon Route Railroad in 1899. Just four years later, only a half-dozen people lived in Dyea.

Little remains to be seen at Dyea except for the **Slide Cemetery,** where 45 men and women who died in the Palm Sunday avalanche of 1898 are buried. Walk through the forests that now cover old Dyea to find a few crumbling buildings and wharf pilings extending into the bay. Hard to imagine that this was once Alaska's largest city! The town site is now part of Klondike Gold Rush National Historical Park, and not far from old Dyea is the trailhead for the Chilkoot Trail and the free **Dyea Campground.**

The Park Service leads free 1.5-hour **walking tours** (907/983-2921) of the old Dyea town site Wednesday–Sunday at 2 P.M. in the summer, but you'll need to find your own transportation from Skagway.

ENTERTAINMENT AND EVENTS
Entertainment

Skagway's best-known boozing establishment, the **Red Onion** (2nd Ave. and Broadway, 907/983-2222), delivers live tunes most summer afternoons courtesy of musicians off the cruise ships. The bar, mirrors, and stove are from the time it served as both a saloon and brothel. But don't believe any tall tales about ghosts; they're all made up for the tourists. The Red Onion is now entirely non-smoking. If you want to get down and dirty and start drinking with the locals at 10 A.M., head across the street and up the block to **Moe's Frontier Bar. Bonanza Bar & Grill** (3rd Ave.

and Broadway, 907/983-6214) has pool tables, microbrews, and sports on the TVs—if you can tolerate the pall of smoke.

The most fun thing to do at night is to attend the **Days of '98 Show** (6th Ave. and Broadway, 907/983-2545, www.alaskan.com/daysof98) in the Fraternal Order of Eagles building. The great-granddaddy of them all, this production is the oldest running theater in Alaska—over 80 years! Matinees are offered most summer days at 10:30 A.M. and 2:30 P.M., and full evening performances start at 7 P.M. Warm-up gambling with "Soapy money" comes first, then the show goes on at 8. The cost is $16 for adults, $8 for kids under 16. Splurge on this one—it's worth the cash.

"Buckwheat" Donahue, a memorable local character (and head of the Skagway Convention and Visitors Bureau), occasionally recites "The Cremation of Sam McGee," "The Shooting of Dan McGrew," and other Robert Service ballads at the Park Service building on Broadway. It's a first-rate show, and Buckwheat always knows how to make people laugh. Free, and worth every penny.

Events

Skagway's first July 4th in 1898 was celebrated with the outlaw Soapy Smith leading the parade on a white horse; he was dead four days later. **July 4th** is still a big day, with a huge parade (locals call it the best in Alaska) and other events. **Soapy Smith's Wake** on July 8 toasts the conman's life and death at the Eagles Hall. The less savory aspects of the wake have been (officially at least) deleted from the program, but certain individuals may still join in after massive consumption of cheap champagne.

The **Klondike Trail of '98 International Road Relay** (www.sportyukon.com) takes place in early September, with more than a 150 teams composed of 10 runners each competing over a grueling 110-mile course from Skagway to Whitehorse.

The main winter event is the **Buckwheat Ski Classic,** a cross-country ski race that attracts both serious competitors and rank amateurs (including the "lazy and infirm") each March.

RECREATION

Rent a quality mountain bike from **Sockeye Cycle** (5th Ave. near Broadway, 907/983-2851, www.cyclealaska.com), which also offers a speedy ride down White Pass: Sockeye drives you up and you roll back down on the bikes for $75. Another popular option includes a train ride up to Fraser, followed by a downhill ride to town for $175. A 2.5-hour Dyea bike tour is $75. **Sourdough Car Rental** (6th Ave. and Broadway, 907/983-2523) also rents bikes, including tandems.

Chilkoot Horseback Adventures (907/983-3990, www.chilkoothorseback.com) has 3.5-hour horseback rides up historic Dyea Valley for $155. The same folks (www.alaskasleddog.com) also offer sleddog cart rides at Dyea for $109.

Nearby Hiking

A network of well-marked trails on the slopes just east of town offers excellent day hikes and a place to warm up for the Chilkoot Trail. Cross the small footbridge and railroad tracks beyond the end of 3rd and 4th Avenues, then follow the pipeline up the hill. **Lower Dewey Lake** is a 20-minute climb that gains 500 feet in elevation. A trail right around the lake branches at the south end off to **Sturgill's Landing** (3.5 miles) on Taiya Inlet. **Upper Dewey Lake** and the **Devil's Punchbowl** are a steep 2.5-mile climb from the north end of the lower lake. Icy Lake is a relatively level two miles from the lower lake, but the trail to **Upper Reid Falls** is steep and hard to follow. A number of clearings with picnic tables surround the lower lake where camping is possible; more are at the other lakes and Sturgill's Landing.

At 2nd Avenue and Alaska Street, go around the airport and take the footbridge over Skagway River. A short hike goes left to beautiful **Yakutania Point,** with views down Taiya Inlet. Go right and head steeply up to the Dyea Road; you'll see the trailhead in a mile for **A.B. Mountain,** named for the Arctic Brotherhood—the letters *AB* are supposedly visible in snow patches each spring. This five-mile hike is steep and strenuous; the summit is 5,100 feet above your starting point (sea level).

The Forest Service maintains a refurbished rail car as the **Denver Caboose Cabin** ($35). This attractive old caboose is six miles north of Skagway near where the railroad crosses the East Fork of the Skagway River. Access is by foot, or the WP&YR train will drop you off for $60 round-trip. Take your binoculars to scan nearby slopes for mountain goats. The **Denver Glacier Trail** begins right beside the caboose, and climbs five miles and 1,200 feet to Denver Glacier. It's a beautiful hike through subalpine fir, paper birch, cottonwood, spruce, and other trees.

Another excellent hiking option begins at Glacier Station (14 miles north of Skagway). Have the WP&YR train drop you off here, and then hike up the easy two-mile trail that leads to a Forest Service cabin near **Laughton Glacier** ($35). Flag down the train to return. Make cabin reservations for either the caboose or cabin at 518/885-3639 or 877/444-6777, www.reserveusa.com.

Located at the Mountain Shop in Skagway, **Packer Expeditions** (907/983-2544, www.packerexpeditions.com) leads guided hikes in the Skagway area, including day trips, and multi-day hikes over Chilkoot Pass. Its most popular trip combines a helicopter flight over the Juneau Icefield with a four-mile hike to Laughton Glacier, followed by a train ride back to town. The cost is $300 for this 5.5-hour trip that is mainly for cruise shippies.

On the Water

A number of companies offer charter fishing out of Skagway; get their brochures in the downtown visitor center or find them at www.skagway.com.

Skagway Float Tours (907/983-3688, www.skagwayfloat.com) has easy three-hour float trips down the Taiya River for $75 ($55 kids). A combination trip that includes a one-hour hike up the first part of the Chilkoot Trail followed by a float down the river is $85 for adults, $65 for kids. The company also has a variety of other hiking, floating, and tour options.

Flightseeing

Skagway Air (907/983-2218, www.skagway air.com) does 90-minute Glacier Bay flightseeing trips for $150 per person, and 45-minute gold rush tours to Lake Bennett for $100. **Temsco Helicopter** (907/983-2900 or 866/683-2900, www.temscoair.com) offers 80-minute "glacier discovery" flights ($250) that include a guided 40-minute glacier hike, and a tour that includes an hour on the Denver Glacier where you get to practice dogsledding ($420).

ACCOMMODATIONS

If you're heading here in midsummer, try to make reservations at least two weeks ahead of time to be sure of a room. Visit www.skag way.com for links to local lodging places.

Hostel

The delightful **Skagway Home Hostel** (3rd Ave. and Main St., 907/983-2131, www.skagway hostel.com) is right in town. Built more than a century ago, the home was once owned by the marshall who arrested the Soapy Smith gang after the shoot-out. An 11 P.M. curfew may put a crimp in your social life, but the owners are very friendly and the hostel is open year-round. There's space for only 12, so reserve ahead. Registration is 5–9 P.M., but late ferry arrivals are accommodated. The hostel has a kitchen, commons area, showers, laundry, bag storage, and free guest computer. Bunks are $15–20, and a couple's room costs $50 d. The owners offer family-style, shared lunches, and mostly vegetarian dinners ($5). Reservations highly advised.

Hotels

Sgt. Preston's Lodge (6th Ave. and State St., 907/983-2521 or 866/983-2521, www.sgt prestonslodgeskagway.com) is a tidy 35-room motel right in town, with clean, nicely remodeled rooms, and free Wi-Fi. Budget units are $80 s or $90 d, and moderately priced spacious rooms cost $95–108 s or $105–115 d. Families appreciate the two-bedroom apartment units ($150 for up to five) with full kitchens.

You might also check out the new units at **4th St. Hotel** (444 4th St., 907/983-3200, www.skagwaypizzastation.com, $75–120 d), located over Pizza Station Restaurant. No TVs or phones, except in the suite ($200 d).

Skagway's largest lodging place is the seasonally open **Westmark Inn** (3rd Ave. and Broadway, 907/983-2291 or 800/544-0970, www .westmarkhotels.com, $119 d) with all the charm of a retirement home; you might feel you were in one, given the cruise ship folks. Grossly overpriced.

Bed-and-Breakfasts

Hosted by longtime Alaskan Tara Mallory, **Mile Zero B&B** (9th Ave. at Main St., 907/983-3045, www.mile-zero.com, $135 d) is a modern seven-room B&B with six large rooms, private entrances and baths, covered porches, a cozy parlor, continental breakfast, and Wi-Fi.

Located within one of the town's oldest buildings, **Skagway Inn B&B** (7th Ave. and Broadway, 907/983-2289 or 888/752-4929, www.skagwayinn.com, open mid-May–mid-Sept.) served through the years as a bordello, a residence, a boarding house, and now as a delightful inn. Six guest rooms ($149–189 d) have private baths, and the others (99–$119 d) share three baths. A full hot breakfast is served downstairs.

Built in 1902 and completely rebuilt after a fire, **The White House Inn** (8th Ave. and Main St., 907/983-9000, www.atthewhitehouse.com, $120–145 d) is a large plantation-style home with 10 guest rooms, one of which is wheelchair accessible. All rooms feature a country Victorian decor, with private baths and continental breakfasts.

Chilkoot Trail Outpost (907/983-3799, www.chilkoottrailoutpost.com) is a modern lodge eight miles out Dyea Road. Eight cabins are available, all with private baths and kitchenettes; $138 d in duplex cabins, or $165 d for deluxe units with queen beds. A full buffet breakfast is included, along with evening campfires, but you'll need to find your own transport from town. Guests can use the screened-in gazebo cooking area for other meals, or pay $25 for a tasty picnic dinner. Because of its location, this lodge is popular with hikers setting

out for the Chilkoot Trail; the trailhead is just a half-mile away. Free Wi-Fi too.

Cabins

Two miles from downtown Skagway, **Cindy's Place** (907/983-2674 or 800/831-8095, www .alaska.net/~croland, open May–Sept.) includes two modern cabins with private baths, microwave, and mini-fridge for $120 d. Also available is a tiny cabin with a toilet (but no shower) for $35 s or $49 d; it will look like luxury if you just got off the Chilkoot Trail. Breakfast fixin's are provided, along with a courtesy shuttle to town, and access to the hot tub.

Another place with cabins on the way to Dyea is **Skagway Bungalows** (907/983-2986, www.aptalaska.net/~saldi, open March–Oct., $125 d). It's a mile from town, and the two in-the-woods cabins have private baths, fridges, and microwaves.

CAMPING

The Park Service maintains a peaceful campground ($6) at **Dyea,** northeast of Skagway. It is especially popular with hikers along the Chilkoot Trail. You'll need to bring water or filter it from the river. For those without wheels, hitching is possible, or contact one of the local taxi companies for a ride. Showers are available from local RV parks or at the small boat harbor.

Skagway's three private campgrounds are all priced around $16 for tents and $29 for RVs, and are open seasonally. **Skagway Mountain View RV Park** (14th Ave. and Broadway, 907/983-3333 or 888/778-7700, www.alaskarv.com) is the in-town tenters' campground, with wooded sites, toilets, showers, and Wi-Fi. The narrow-gauge tracks border the grounds, making this a good place for photo opportunities. **Pullen Creek RV Park** (907/983-2768 or 800/936-3731, www.pullencreekrv.com) is next to the harbor and cruise ship dock. This is great if you like being in the heart of the action, with steam engines, cruise ships, and shopping, but not so great if you're looking for a quieter, more natural setting. **Garden City RV Park** (16th Ave. and State St., 907/983-2378 or 866/983-

2378, www.gardencityrv.com) is little more than a parking lot with bathhouse.

FOOD

With so many visitors flashing the cash, Skagway's high meal prices should come as no surprise. But at least the variety and quality are considerably higher than what you'll find in Wrangell!

Breakfast and Lunch

Corner Café (4th Ave. and State St., 907/983-2155) is the local greasy spoon, with burgers and pizzas, plus reasonable breakfasts and fast service—if you don't mind all the cigarette smoke. A better bet (smoke-free) is **Sweet Tooth Café** (3rd Ave. and Broadway, 907/983-2405, daily 6 A.M.–3 P.M.), with good all-American breakfasts and lunches. Both Corner Café and the Sweet Tooth stay open year-round; most other eateries close when the cruise ships flee to the Caribbean.

At **◖ Alaska Gourmet Café** (361 5th Ave., 907/983-2448, www.akgourmet.com, $7–11) owner Lara Cavanelli serves up an eclectic world of flavors: enormous bowls of kosher sockeye salmon chowder, Indian samosas with chutney, Aussie meat pies, smoked turkey sandwiches on homemade bread, fair-trade espresso (best in town), and even fresh sushi. Great breakfasts, too. Locals know about this place, so it gets packed for lunch.

Haven Café (9th Ave. and State St., 907/983-3554, www.haven-cafe.com, open year-round, $7–10) is far enough off the tourist path to be mainly for locals, and they like it that way. It's a great place for homemade granola, breakfast sandwiches, paninis, salads, soups, espresso, and even Wi-Fi (fee). Come back Sunday evenings for live music.

Other places worth a visit include **Glacial Smoothies & Espresso** (336 3rd Ave., 907/983-3223) and **Skagway Pizza Station** (444 4th Ave., 907/983-2220, www.pizzastation.eskagway.com). Both are open year-round.

Dinner

Skagway Fish Company (907/983-3474, daily May–Sept.) is the tent-like structure near the cruise ship dock and facing the small boat harbor. The menu includes T-bone steaks, pork chops, BBQ ribs, oysters, and fresh salmon or halibut, but I recommend the halibut fish and chips ($13). The fish is locally caught, and it comes with a pile of fries and homemade coleslaw. Good strawberry cheesecake too.

Skagway Inn (7th Ave. at Broadway, 907/983-2289 or 888/752-4929, www.skagwayinn.com) puts on a three-hour **Alaska Garden and Gourmet Tour** for $60 where you can watch chef and owner Karl Klupar prepare a delicious three-course seafood meal. **Red Onion Saloon** (2nd Ave. and Broadway, 907/983-2222) serves surprisingly good pizzas, chili, and sandwiches in a historic setting.

Stowaway Café (907/983-3463, $16–27 entrées) is where locals (and tourists) go for good food in a harborside setting. There's even a big deck for sunny days. The café specializes in seafood of all types, and the wasabi salmon is always great, but also serves everything from smoked ribs to steaks. Be sure to ask about the daily specials. Reservations advised for dinner.

Starfire Grill (4th Ave. and Spring St., 907/983-3663, $11–13) serves excellent Thai lunches, chicken satay, curries, potstickers, soups, and pad Thai. The express menu is great if you're in a hurry. Starfire closes at 4 P.M.

Groceries

Fairway Market (4th Ave. and State St., 907/983-2220) is Skagway's grocery store. Fresh produce arrives on Tuesdays, and may be wiped out by the weekend.

You Say Tomato (2075 State St., 907/983-2784) is a little natural-foods market with freshly baked breads and locally grown produce for reasonable prices.

INFORMATION AND SERVICES

Both the Park Service Visitor Center and the Skagway Visitors Information Center are described in *Sights*. The small **town library** (8th Ave. and State St., 907/983-2665) offers free reading material on the paperback racks inside, and you can check your email on its computers. Rent computer time at **Glacial Smoothies** (336 3rd Ave., 907/983-3223) or **Ports of Call** (363 2nd Ave., 907/983-2411). Both places also serve light meals.

Mountain Shop (4th Ave. between Broadway and State St., 907/983-2544, www.packerexpeditions.com) is the outfitter in town, and also sells supplies for the trail. Books are available from **Skaguay News Depot** (Broadway, 907/983-3354, www.skagwaybooks.com).

One of Alaska's oldest bank buildings, **Wells Fargo** (6th Ave. and Broadway), changes green dollars into multicolored Canadian dollars, and has an ATM.

The **Skagway Recreation Center** (13th and Main Sts., 907/983-2679, www.skagwayrecreation.org, $5/day) is a surprisingly impressive place in such a small town, with a gym, weight room, cardio room, climbing wall, skate park, and various classes.

For medical emergencies, **Skagway Medical Clinic** (11th Ave. and Broadway, 907/983-2255) has a physician's assistant on staff.

GETTING THERE
On the Water
Skagway is the northern terminus of the Alaska Marine Highway ferry system (907/465-3941 or 800/642-0066, www.ferryalaska.com), and ferries arrive daily during the summer, stopping at the **ferry terminal** (907/983-2941), just a block from downtown.

Alaska Fjordlines (907/766-3395 or 800/320-0146, www.alaskafjordlines.com) operates the *Fjord Express,* a large and stable high-speed catamaran with daily summertime runs from Skagway to Haines and then on to Auke Bay in Juneau. The boat leaves Skagway at 8 A.M., arrives in Juneau at 11:30 A.M., and then heads back at 5 P.M., returning to Skagway at 8:15 P.M. The cost is $139 round trip, including a bus to downtown Juneau. A light breakfast and dinner are included, and the boat stops for wildlife and photo opportunities. This passenger-only ferry is very popular with RVers who want to see Juneau in a day. One-way trips and overnight stays in Juneau

are allowed; reservations recommended. This is an efficiently run and friendly operation.

Chilkat Cruises (907/766-2100 or 888/766-2103, www.chilkatcruises.com) offers high-speed catamaran service between Haines and Skagway, with several departures a day mid-May–mid-September. The cost is $51 round-trip ($25 for kids). The boat does not stop on any of these trips for wildlife viewing or photos, but does have a few snacks on board.

Air
Three companies have daily flights connecting Skagway with Juneau and Haines: **Skagway Air** (907/983-2218, www.skagwayair.com), **Wings of Alaska** (907/983-2442, www.wingsofalaska.com), and **L.A.B. Flying Service** (907/983-2471, www.labflying.com).

Long-Distance Buses
Yukon Alaska Tourist Tours (867/668-5947 in Whitehorse or 866/626-7383, www.yatt.ca) has a daily bus to Whitehorse ($65), along with a mix of bus/train combo tours. In Whitehorse, catch the **Alaska Direct Bus Line** (867/668-4833 in Whitehorse or 800/770-6652, www.alaskadirectbusline.com) for service north to Anchorage or Fairbanks.

GETTING AROUND
City-run **SMART** (Skagway Municipal and Regional Transit) buses (907/983-2743, www.skagwaytransit.com) run daily, shuttling from the cruise dock into town out to 23rd Avenue (access to the gold rush cemetery). The one-way cost is $1.50. Buses run continuously 7:30 A.M.–9 P.M. May–September.

Several local tour outfits offer drop-off services for hikers heading up the Chilkoot Trail and for campers staying at Dyea: **Dyea Dave's** (907/209-5031), **Frontier Excursions** (907/983-2512 or 877/983-2512, www.frontierexcursions.com), and **Klondike Taxi** (907/983-2400).

Rent new cars from **Avis** (2nd Ave. and Spring St., 907/983-2247 or 800/331-1212), or used vehicles from **Sourdough Car Rental** (6th Ave. and Broadway, 907/983-2523). If you're driving to Whitehorse, stick with Avis since Sourdough hits you with $0.25 per mile after 100 miles. **Skagway Classic Cars** (907/983-2886, www.skagwayclassiccars.com) has immaculate cars from the 1950s and '60s, with chauffered trips around town for $33 per hour.

Tours

Given the influx of tourists to Skagway, it's no surprise to find a multitude of tour options. The most unique local tours are aboard the canary-yellow 1920s vintage White Motor Company cars run by **Skagway Street Car Company** (907/983-2908, www.skagwaystreetcar.com). The complete two-hour trip costs $40 ($20 kids), but most seats are pre-sold to cruise ship passengers. To be sure of a spot, book a week in advance. This is one of the few Alaskan guided tours that I'd actually recommend.

A number of other companies also offer van tours around the area; get their brochures at the visitor center. These typically cost $25 for a 2.5-hour trip that includes the town of Skagway and White Pass Summit; some take an alternate route to the Chilkoot Trailhead and Dyea, or a longer trip into the Yukon.

Skagway Carriage Company (907/723-3117) provides a completely different sort of tour: horse-drawn carriage rides around town. Just look for the carriages on Broadway.

CHILKOOT TRAIL

One of the best reasons for coming to Skagway is the historic and surprisingly scenic 33-mile Chilkoot Trail. During the gold rush of 1897–1898, what had once been an Indian route from the tidewater at Dyea to the headwaters of the Yukon River became a trail for thousands of men and women. Today, the trail is hiked by several thousand hardy souls each summer, along with a few insane wintertime trekkers. The western portion of this route lies within **Klondike Gold Rush National Historical Park,** while the eastern half is managed by Parks Canada as **Chilkoot Trail National Historic Park.** All hikers crossing the border must clear Canadian Customs, so an official ID (preferably a passport) is needed.

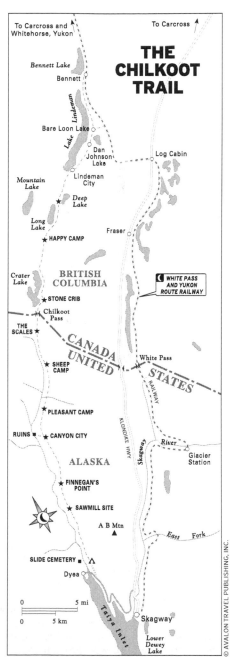

THE CHILKOOT TRAIL

To Carcross and Whitehorse, Yukon

To Carcross

Bennett Lake

Bennett

Lake Lindeman

Bare Loon Lake

Dan Johnson Lake

Log Cabin

Mountain Lake

Lindeman City

Deep Lake

Long Lake

Fraser

★ HAPPY CAMP

Crater Lake

BRITISH COLUMBIA

★ STONE CRIB

Chilkoot Pass

THE SCALES ★

WHITE PASS AND YUKON ROUTE RAILWAY

CANADA
UNITED

White Pass

STATES

RAILWAY

★ SHEEP CAMP

★ PLEASANT CAMP

RUINS ★ CANYON CITY

KLONDIKE HWY

Skagway

River

Glacier Station

ALASKA

★ FINNEGAN'S POINT

★ SAWMILL SITE

A B Mtn

East Fork

SLIDE CEMETERY

Dyea

0   5 mi

0   5 km

Taiya Inlet

Skagway

Lower Dewey Lake

© AVALON TRAVEL PUBLISHING, INC.

A minimum of three days and nights (but preferably four or five) is needed to hike from Dyea to Bennett over 3,246-foot-high Chilkoot Pass. This is no easy Sunday outing: You must be fit and well prepared. It is best to hike north from Dyea rather than south from Bennett since this is the historic route, and a descent down the "Golden Stairs" can be dangerous.

You will be above the tree line and totally exposed to the elements during the 11 miles from Sheep Camp to Deep Lake (the hardest stretch). Weather conditions can change quickly along the trail, and hikers need to be prepared for strong winds, cold, low fog, rain, and snow, even in mid-summer. Because of the rain-shadow effect, the Canadian side is considerably drier than the Alaskan side. Mosquitoes and other insects are an annoyance, and snowfields linger between Sheep Camp and Happy Camp well into the summer. Despite these challenges, for scenery and historical value the Chilkoot Trail is unsurpassed in Alaska and western Canada.

Flora and Fauna

The vegetation changes from coastal rainforest up the Taiya Valley to alpine tundra as you approach the pass and rise above the 2,700-foot level. On the drier Canadian side you'll find an open boreal forest of alpine fir and lodgepole pine. Although black bears are often seen along the trail, there has never been an attack on a hiker. Help keep it this way by storing food and garbage properly.

History

It took each would-be miner an average of three months and dozens of trips back and forth from cache to cache to pack his required ton of supplies into Canada. By the spring of 1898, three aerial tramways were operating on the Chilkoot. The thousands of stampeders stopped at Lindeman and Bennett, built boats and rafts, and waited for spring break-up, which would allow them to sail the 900 kilometers to Dawson City along a series of lakes and rivers. When the ice broke up in May 1898, some 7,124 boats and rafts sailed from the shores of Lakes Lindeman and Bennett. Mounted Police records show 28,000 people traveling from Bennett to Dawson in 1898. Ironically, by the time they got to Dawson every claim in the Klondike was already staked. By 1900, the railway had opened from Skagway to Whitehorse, and Dyea and the Chilkoot Trail became ghost towns.

The Route

The Chilkoot Trail begins just before the bridge over the Taiya River at Dyea, nine miles northwest of Skagway. The first section of the trail traverses lush rainforests along the Taiya River. Artifacts from the gold rush litter parts of the path here, including bits of clothing, rusting stoves, pulleys, cables, and old wagons. At **Canyon City,** 7.5 miles from the trailhead, a short side trail and a suspension bridge across the Taiya River provide access to the remains of one of the settlements that sprang up during the rush to the Klondike. You'll find a number of artifacts here, including a boiler that powered tramways to haul supplies over the summit. Beyond this, the trail climbs steeply to another long-abandoned settlement, **Sheep Camp** (Mile 13), where a ranger is in residence nearby all summer.

Beyond Sheep Camp, the trek becomes far more challenging as the route takes hikers through a narrow valley before heading above tree line. Artifacts—including metal telegraph poles and pieces from an old tramway used to haul goods up the mountain—become more common as you climb past "The Scales" (Mile 16), where packers reweighed their loads and increased their fee for the difficult final climb. Modern-day hikers start to wonder about their sanity at this point, since the infamous "Golden Stairs" lie ahead; the name came from the steps carved in the ice and the snow by the miners. During the winter of 1897–1898 thousands of prospectors carried their heavy loads to the 3,535-foot summit of **Chilkoot Pass.** Photos of men going up here in single file are still the best-known images of the gold rush. Today, hikers struggle up this 45-degree slope with full backpacks. Snow generally covers the pass until mid-July, and can be waist-deep early in the summer.

Avalanches can occur before early July, and avalanche transceivers are recommended. Ask at the Trail Center for current snow conditions and other hazards. A warming hut provides protection from the weather once you cross into British Columbia; Parks Canada wardens here check to make sure you have a permit.

After the challenging summit climb, hikers are rewarded with easier hiking and spectacular vistas (when weather permits), but it's still a long distance to the end of the trail. Many hikers camp at **Deep Lake** (Mile 23), while others continue on to **Lindeman Lake** (Mile 26) for the night. A Canada Parks warden station and warming huts are at Lindeman. During the stampede, thousands of miners halted along the shores of this lake, quickly forming the town of Lindeman City. Here they built boats for the journey down the Yukon River to the Klondike gold fields. Reminders of the gold rush can be found in the countryside here, and a small cemetery marks the final stop for those who never made it to the Klondike.

Beyond Lindeman, the trail climbs a ridge overlooking the lake and then splits, with one path turning south to meet the Klondike Highway at **Log Cabin,** where you can catch a bus back to Skagway or Whitehorse. Those who continue straight at the junction will reach a pretty place called **Bennett** on the shores of Lake Bennett. Only one family lives here today, but hikers will enjoy exploring the log church built by the miners and a grand White Pass & Yukon Route Railroad depot. Most hikers end their trip here, catching the train back to Skagway.

Hiking Permits

Backcountry permits are required of hikers on the Chilkoot, and the number of hikers is limited. The U.S. permit is C$20, and permits for the Canadian side cost an additional C$35. For trail information, maps (including an excellent *Hiker's Guide to the Chilkoot Trail*), a helpful listing of transportation options, and backcountry permits, contact the Park Service's **Chilkoot Trail Center** (907/983-9234, www.nps.gov/klgo, daily late May–early Sept.

8 A.M.–5 P.M.) in the historic Martin Itjen house in Skagway. You can also buy trail permits through Parks Canada in Whitehorse (867/667-3910 or 800/661-0486, www.pc.gc .ca/chilkoot).

Most permits are reserved months ahead of time (C$12 extra), but eight permits are reserved for walk-ins each day at 1 P.M. In July and August, folks without permits start lining up at the Trail Center by 11 A.M. to be sure of a spot. At other times you won't have a problem getting onto the trail even at the last minute, but call the Trail Center for the latest situation.

Practicalities

Official campgrounds—most with tent platforms, outhouses, cooking shelters, and bear-proof food storage—are at nine sites along the Chilkoot Trail in addition to the one at the Dyea Trailhead; most popular are those at Canyon City (Mile 7.5), Sheep Camp (Mile 12), Happy Camp (Mile 21), Lindeman City (Mile 26), and Bennett (Mile 33). Campfires are permitted only at Canyon City and Sheep Camp. There are shelters with woodstoves at Canyon City, Sheep Camp, and Lindeman, but these are for drying out only (not overnighting). Everything along the trail dating from the gold rush (even a rusty old tin can) is protected by law, and there are severe penalties for those who damage or remove items.

Everyone entering Canada must clear Canadian Customs. If you come in along the Chilkoot Trail and do not speak to an official at either Whitehorse or Fraser, you should report at the first opportunity to either the RCMP in Carcross or the Immigration Office (open Mon.–Fri.) at the Federal Building in Whitehorse.

Getting There

Several Skagway companies offer drop-off services ($10) from town for hikers heading up the Chilkoot Trail. Best known is **Dyea Dave's** (907/209-5031), but similar services are available from **Frontier Excursions** (907/983-2512 or 877/983-2512, www.frontierexcursions .com) and **Klondike Taxi** 9907/983-2400).

The WP&YR's **Chilkoot Trail Hikers Service** (907/983-2217 or 800/343-7373, www.whitepassrailroad.com) provides a shuttle train on Fridays, Sundays, and Mondays from Bennett to Fraser ($50) or Skagway ($90). Make advance reservations since space is limited. Meals are available at the Bennett station.

Although most hikers choose the train, some prefer (or have no option because the rail bus is full or the timing doesn't work out) to hike out along the railroad tracks from the Lindeman area to Log Cabin, where they catch a **Yukon Alaska Tourist Tours** (867/668-5947 in Whitehorse or 866/626-7383, www.yatt.ca) bus, or get a ride with Dyea Dave, Frontier Excursions, or Klondike Taxi for around $25; advance reservations essential. A final option is to fly by floatplane from Lake Bennett to Whitehorse via **Alpine Aviation** (867/668-7725, www.alpineaviationyukon.com).

THE KLONDIKE HIGHWAY

This 98-mile road from Skagway to the Alaska Highway 21 miles south of Whitehorse closely follows the White Pass & Yukon Route rail line built at the turn of the century. The 65-mile stretch north to Carcross was opened in 1981, completing the route started by the U.S. Army in 1942 from the Alaska Highway south to Carcross. The road ascends quickly from sea level at Skagway to White Pass at 3,290 feet in 14 miles. Many turnouts provide views across the canyon of the narrow-gauge White Pass & Yukon Route track, waterfalls, gorges, and long drop-offs—if you're lucky and the weather cooperates. At the summit, **Canadian Customs** welcomes you to British Columbia, and is open 24 hours a day in the summer, and 8 A.M.–midnight at other times; set your watch ahead an hour to Pacific Time on the Canadian side. U.S. Customs is open 24 hours a day year-round.

MOON SOUTHEAST ALASKA

Avalon Travel
A member of the Perseus Books Group.
1700 Fourth Street
Berkeley, CA 94710
www.moon.com

Editor: Sabrina Young
Series Manager: Kathryn Ettinger
Copy Editor: Kate McKinley
Graphics Coordinator: Elizabeth Jang
Production Coordinator: Tabitha Lahr
Map Editor: Albert Angulo
Cartographers: Aaron Dorden, Kat Bennett
Proofreader: Valerie Sellers Blanton

ISBN-13: 978-1-59880-343-3

Text © 2007 by Don Pitcher
Maps © 2007 by Avalon Travel Publishing, Inc.
All rights reserved.

Some photos and illustrations are used by permission
and are the property of the original copyright owners.

Front cover photo © Don Pitcher
Title page photo: Eldred Rock Lighthouse, Lynn Canal
south of Haines, Alaska © Don Pitcher

Printed in USA

ABOUT THE AUTHOR

Don Pitcher

Perhaps Don Pitcher's love of travel came about because he moved so much as a child; by age 15 he had lived in six states and two-dozen East Coast and Midwest towns. Don's family hails from Maine, but being born in Atlanta made him a southerner with New England blood. He moved west for college, receiving a master's degree from the University of California at Berkeley, where his thesis examined wildfires in high elevation forests of Sequoia National Park. When his first (and only) scientific paper was published, he appeared headed into the world of ecological research.

Shortly after grad school Don landed what seemed the coolest job on the planet: being flown around Alaska's massive Wrangell-St. Elias National Park in a helicopter while conducting fire research. Over the next 15 years he built backcountry trails, worked as a wilderness ranger, mapped grizzly habitat, and operated salmon weirs. After that first season in Alaska, Don spent three months in the South Pacific, and quickly found himself addicted to travel. These explorations eventually took him to 35 countries and all 50 U.S. states.

In addition to this book, he is the author of Moon Handbooks to Washington, Wyoming, Yellowstone & Grand Teton, and the San Juan Islands. He has photographed three popular travel books for Compass American Guides and served as editor for *Best Places Alaska*. Don's photos have appeared in a multitude of other publications and advertisements, and his fine-art prints are sold in many Alaska and Washington galleries.

Don lives in Homer, Alaska, with his wife, Karen Shemet, and their children, Aziza and Rio. Find details on his latest writing and photography projects – along with web links to places mentioned in this book – at www.donpitcher.com.